TROJAN HORSE

The Unseen Solution to Critical Business Problems

ISBN 979-8-9922116-2-7

Emissary
PUBLISHING

Published in Phoenix, Arizona by Emissary Publishing.
Emissary is a business trade name of Ed's Voices, LLC.
The views expressed by the author are those of the author and do not necessarily reflect the views of the publisher.

Table of Contents

Foreword

If you own or run a business, or work in business management and want to do a better job, it's my privilege to introduce you to Dean Svarc.

I have known Dean for several years, and worked as his controller and CFO in his business ventures. I come from a professional financial background and owned my own business for more than ten years. I worked as a controller and as a CFO for companies private and public, including one with more than $9.6 billion in sales.

As a finance guy who hates to spend money, I'm pleased to say Dean is one of a handful of owners I trust to make good decisions, even when they sometimes go against my instincts. He's a forward-thinking visionary who loves innovation and outside-the-box thinking, as well as a no-nonsense manager of both people and product.

After I sold my business, Dean reached out for help. He needed a controller for a company he had recently purchased. My experience in the manufacturing industry was disappointing; most owners and management I knew focused solely on the bottom line, often at the expense of caring for employees.

Dean's approach is different; he believes in attending to each and every detail, to create an environment where employees look forward to their workdays.

For most business leaders, "change" is the most evil word in the English language. Not so for Dean! He welcomes change; in fact, he *insists* on it, to improve the strength of the business and the workplace culture. His B.A.S.I.C.S framework takes you through multiple levels of change, ranging from the simplest to the most complex maneuvers required to grow, scale, or turn your business around.

Trojan Horse tells the backstories of Dean's incredible success with turnarounds. He gets tremendous results, and takes his companies from losing money to profitability, and (in company culture) from fragmented to unified. He has an uncanny ability to visualize a brighter future where others fail to see it.

I hope you enjoy Dean's ideas and implement them, because when you're ready for change, you'll see what a difference it makes.

George R. Thompson

Dedication

To Dominique

For the years we shared, the love and belief you once gave so freely, and the strength you helped me find within myself. Though our paths have diverged, the foundation you helped build will always remain a part of who I am.

To Justin

For a lifetime of friendship that has weathered every season of life. Through challenges and triumphs alike, your loyalty, patience, and faith in me have never wavered. You've been more than a friend — you've been family, and I'm forever grateful for your presence in my journey.

To George

For your steadfast guidance, patience, and quiet wisdom. You were a mentor, a teacher, and a grounding presence through every storm. Your influence continues to echo in the way I lead, think, and live.

A Note to the Reader

There are two ways to read this book: the right way… and the other way.

The book is divided into two parts: **Prerequisites** and the **B.A.S.I.C.S** framework. If you want this book to work for you, *you should not* skip ahead to Part Two.

If you're a founder, business owner, management, or leader, you are the "core" of your company. Everything rises and falls on the condition of the core. If you're compromised in some way, your company will follow.

You should also borrow a concept used by the U.S. Navy: the captain of the ship is *accountable*, even if the problems are caused by the sailors running the engine room. You may not be directly *responsible*… but you are accountable, whether you acknowledge it or not.

That's why you need to go through Part One—several times. Soak up every word of it. Take immediate action to make your business' core the strongest it can be.

If you want your company to grow, change, improve, and succeed… it will only do so if *you* do those things first.

You'd have to search long and hard to find a successful, profitable, and efficient company with a healthy culture… *and* a bad leader.

The two don't go together. I know, because every distressed company I've ever bought or managed had leaders with huge deficits in personal growth and improvement. Not *one* had a noble, visionary CEO or founder with purposes higher than their pocketbook.

So go through Part One *multiple times*. Always assume you can dig deeper into your own problems if you're trying to grow or rescue your business.

And you can always reach out to me if you read and try my methods and something doesn't work. That's my specialty—finding the real problem and fixing it... fast.

Dean Svarc

Introduction

According to tradition, the ancient Greeks used the Trojan Horse to gain entry to the city of Troy after ten years of failed siege warfare. They delivered the horse as a peace offering, but inside hid a detachment of Greek soldiers who snuck out at night, opened the city gates, and let the Greek army into the city, which led to the fall of Troy.

Many business owners and managers I've met over the years fall prey to a parallel problem. They lack the growth and maturity they need to succeed in business beyond a certain level. When circumstances change, seemingly for the better, they receive that change gladly, like the Trojans received the Greeks' "gift." But they have no idea what waits for them inside.

My name's Dean. The two things I do best are improve companies and change people's lives. But I'll never forget the day I learned that my first business, which generated millions in top-line revenue at the time, had only $10,000 in the bank.

I felt like the only life changing was my own... and not for the better. It rang in my head like a bell:

I don't know what went wrong...
I don't know who to talk to...
I can't decide which way to go to fix it!

If you've ever run a business, you'll find this easy to imagine. In the room sat my wife, an MBA and CPA; David, a friend and fellow business owner; George, the controller I'd hired to dig into our numbers; a counselor friend; and me. The account had an approximate starting balance of around $250,000. I knew it had gone down, but after a while, I felt shocked to discover how low it went. Our sales were great! How could we possibly lose that much cash?

When I bought the company, I knew I could lead it. I was in my late thirties, and I had work and management experience in several industries. I'd been an auto mechanic, a machinist/journeyman, an electrician, a plumber, and a carpenter. Then I moved into the world of technology: software development and corporate IT. I soaked up a ton of training in philosophies like Six Sigma, LEAN Manufacturing, Project Management, and human psychology. I got promoted into positions of management, then eventually leadership. We later purchased a manufacturing company. Three years after I took over the business, the Rockford Chamber of Commerce voted me Manufacturer of the Year. Personally, I was happily married for fifteen years and raising two sons. Life seemed... *great*.

When I first took over, everything went mostly... good! We improved efficiency and productivity, and sales increased. If you've owned a business, you know—when things go well, you get the credit, and when things go poorly, you get the blame. I enjoyed the success, but couldn't shake the unease I felt about our cash situation. We had just moved the business to a new facility so there were a lot of outstanding expenses that were not accounted for, yet. I needed outside eyes because I couldn't figure out where the money was going. If you ever meet me or follow my content online, you'll hear me say this repeatedly (and you'll read it several times in this book)...

The hardest question for business leaders to answer is this:

**WHAT'S THE
REAL PROBLEM?**

Most of the time, when I talk to leaders, they confuse the real problem with surface issues. "My company bleeding cash" was the *symptom* of the problem. But that's like a mechanic diagnosing a stalled vehicle as "engine failure." Some cars stall because they simply run out of gas! We're accountable to watch the details closer than anyone else and figure out the issues when something doesn't work. But before we can get to that, we have mindset problems of our own that need to change.

I listened as the controller talked about the problems in the company's finances. We were losing money on some parts we ordered regularly. Elsewhere, our prices were too low. That meant the revenue those products generated resulted in dishing out the employee payroll from a break-even financial position. You can't run a company on fumes like that.

I kept it together, but I had too much personal and professional pressure. The straw that broke the camel's back was the sound of my wife crying in the background. She had seen the bank account get lower every month and felt the pressure, too, but she couldn't solve the problem. I had no answers for what had gone wrong and no escape from accountability. Watching my wife cry due to financial stress in the business struck me like nothing else.

I'm thankful David was in the room that day. As a fellow business owner and friend, he threw me a lifeline when he said, "Dean, don't panic. I've been in your shoes. I've nearly gone broke five times in twenty years of owning my business."

David's intervention didn't solve the issue or relieve my stress... but at least I knew I wasn't the first (or only) business owner to go through something like this. His words stopped me from losing perspective and going into complete freefall. I respected David; he seemed to have his life much more put-together than I did. From the way he spoke, I sensed he was telling me about my future.

Looking back today, as the owner of several multimillion-dollar companies... I *know* David predicted my future.

I can also, now, name the real problem in that company. At the time, I *thought* it was the general manager, who'd worked there for twenty-five years. He was toxic toward the staff and hostile to my plans for the business. We discovered that he'd sabotaged the company at a cost of over $250,000 in two years. If I'd known then what I know now, I'd have caught it and fired him immediately. No doubt, that manager was a contributing factor.

Unfortunately, I had bigger problems than a lousy GM. The business' crisis unleashed chaos elsewhere in my life. Due to old family trauma and financial stress, my marriage ended. Overnight, my entire personal social circle and business network evaporated, leaving me completely alone and isolated. I looked around for someone to blame, but I couldn't find *anyone*. I could barely find any person to talk to about anything!

The only one I still had... was myself. As I look back, I realize the real problem was *the man in the mirror*. That general manager was a jerk... but *I* failed to fire him when it could have helped. I feared of the impact to the business and how the rest of the team would react.

I've coached and mentored enough business leaders to know that no matter what happens, when you're the captain of the ship, you can't blame others for your failure to act. You can't even blame them completely for *their* failures. If you're willing to tolerate bad behavior from a general manager... you shouldn't blame them for behaving badly! As long as they're on your payroll, you're accountable for what they do.

I didn't think I could tell anyone about any of this at the time. I thought I had to keep my fears to myself and keep absorbing the sabotage from a man below me on the hierarchy. I paid a huge price for bottling up my emotions and fears. I had to walk around my company every day, acting like I had things under control, and it took a toll on my mental health.

If I've noticed one thing in all my years in business, it's that *no one* ever asks the leader, "How are you doing?" They assume, because you're the leader, you must be doing fine. It creates a vicious loop for leaders: you think you have to bottle everything up, because no one cares... and it turns out, from people's everyday behavior, that you're right! They don't care. You have to care for yourself, because no one else will.

It might sound crazy, but after considering the situation years later, I see how that time of my life turned out to be one of the best things that ever happened to me. With everything stripped away, I made a radical decision: I was finished with the "matrix" of my old life and ready to do whatever it took to rise from the ashes. I went through a multi-year transformation where I rearranged *everything* about how I think, speak, and act. I emerged a very different man. That hard season should have been enough to send me off the ledge. Instead, it turned into a rebirth—a life and career of success beyond anything I could imagine. I'm finally free to be the business owner and leader I'm supposed to be.

Chances are, you picked up this book because you want or need your business to change and grow. Maybe you've spun into chaos like I did, and you don't know where to turn. Or maybe you're doing "good, not great," and you have no idea how to move forward. It doesn't matter. Wherever you are, right now, I want to be for you what David was for me. I'll tell you just as he once told me: "I've been where you are!"

You, too, have the power to change how you think, speak, and act. You can also help the people you lead to change. But the big question throughout this book is this: **"Are you ready for change?"** Some people are not; they want to put a Band-Aid™ over their problems and keep running, hoping the problems will fix themselves. They're fixated on the sparkle of the Trojan Horse, and they haven't figured out that enemy forces hide within.

I'm going to show you how true change takes place in this book. I'll share how I did it—not once, not twice, or even three times. I've done numerous acquisitions and business turnarounds for many years. I excel at changing cultures and making businesses profitable and prosperous, and though I'm paid well for it, I've discovered a purpose far greater than financial reward.

I do what I do to help fellow business leaders. Too many owners and managers start their journey without clear roadmaps on how to build successful companies. You can take *Trojan Horse* as your blueprint, your roadmap. It's tested, proven, and timeless. It works every time.

Too many leaders get stuck, going in circles, because they read books about high-level business theory without task-driven guidance. *Trojan Horse* has an entire second half dedicated to the step-by-step process I've used at every company I've bought and turned around.

Too many leaders crash and burn under the weight of roles and responsibilities they're not equipped to handle. Most of them feel completely alone, watching their dreams die because they don't have anyone they can talk to. You will find solace in the pages of *Trojan Horse*, and you are welcome to reach out to me as well.

I also do what I do because of the people who come into my office and hug me, or who cry as they share personal struggles, or who put up Post-It™ notes around the office that read "WWDD?" ("What Would Dean Do?"). I never told them to do it, and they never asked my opinion. But if you've stood in an office like I did on that day and survived, you'll be surprised at what you can handle. You'll be amazed at what you can create, and that you can inspire others to follow. In *Trojan Horse*, you'll hear plenty from me. But some of my key employees chimed in as well, to give you up-close and personal accounts of working at our companies. You'll feel the difference.

Let me help you, too. I didn't gain all this experience and knowledge to keep to myself. Life is about sharing good things we learn and helping people dodge bullets we took along the way. When I consider my experience, it gives me hope for you, the reader. If a guy like me can overcome all of that and become successful as well as significant… I believe you can, too.

So let's look forward to change. Are you ready?

Dean Svarc

Part One - Prerequisites

Chapter One

Are YOU Ready for Change?
Part 1

"Human beings solve zero percent of
problems they don't think they have."
Unknown

O ver the last decade, American TV audiences enjoyed the series
"Undercover Boss," where owners and managers at large
companies go "undercover" as entry-level employees followed around
by camera crews.

I don't watch much TV, but I found the concept interesting for real-life
application. While most critics saw the show as a glimpse into the
lives of the working class, I saw something different: a made-for-TV
opportunity that compels business leaders to identify and address
problems in their organizations at a granular level.

To do this, they assume an alias and a fictional backstory. "Hi, I'm
Mike," they might say. "I just quit my last job because they cut my

hours." Older leaders might tell co-workers that they had a hard time finding a job because of ageism, and took the job to participate in a competition series aimed at retirement-aged workers.

Producers also developed explanations for the presence of the camera crew. The undercover bosses would tell co-workers, "I took this job because they said they wanted to film me in a documentary for training purposes. I thought it would be interesting to have a job where someone followed me around with a camera all day."

This is funny to me because of what I do—and more importantly, how I do it. Business leadership is complicated because leaders make it complicated. When the only way they can find out what's wrong with their companies is by going undercover and posing as an employee, you know it's time to hit the "refresh" button.

That's why I decided to name this book *Trojan Horse*. It'd be great if every leader could take a turn as an undercover boss on a reality TV series, but that's not going to happen. The good news, however, is that you don't need to be on TV. You can become your own Trojan Horse without adopting a phony name or backstory. A camera crew would be nice... but you can document what you do without one. For our purposes, a pen and paper work well enough.

At the same time, the person you become will be different from the person you currently are. So in one sense, your new identity will catch your employees, customers, vendors, and shareholders by surprise. They'll recognize your face... but the way you communicate and show up at work becomes different—*radically* different. Like the leaders on *Undercover Boss*, you will take on an alternate (upgraded) identity. You'll also imitate the TV show by documenting everything you do, which departs from how most leaders run their businesses.

A majority of business owners and managers stay safely in the audience of a show like *Undercover Boss*. This is where *Trojan Horse* will challenge and reward you. Ironically, changing (improving) your identity and documenting it from start to finish is how you move away from the crowd of spectators and into the arena where you face the music. You gain experience and confidence that most of your peers don't know they need. I'm fond of President Theodore Roosevelt's famous quote:

> *It is not the critic who counts; not the man who points out how the strong man stumbles, or where the doer of deeds could have done better. The credit belongs to the man who is actually in the arena, whose face is marred by dust and sweat and blood, who strives valiantly, who errs and comes up short again and again, because there is no effort without error or shortcoming, but who knows the great enthusiasms, the great devotions, who spends himself in a worthy cause; who, at best, knows, in the end, the triumph of high achievement, and who, at the worst, if he fails, at least he fails while daring greatly, so that his place shall never be with those cold and timid souls who know neither victory nor defeat.*

I believe most owners and managers on this planet live and work like **spectators** when it comes to growing and maturing their companies. They stay safely on the surface of issues and try to solve them without understanding them. They fail to invest in themselves or their teams, which makes them weak when things go wrong. If you want to know whether you're ready for change, a good place to start is to ask yourself if *you* live like a spectator. I lived that way for a long time, both at work and at home. Ironically, it was the biggest roadblock to the change I needed to make.

Spectators exist at every level, including leadership. You don't escape the trap just because you have a corner office. It just looks different for a CEO than for a janitor. Spectators exist on a spectrum. They function well in some areas, just like sports fans have jobs and own businesses. But get them onto the field or the court, in zones where they lack competence, and they become ineffective and incapable of learning. They become their own worst enemies.

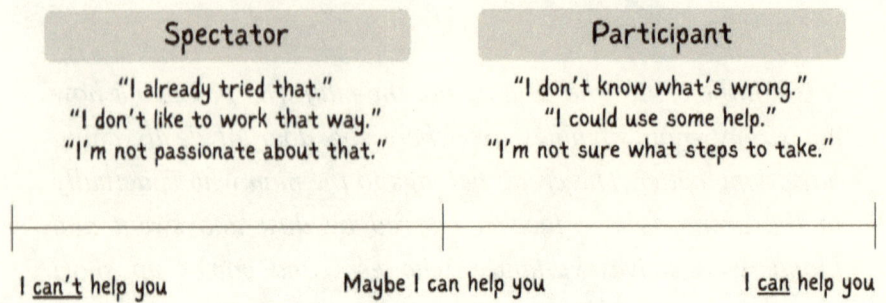

The Spectrum of Business Owners

Spectator	Participant
"I already tried that."	"I don't know what's wrong."
"I don't like to work that way."	"I could use some help."
"I'm not passionate about that."	"I'm not sure what steps to take."

I *can't* help you   Maybe I can help you   I *can* help you

Different Kinds of Spectator Leaders

On one end of the spectrum, spectator leaders have "all the answers." Like an armchair quarterback, they talk in circles—they say a lot and accomplish very little. I sense this quickly when I meet them by how they answer my questions:

Owner: "My business is not doing well."
Me: "Have you tried [XYZ]?"
Owner: "Oh, yeah, we already tried that and it didn't work."

Do you know people like this? Does it describe you? If you answer "Yes," I can tell you're not ready for change. You've done it all, tried it all, and know it all. We can't even discuss the problems in your business because *you are the problem* and can't admit it. We will never find enough time to have heavy conversations, get your buy-in, reshape your entire mindset, *and* rescue the company.

When things go bad, spectators blame everyone but themselves—vendors, customers, employees, the economy, taxes, regulations, overseas wars... you name it. They reject any outside perspective. It's (sadly) funny because if they could admit they don't know everything, you could hold them accountable and help them change. But spectators run away from accountability. In the end, they sound like a narcissistic divorcee whose memory of their divorce gets worse every time they tell it. They go from having "a few bad years" in their marriage to having "no good years at all."

I once purchased a tool company from a woman who knew *everything*. She inherited the business from her late parents. It didn't take long to figure out no matter who she dealt with, she fixated on drama at the expense of facts. She answered every question I asked her with complaints about other people's personalities and temperaments:

"Oh, that guy's a jerk!"
"They just cheated us."
"They're just difficult to deal with."

Her attitude told me what I needed to know. I could tell there was more to the story. I dug into the financials and receivables and discovered that the guy she labeled a "jerk" never got paid for his services. The people she derided as "cheaters" insisted on cash-on-delivery because otherwise she'd make them wait forever to pay her bill. The "difficult to deal with" company refused to accommodate her immature interpersonal style. She lacked the skill set to own or lead a business, and it showed. The most important quality any business leader can have is the ability to grow and improve themselves and how they interact with the world around them.

Another company where I worked had unionized employees. The union leaders hated the management, and vice versa. I disagree with the idea of hating a group of people you've never tried to work with, but as I dug in to change the company culture, I saw the same excuses emerge: "We've tried working with them, and they're just difficult." It wasn't true! I was there for a year and a half, and the union never filed a single grievance while I managed operations. All it took was *not being a jerk* from the start.

But you can be a nice person and still make bad decisions. I bought a manufacturing company from a very nice couple who made the mistake of hiring the wife's brother to work there. The husband was kind and pleasant to a fault, but he was terrified of firing his brother-in-law because of what might happen to his relationship with his wife. When I took over, the husband tried to dump the responsibility of firing the brother-in-law onto me. He said, "Dean, you gotta fire him right away. He's nothing but a problem. He's going to hurt you, I promise." So much for being a "nice" guy!

When I asked him why he hadn't pulled the trigger for all those years, he said, "Well, you know, it's my wife, and my wife's brother…"

Spectators prioritize emotions over logic and are not ready for change. There's no place for you, as captain of the ship, to let emotions drive your decisions. If you can't tell the difference between feelings and facts or control your own impulses, change will not work for you.

When I say "emotions," don't think only of the obvious ones, like anger or fear. Indifference is an emotional message, too. You can send very clear messages to employees, customers, and anyone you care about through **indifference**.

There are two kinds of indifferent leaders in business: the ones who run a company as it declines, and the ones who run it into the ground because they just don't know how to run a business.

Declining or stalled companies usually have an aging leader who got used to running his business a certain way. He's made his money, and he's happy with how things operate. As time passes, profits begin to go down, but he doesn't make any changes. Technology and delivery methods improve, but he prevents his company from keeping up with the times. In manufacturing, that's like insisting a team use manual machines long after the invention of CNC (computer numerical control) machines. He might have a great team of employees, but they'll never go as fast as a competitor with superior technology.

Inefficiency grows while profits continue to shrink. He can only raise prices so much before his customers give up and turn to his competitors... who can get the job done faster and cheaper. Then comes the day he has to lay off employees. They've been loyal for years, and he treated them well... but he can't afford to keep them. What changed? Everyone's doing the same thing they've always done. The truth is he, the owner, refused to keep up with change because he's afraid of it. If you dug deep enough into his story, you'd find that he craves stability and consistency because of a wild and chaotic early career or childhood. To this leader, the idea of changing anything feels extremely scary.

But his employees don't care, as he lays them off one by one. Do you think they'll accept the excuse that he feared change? Do you think they care about his difficult career or childhood? Not a chance!

Other owners and managers run their businesses into the ground because they have no clue what they're doing. Some businesses die because leaders put all their eggs in one basket. For instance, say a dealership stocks most of its product from one major manufacturer and suddenly, that manufacturer pulls out of the area. The leadership says, "We stock ninety percent John Deere tractors because they're the best and everybody uses them!" Uh... no! People don't buy John Deere if John Deere doesn't have service or support within one hundred miles!

Other instances include family-owned companies where the parents leave the business to their kids—who did nothing to make the business work (or they work there, but they don't really have any interest in it). "It's our legacy, what we leave behind for our kids," say these parents.

No! It's not "legacy" if your kids don't want or don't know what to do with it, and they only see it as a piggy bank! These parents are indifferent to *reality*. Reality deals in facts, not feelings.

Then you have leaders who get into business because they have a passion about something for its own sake. They do what they do for themselves, rather than what's right for a business. They start a flower shop and spend hours making the perfect arrangements… but they don't know how to market themselves, so they lose money and go out of business. Or they start a bakery where they make the most delicious cookies, the same ones they enjoy at home… but nobody buys them. These people ignore market demands because they're caught up in their own ideas of value, worthiness, or interest. They run on feelings, but in the math behind the business, feelings don't matter.

Sometimes, the market doesn't want John Deere or homemade cookies. It might want Caterpillar and Mrs. Fields! If you prefer the first options but no one else does, buy them for yourself and use them on your own time!

Don't offer what you *think* is right;
offer what the market <u>wants</u>.

If 90 percent of my customers at my box company tell me they want a blue box… guess what we're making? Blue boxes! You can learn what the market actually wants if you're willing to ask. You might have a great degree of self-awareness as an owner or manager. But the next level of self-awareness is to risk learning what people really want from you and how they perceive you.

The worst kind of leader, however, pays for advice so they can resist it anyway. If you pay me to consult for you, and I show you what's wrong and how to fix it, the one thing you should *not* say is:

"Well, I don't work like that. I like to work this way."

If that's how you respond to good advice, you're definitely not ready for change. The problem is obvious: *your way isn't working or you don't know your way isn't working!* Nobody cares how you like to work. Not your spouse, kids, employees, customers… nobody. Your only concern should be whether you do the right thing for your company. You're the only person who can care enough to do it!

On the other end of the spectrum, some owners can admit they *don't* have all the answers. The closer you are to this mindset, the greater your chance of survival and growth. Pay attention to some of the differences, however. For example, you can be:

- A leader who has absolutely *no* idea what went wrong.
- A leader who knows something's wrong, but has no idea how *badly* it's damaged them.
- A leader who knows something's wrong, but isn't sure which steps to take to fix it or what order to follow.

If you see yourself in these examples, I can help.

But before we go on, beware:

If you accept accountability for problems in your business, be prepared to do it for everything else in your life.

You don't get to pick and choose between business and personal problems; one ties directly to the other. Just as you don't shed difficulties in your personal life by walking through the doors of your office, work doesn't stay "at work" when you get home to your family. So be ready for change at *every* level.

You Don't Need a Band-Aid™

During long winters in Illinois, I used to enjoy snowmobiling in my spare time. Sometimes, it gets dangerous, and you can get hurt. Blood and pain don't bother me much. I've taken a few bad turns and falls, and I've stitched and bandaged myself up in freezing cold weather. It goes with the territory of high-speed fun on slippery surfaces like snow and ice. Most of the cuts I take are small enough that a simple Band-Aid™ does the trick.

But you shouldn't put a Band-Aid™ on *internal* bleeding. If you have that problem, you need to see a doctor immediately. Internal bleeding usually means something is seriously wrong. It's often caused by severe trauma, a disease like hemophilia, or complications from surgery. The strange thing about internal bleeding is that outwardly, you can look completely normal... but on the inside, you're on a fast track to life-threatening conditions—or even death.

Business problems are like internal bleeding. They give off pain signals the same way the body does when you're in trouble. You can trigger them by severe external traumas like economic downturns or disruptions like pandemics. But most business problems are more like hemophilia or complications from surgery. Bad employees and cultural dysfunction chip away at the inside of your company, just like diseases. Leaders operate surgically... on the wrong areas, and they only make problems worse.

Take an example of two employees who have some kind of disagreement, to the point that they disrupt work for each other and the rest of the team. They hurt morale, and they slow down production and efficiency for the company. Would you like to guess what most owners and managers do when situations like this arise?

If you guessed "they separate the employees," you are correct. Most leaders think the best way to deal with conflict between employees is to put physical distance between them. In the heat of the moment, that might break up a shouting match or keep things quiet... but it doesn't solve the problem. People aren't objects. You don't fix conflict by simply moving to a different room! That's an example of how leaders try to put a Band-Aid™ over problems that run much deeper than the surface.

Many leaders in my industry struggle with this. They rise through the ranks as an electrician, plumber, mechanic, or machinist. The easiest way to stop objects from malfunctioning is to switch them off or stop using them. Typically, owners and managers in manufacturing and the skilled trades have below-average skills for managing people. They start out on their own, get busier over time, and eventually hire people to work for them. But if you lack the soft skills to deal with and understand people, watch out! The bigger your company gets, the more people you need to hire... and the more people you hire, the more conflict you'll face.

Here's another example of the Band-Aid™ mentality: leaders' reactions to workplace accidents. Let's say an employee, Joe Schmoe, backs up a company truck, hits a pole, and damages the door. How do you think most leaders respond?

If you guessed, "They ask one or two simple questions, tell the employee to 'Take it easy,' and then walk away," you're correct.

Of course, it's better to keep calm than scream and yell. I'll give them that. But keeping calm alone doesn't solve the problem. Say the leader asks the employee, "What happened?" and the employee gives a truthful answer, like "I wasn't paying attention." If that's the end of the matter... the problem remains unsolved. Don't be surprised when a week or two goes by and Joe Schmoe causes more damage and accidents. If it becomes enough of a recurring problem, you're forced to take action by writing up, and eventually terminating, a good employee because his boss failed to dig deep and find the *real* problem. There could be a systemic issue, such as a lack of proper training or procedures.

But more likely, Joe Schmoe failed to pay attention because he's stressed at home, stressed at work, or something is affecting his ability to concentrate. When things like this happen, the *leader* has the responsibility of asking probing questions and finding the root of the problem. But most leaders are out to lunch, and that's sad because they have a powerful tool at their disposal: their own vulnerability.

Be Vulnerable

Vulnerability seems uncomfortable—until you do it the right way. Don't picture crying at meetings or turning your workplace into a group therapy session. Vulnerability involves showing your employees that you're a human being just like them. Yes, you have strengths, and you're the leader… but you also have weaknesses, and you have more in common with them than they think. You show the team that you're there for more than money, and that even though your life might *appear* perfect… it's not.

Don't turn vulnerability into a formal process. I usually do it in one-on-one settings, and I'll share something about myself that the employee doesn't know. I want to find out how they've been treated in the past because I'm rarely their first boss. I'll talk about some of the jobs I used to have and emphasize the ones where I had toxic bosses or co-workers. Then I'll ask, "What about you? Did you have lousy bosses or co-workers at your old job?" With some of the companies I've bought, I already know the answer because I meet the previous owners—but I ask the employees anyway. I want them to know that they're moving into an environment of safety.

I'm always amazed at how well people respond to this, and it unlocks deeper connection with them. If an employee says, "The previous owner screamed and yelled in my face," or "I wasn't appreciated at my last job," I start digging. "'Not appreciated'?" I ask. "What do you mean?" Then they'll go on to tell me how their bosses and co-workers made fun of them or treated them inappropriately. Now I know a little more about what drives that employee; I know that they expect to be treated poorly. It tells me what to look out for and what I may have to address. If I do it successfully, I know I'll get an employee for life.

Another way you can do this is to share personal stories. I'm not saying you need to get into the weeds, but you can show people that you have your own problems. As I get to know my employees, I'll usually share, at some point, how my marriage ended in divorce. Just take a look around your office or factory. If there are people working there, you can bet your bottom dollar they have personal problems they're dealing with, on top of working forty or more hours a week for you. Wouldn't you want to make work a place where they feel safe if their personal lives aren't going so well?

Vulnerability will give you more insight into your employees than any amount of money could buy. You'll form a bond of sincere trust and care with them, which they want from you even more than their paycheck. Remember—we're not talking about whining or complaining, or disclosing to your team that you're feeling bad about yourself. But sharing stories from your past that dovetail with what people are going through makes you more relatable and less like a machine to them.

The Way You Treat People

How you treat people matters. Write that down, because it sets limits on their ability and willingness to work with you toward a vision of success.

I once got a job working at a machine shop for a manager who berated me nonstop the entire time I worked there. But a woman who worked in the assembly department, Tamika Brown, was a friend and treated me kindly. She was awesome. After a few years, she caught me off-guard one day when she said, "You know, Dean, you're not who you were when you started working here."

"Really?" I asked. (I felt fine.) "What do you mean?"

"You aren't as confident as you were when you started," she said.

The light went on for me. The constant put-downs from my manager had knocked my confidence down a few notches, even though I'd acquired a lot of experience. This is the number one way leaders fail employees—putting people down and mistreating them. The more poorly you treat people, the lower expectations they have for their success and future at your company. It sounds obvious… but you'd be surprised how many owners and managers feel entitled to speak to their employees with a negative or abusive tone.

This is what happened in my role at the company with the labor union, a gear box manufacturer. The management team simply had a bad attitude about the workers. They thought the employees were a bunch of "idiots" who focused on stealing from the company. The president, I soon learned, had risen through his career as a sales manager. You'd think he would have good people skills, with a sales background… but plenty of salespeople don't. He was arrogant and inconsiderate. By the time I got there, they'd stopped even trying to resolve simple issues, like employees showing up late. They didn't bother to talk to the employee or the union leaders; they simply wrote the employee up, and then the union would react by filing a grievance.

Abusive leaders lack "soft" skills (like communication and empathy) because they get their start with "hard" skills (like math or engineering). They start their companies by mastering a trade and eventually get too busy to work alone. Demand for skills with making toilets or wiring homes means you excel with *things*… but not necessarily with *people*. You can't truly learn business or project management in trade school or college; you have to learn on the job. So even if you make toilets really well… you're in trouble if you talk down to your staff or belittle them. You'll face severe obstacles if you refuse to train them or take time to learn about their lives.

Others short-circuit their potential by silence or by acting pleasantly indifferent to employees' performance. Instead of being loud, obnoxious, or degrading… they stay quiet and reserved. They never say anything, one way or the other, to employees. In some ways, this is worse than being a loud tyrant. At least you know where you stand with a tyrant, but with super-calm and laid-back employers, you never know where you stand. One of my employees, Melissa, described her previous job this way:

> *We were put in a box, and that's where we stayed, so I didn't really grow in any area of life. They were a large, well-known company with high standards, but their annual reviews felt like a chit-chat session because I liked my boss, and my boss liked me. There was no feedback or constructive criticism on how I could improve. They would promote me because they liked me, but it was based more on politics than performance. They expected me to think on my own; if there was progress, they said, "Great!" and if it stayed the same, they'd say, "Well, at least it didn't go down."*

So you can be a kind and gentle person… while still being far less of a boss than your employees deserve. Neither "loud" nor "quiet" will build strong bonds between you and the people who work for your company. Although there are exceptions, most employees quit because of *lousy management* rather than pay or amenities. Just because they *say* they found a higher-paying job doesn't mean they're only motivated by money.

"But Dean," you say, "I'm not a loudmouth, and I'm not quiet either! I'm nice, and I want to perform and do well, but my people are still quitting!"

Okay… re-read what I said about being a spectator and the dangers of indifference. Your behavior tells me what you really care about, 100 percent of the time. You might be a very nice person to work for… *who hasn't got a clue about what the market wants*, so you offer cookies when they want pizza. You might be a laid-back employer who loves to chew the fat… *who also manages a company in decline*, which makes your competitors look more appealing as potential employers. Do you see how being "nice" doesn't cut it? You can be a poor leader without being rude or unpleasant. This world has plenty of kind, pleasant people; not all of them are cut out to lead companies through meaningful change.

Here's something to remember about employees: unless you're hiring a teenager for their first job, **you aren't their first boss**. Maybe that sounds obvious, but you'd be amazed how many leaders act like their employees have no prior work history. Here's what I mean:

After I left that machine shop with the abusive manager, I found a new job with a new boss. Unfortunately for the new boss, he had to deal with a different Dean—one who was beaten down a little. Should this be any different for your employees? You don't truly know who you're hiring. A lot of employees bring trauma from previous bosses into their new jobs, and just like me in the years before my transformation, they have something to prove.

As leaders, we need to change the game:
from proving to *im*-proving.

Be humane, even if you've got one thousand employees. Walk the floor, and treat your people like you would treat a group of friends or relatives. It matters.

"Proving" versus "Improving"

I've sold a few of the companies I've owned over the years. When I sold the first one, I wept. It was the classic owner's case where the company was "my baby," and I'd put my heart, soul, blood, sweat, and tears into it. It was hard to let go. Somehow, that company was supposed to act as "proof" of my value and goodness… even though it never really did.

When I went through my transformation, I left my old social circles and went through a period that looked (to some) like isolation, depression, withdrawal, or a midlife crisis. (*Funny how people's perceptions clash with reality.*) As I went, I learned to walk away from proving myself. I focused instead on *improving* myself. Have you heard the saying, "The journey *is* the destination"? That's the kind of shift I went through. I learned that by constantly improving myself, I could truly focus on the business instead of focusing on my insecurities. I could genuinely care for employees, make them a priority, and build strong bonds with them. My business grew much faster once I made that decision. When you walk consistently down the path of self-improvement, your business has to grow with you. It's a reflection of you, just like your shadow on a sunny day.

But don't be fooled: growth is not easy—or painless.

The Way of the Eagle

There is a story about eagles when they reach the midway point of their lives. As they age, eagles' talons and beaks become dull, which makes it more difficult to capture and eat their prey. So they face a choice: they can let the progression happen and die within 1-2 years. Or they can retreat to high mountain country, where they are less susceptible to predators, and slowly pluck out their own talons and feathers with their dulled beaks. Once they finish with the talons and feathers, they smash their beaks against rocks, until the beaks are completely broken off.

Then, miraculously, the birds grow new beaks, talons, and feathers. It's as if they get a new lease on life and exchange a slow death for a lifespan that can last as long as thirty more years. Do you see the parallel to human transformation? It's like what happens to us, as business leaders. It's exactly what happened to me, when my life crashed and burned. If you never break your beak, pull out the talons, toss the old feathers, and get "reborn" at least once in your life… you'll die. But a painful transformation can make you soar higher than you ever thought possible.

I've learned four magic words:
"Pain is my friend."

Even today, the purchase of a new company carries huge consequences. I sense a ton of uncertainty every time I do it, because I don't yet know what the real problem is. Worse—I *choose* this fear and uncertainty purposefully. I don't "need" another business. I don't need the stress, work, or even the financial rewards and excitement that come at the end of B.A.S.I.C.S. I do what I do because of the *people* in the company, and I welcome the pain and unease it brings.

To become the kind of leader you're capable of being, you need to reach a place where you feel the same way: the pain and struggle are not only worth it but *good* for you. They teach you in a way you never forget. Be like the eagle, and learn to soar.

The Right Voices Lead to the Right Choices

You're ready for change when you start to question the company you keep in your spare time. Before my transformation, I was open to advice from people I had no business listening to, whose lives I wouldn't want to live. When you're ready for change, you build a healthy distance between yourself and people you've listened to in the past. The sad part is that most of these people are average, decent ones. They might even be members of your family or friends you've had for a long time.

Don't get me wrong—we're not talking about cutting people off or telling them to get lost. Instead, you have to understand the value of your time. Every time you screw around by listening to someone who can't help you, it's like spending that time drinking alcohol, doing drugs, or binging on movies and TV.

I've had people object to this. "But Dean!" they protest, "I want to enjoy my life!"

You will always be able to "enjoy life." If you truly want to spend your time listening to people who can't help you, be my guest. Just understand: every time you say "Yes" to one thing, you say "No" to something else. Do you want to enjoy life? Then enjoy it… but don't expect to be successful. Do you want to be successful? Then become successful… but don't expect to do what the average person calls "enjoying life."

Do I sound like someone who doesn't enjoy his life? Pursuing success means doing *everything* you'd rather not do. Sure, there are many things I'd rather not do, and I do them anyway… but that doesn't mean my life sucks! Maybe snowmobiling across fresh powder on a beautiful winter morning sounds "boring" to you. Maybe you think I grit my teeth and groan when I book my family on a getaway trip to Europe or take my boat out with friends and family. All I can say is, "Don't bet on it."

The funny part is, if you're prepared to put in two to three years of doing the really hard work… you get to do both: hard stuff and enjoying life.

For the record, I was never lazy, nor a drinker/smoker/partier (except in my younger years), even before my transformation. I've always been a hard worker and a professional. But I'll admit: I spent a lot of time watching TV and movies, found plenty of distractions, and listened to a ton of bad advice. That's what people do when they don't know the value of their time.

I thought I was obligated to listen to friends, neighbors, and family... even if they didn't have a clue what they were talking about. I'd think, "Well, ya know, it's Uncle Ed, so just let it go..."

NO! I don't care how well-meaning Uncle Ed is. I'm only interested in his opinion if I can look at his life and say, "Someday, that's how I want to live." Respect yourself enough to look honestly at how Uncle Ed lives and say, "This is not acceptable in my eyes."

When you're ready for change, you become more discerning about who gets your attention.
The right voices lead to the right choices.

The first signs you're ready for change take place internally with how you think. You're ready for change if:

- You can admit **you don't know** what your problem is, how much damage it causes, or what to do about it.
- You're willing to **ask the people you lead** about their perspective on the problem(s)
- You're tired of putting **Band-Aids™** on bone-deep cuts and diseases in your business
- You care about **treating people well,** and you recognize that you're not their first boss
- You're tired of trying to "prove" yourself, and you'd rather focus on **improving** yourself
- You're willing to do **painful, solitary work,** like an eagle, to extend your lifespan and regain your effectiveness

- You're willing to **walk away from the voices you've listened to** and seek advice and guidance from people whose lives you truly want to live

In the next chapter, we're going to get more into the brass tacks of change—practical and habitual moves you can take *right away* to set a new course for yourself and your business.

Chapter Two

Are YOU Ready for Change?
Part 2

"Thinking will not overcome fear, but action will."
W. Clement Stone

W ithout concrete action, there's no change. You'd think that would be obvious, but you'd be surprised how many people back away when it's time to get to work. I'm different because I've learned to go full-bore into the deep work it takes to effect change.

Act Now to Combat Stress

I hate business books that stay up in the clouds, talk in circles about theory, and never give readers concrete actions they can take immediately. We're going straight to work in this book! I assume you've read Chapter One, you're ready to improve, or maybe you're under some stress, and you wonder what you can do *right now*. So here's your action blueprint.

Resolving stress is like sorting between your Circle of Influence and Circle of Concern, if you're familiar with Stephen Covey's concept in *The 7 Habits of Highly Effective People*. In the Circle of Influence, you focus on things truly within your control; everything else goes in the Circle of Concern. Even though the stress you deal with might affect you personally, you have to be honest about how much control you have over it. If you can't fix something straight away, you have to release it, so you can think and focus. Otherwise, it'll eat you alive.

First, I want you to **write down everything that stresses you out**. Whether it's employee problems, low margins, supply chain issues, grouchy customers, lawsuits, or the never-ending mystery of marketing and sales… write it down. Get it on paper so it's all documented and accounted for. This will help you to take it off the forefront of your mind without forgetting about it completely. Now your mind is clearer, and has more capacity to think and make good decisions.

Next, you're going to write down a simple header phrase, a **one sentence** high-level summary of the issue, and then a couple of **bullet points** detailing the symptoms, impact, or examples of the problem. If you feel anxious, for example, you can write a few sentences about certain triggers to your anxiety. You might list the wrenching feeling in your gut every time your wife wants to talk about the family finances or the anger that wells up inside you when your children argue with each other.

You know how you write down your to-dos so you don't have to remember them? Stresses work the same way. Here's the trick:

Write down your stresses,
so you don't have to remember them.

Stress list

Not enough money
Hate the feast-famine cycle and stress about
customer payments.
- Billing is always late
- Can we travel for Christmas?
- Daughter needs braces
- Wife is feeling stressed: 3 conversations!

John's bad attitude
Is John bringing the whole team down? He's been
here a long time, but front office seems to have bad
blood with him.
- Rachel mentioned John's attitude
- He arrived late twice last week
- He's been leaving earlier than normal

Daughter's bad grades
Says she's studying, but grades are going down.
- Will she get into college?
- What changed at school?

When I went through my transformation, this became my habit. I'd write down stresses from the past that caused anxiety or concerns that made me worry about the future so I could live in the moment and focus on the present. I'd put them on a piece of paper and leave them next to my bed or attached to my desk, the walls, and the bathroom mirror. As I did this, I noticed I stopped thinking about my stress. The practical effect of writing it down pushed it to the back of my mind so I could focus. If you do this, you can expect your stress level to drop right away by at least 50 percent. It's like having your computer's cache memory wiped.

Once you take care of distant stresses, you can move on to more immediate concerns. Just remember the rule from Chapter One: "If it's not a problem one year from now, it's probably not a problem at all." The main reason you're stressed is fear of the unknown, and this usually shows up as either *depression* (the past) or *anxiety* (the future).

Have you ever been around a depressed person? **Depression** makes all of life and work miserable—for that person and others. What makes you think it's any different for the rest of the world if *you're* the one who's depressed? As Dennis Prager once said, "Happiness is a moral obligation." Nobody wants to be around you if you're moping around, whining, feeling sorry for yourself.

For depression, the solution is simple:
"GO. WORK. HARD."

Hard work. That's it. I've never met someone working sixty-to-seventy hours a week toward *their goals* who's depressed. I've never met someone working hard on fitness, marriage, or friendships who's depressed. I've worked hard all my life; I don't know what it's like to be depressed. I've been sad, even hurt... but not depressed. I'm not sure depression even truly exists. People who bust their tails on the most important things don't have time to be depressed. Make sure you're one of them.

You don't work hard to "run away" from problems. You work hard because sitting still and dwelling on problems only makes them worse. When you take action, you stem the tide of negativity in your mind, as well as in what you produce. Negativity grows automatically unless you fight back and do something positive and productive. So, if you want to avoid depression, get outside in your yard and pull weeds. Fix something, build something, or work on a sport or hobby. It builds confidence and self-worth—two essentials you'll need to tackle your real problems. You'll even feel it in the moment, because when you work hard at something, your brain releases positive chemicals like dopamine and endorphins.

Now, **anxiety** is a little different. Anxiety disrupts your focus by causing you to speculate about the future and where you lack knowledge or control over outcomes. Being around an anxious person, in some ways, is worse than being around a depressed one. (*At least* *depressed people are 100 percent certain their future will turn out poorly!*) Anxious people worry about the future going sideways, but they make it worse by trying to control it! They spend money they don't have. They spend hours and hours trying to research things they don't truly understand. They become paranoid and chase waterfalls, trying to prevent feared outcomes that likely won't happen in the first place.

Would *you* like to be around someone like that every day of your life? I doubt it... so don't do it to others! Worrying about the future is like trying to control your opponent when you're playing chess. Here's a little "pop quiz" to help keep you grounded and make one move at a time:

Q: Let's say you feel a pain in your chest, and you go to your doctor to get it checked out. Should you be stressed?

A: <u>NO</u>. You don't have enough information. Maybe you slept wrong. Maybe you're sore from a workout. Maybe the connection between your brain and heart is getting older, which causes an occasional irregular heartbeat.

Q: The doctor checks the X-rays and says, "We see something funny in your chest." Should you be stressed?

A: <u>NO</u>. Why? He hasn't told you what it is yet! He doesn't know, and you don't know, either. It could be indigestion, and all you need is to take some Tums™.

Q: Now the doctor says, "There's a mass in your chest." Should you be stressed out?

A: <u>NO</u>, because he hasn't told you what kind of mass it is. It could be fat mass, muscle mass, or Midnight Mass for all you know. The point is, *you don't know*. So you shouldn't be stressed.

Q: Now the doctor goes deeper and says, "It's cancerous." Should you be stressed? Will stress help your cancer?

A: <u>NO</u>. Stress will make your cancer worse. They haven't told you what kind of cancer it is.

(I'm not stupid… a cancer lump in your chest will stop you in your tracks. What I'm trying to do is offer a different mindset than the one most people use, because if you want to see change in yourself and your business, you're going to need a different mindset.)

Q: Now the doctor says, "It's Stage Four. You're a dead man walking." Should you be stressed?

A: <u>NO</u>. Why? Because if you're playing chess against anxiety about the future, the only thing you should focus on is *the next right move*. Maybe you can beat this cancer by changing your diet. Maybe you need surgery and chemotherapy. But the only thing you should care about is the next move.

Q: Now they tell you, "The treatment for this cancer is only available in Switzerland." You have to arrange travel and pay for the Swiss medical treatment, which costs $1 million. You don't have $1 million in cash or three months to spend in Switzerland. Should you be stressed?

A: <u>NO</u>, because you're focused on the next right move. It's a game of chess. You need to choose the next best move, even if you're losing.

Maybe the next right move is to find a better price on an earlier date. Maybe you can find dirt-cheap red-eye flights and hostels that let you stay for $20 a day. Maybe you have to beg, borrow, and steal… but you *find a way*, because you only get one life.

Find the Problem … the REAL Problem

If you really had to live through chest pains and Swiss hospitals, that's the remedy: *find the way*.

You find the way because you are the main participant in the one life you have. You're not a spectator. Spectators sit in the stands and wonder why their teams fall apart. They get on the TV sports talk shows and spew nonsense about why teams' strategies fail. Spectators babble endlessly about how they would do things better... but only *participants* stay in the fight and play to the whistle.

Still... let's be real: "the way" you must find rarely sticks out like a sore thumb. It hides behind illusions, dead ends, and false hopes. Believe it or not, this has something in common with the solutions you seek to your business problems. You can go through a thousand fixes; unless you know what the real problem is, none of it will pan out. As the leader, you're going to have to *dig*. Dig down deep, ask questions, and keep going until you get answers you can build on.

The **HARDEST** thing for business leaders to do
is to discover the real problem.

Every company has problems. There isn't a single one free of them. The biggest, wealthiest, most recognizable brand names you can think of have problems: Amazon, Google, Microsoft, Westinghouse, Caterpillar, Tyson Foods, Procter & Gamble, Ford Motor Company... they *all* have problems they can't solve. That's good news because you can be sure you're not singled out.

But where to start? Let's say your problem is financial. Do you spend too much money, or do you not earn enough income? Is someone embezzling from you? Do you have enough sales and recurring income streams?

Or does the issue lie with your team? Do you have the right insurance and benefits package? Do you have a good location? Is morale high, or is your company a terrible place to work?

Your problem might turn out to be embarrassing. It might make you look incompetent or immature. But denial is just as bad as incompetence and immaturity. You know the old saying, "Wherever you go, there you are"? You can't run from these problems because they all trace back to you as the leader. Your employees might be responsible for their roles and actions, but as the leader, you are *accountable* for them.

So what's Step #1 for finding the real problems? Three words:

> # Interview
> # Your
> # Employees

Ask them to answer you honestly about the problems they see, and make sure they understand there won't be any repercussions toward their jobs. In my field of work, it never fails: my employees know *all* the problems I can't see. We occupy huge buildings—tens of thousands of square feet. How could I possibly have eyes on every last inch of each one simultaneously? It makes perfect sense to let your employees be your "eyes and ears" for problems.

Make sure workers know you're not interrogating them or trying to turn them against one another. Tell them the interview will not threaten them or their job. I'll often say something like, "I'm interviewing you to improve the company and find problems. This has nothing to do with you. If you notice a co-worker doing something wrong and you tell me, I'm not going to expose you. I'm not even going to attack them. I just want to fix the problem."

What to Do With Your Opinion

Step #2 is to remember to ask, "**What are the facts?**" What you think or feel about someone or something is irrelevant. Let me give you a simple example:

Let's say an employee sees me wearing a baseball cap and says, "Nice hat."

Did he complement me, or was it an insult?

The only way to know for sure is to ask a follow-up question for confirmation: "You actually like this hat? Really?"

If the employee says, "Yes, I love it!" then I know he's being sincere. But if he says, "Nah, not really," I know he's being sarcastic.

So find out as many facts as you can before you make a judgment. If John Doe backed the truck into the wall last week and tore the door off its hinges, *don't leap to conclusions*. Don't say to yourself, "John was mad at me last week. I think he did it deliberately to get back at me." Find out what the facts are, and remember every time you think you know all the facts... there are more facts. You might have enough facts to make a judgment, but you never have all of them.

On the flipside, **don't listen to the self-critical voice** in your own head: "John was mad at me last week, and I deserved it because I'm incompetent. I deserved to have that truck damaged." That voice is your subconscious mind when it wanders off the reservation. It's there to protect you from getting hurt, but if you shift your focus from facts to emotions, the self-critical voice goes into overdrive.

Throughout my career, I've learned to avoid two things:

(a) jumping to conclusions, and

(b) apologizing early without knowing all the facts.

Eagles Fly Alone

Remember the lesson from the eagle about transformation? Well, there's another side to it: eagles are comfortable **being alone**.

I don't mean *physically* alone, like sitting in a room by yourself or living like a hermit in the desert. What I'm talking about is *standing alone*, when everyone around you disagrees with your decision and they're busy losing their minds. You have to know who you are and be comfortable with the blowback for decisions you make, things you say, and (especially) the times you have to fire people. I guarantee: you'll do it alone.

Back in the early 1980s, President Ronald Reagan blocked a deal between the United States, Western Europe, and the Soviet Union to build a natural gas line from Russia to the West. The Soviets liked the idea because it would give them a revenue stream and a foothold to continue menacing the West. The Europeans, including allies like France, Italy, Belgium, and the Netherlands (among other countries) liked the deal because they needed natural gas and the Russians promised them discounted prices.

Reagan's entire cabinet, the U.S. Congress, and the American manufacturing and engineering industries also liked it. The Soviets agreed to purchase significant amounts of American construction material, equipment, and manpower to do the job. It would have been beneficial to the U.S. economy, which was in a deep recession at the time.

Against all of these voices and forces, President Reagan stood alone and said, "No." He knew that if he agreed, the Soviets would enjoy decades of control, influence, and the ability to hold the Europeans hostage. He risked offending his voters, allies in Congress, loyal cabinet members, foreign allies, and an enemy armed with nuclear weapons. The media went crazy and attacked him for his decision, and the domestic recession continued.

But Reagan was comfortable being alone. The Soviets never got their pipeline. In fact… ten years later, their entire system collapsed.

Learn to be okay with being alone.
You will make unpopular, hard decisions
in your business.

Changing How You Communicate

You're ready for change when you change how you speak. People who grow constantly improve their communication with themselves and others. You'll hear someone phrase something differently than you typically do, and you'll think to yourself, "That's much better! I'm going to use that from now on." Or, more commonly, you'll hear those who make negative, sarcastic, or defeatist comments and you'll want to keep your distance.

One way I changed my speech patterns was to slow down and not interrupt people. My mind usually sees the big picture quickly, and it doesn't take me long to figure out what I want to do. This plays out great when I work alone, but if I need to work with others, I can go so fast that I outpace or confuse them. Personally, I don't need a lot of conversation. But if another person is five steps behind me, it pays to go slowly. As the leader in your business, and especially if you're a "hard-charging" personality, you'll be amazed what you can discover and accomplish if you're slow to speak and quick to listen. You'll also cover more details, more often—which leads to fewer mistakes.

Another way I learned to change the way I speak was to invite my team into the conversation and make them feel valued. The most successful people in the world get "buy-in" from the people they lead.

This doesn't come very naturally, if you have a commanding personality, but take it from me (a commanding personality)—this stuff works. I rarely dictate anything to anyone. Instead, I approach people and say, "Hey, here's something I'm thinking of doing. What do you think?" And then I shut up and listen.

The first few times I tried this, I felt surprised to discover how much interest and enthusiasm it created among my staff. When I seek buy-in from those I lead, several things happen:

- I raise others up and empower them
- I train people to think for themselves rather than depend on me
- I show them their opinions matter
- I also learned back in my consulting days to speak carefully, particularly if I'm dealing with people who don't necessarily work for me and whom I can't fire, such as independent contractors.

Daily Habits, Minute-by-Minute Actions

The events that led to my transformation took away my friends, associates, and lifestyle. So I found and created new ones. I figured that if I wanted to live a completely different life, I had to alter how I did most things. I changed my health habits, wardrobe, and relationships. I restructured my days. Previously, I listened to any and every opinion or idea that came along. Now, I decided, I would "brainwash myself" into becoming who I wanted to be.

To this day, I wake up around 5:00 every morning. I don't need an alarm; I just get up. I devote the first two hours of my day to preparing and reflecting on the man I have become. I leave my smartphone switched off, take vitamins, drink tea, and eat celery and carrots. I turn on the fireplace and sit quietly, writing the top ten things I'm thankful for in my journal. I listen to homemade, audio affirmations I record on my phone, and my personal vision for my life, and I write a paragraph or two about my goals. I read a chapter in a book, followed by fifteen minutes of studying Russian. Almost every day, I exercise. Finally, I examine my schedule and financial dashboards. *Then...* I'm ready to begin.

Your physical condition is important. You may have privacy in what goes on inside your head, but your team observes your health, movement, and body language. If you carry extra weight, eat poorly, take medications for heart problems, drag through the day hunched over in your seat, and so forth... they'll notice. Subconsciously, they'll lose respect for you. But if you stride through your office or your shop with confidence, a high level of fitness, and positive energy, they'll notice that too. It models and sets an expectation of excellence for them.

I challenge employees at every company I own. Each person in the office who sits for most of the day has a whiteboard at their desk or workstation, and they pick a simple exercise and choose the number of reps they think they can do. Once they choose, I tell them, "That's the number of exercise reps you should do every day. Sit-ups, push-ups, crunches, jumping jacks... I don't care. Get up from your desk and take thirty-two steps, if that's all you can do... but you should hit that number every day." Everyone—and I mean *everyone*, including me—does this. When they drop a few pounds, feel stronger and more energetic, it builds morale and confidence.

Casting Vision

Imagine if I told you, "Meet me at Walmart," from my office in Illinois. If you're in Miami or San Francisco, you'd need more specifics. Walmart is so common in America that you could, theoretically, drive around long enough and find one. But if the objective is to meet *me*, you'll be no closer to the goal.

If I'm talking about a Walmart here in Illinois, but you haven't left Miami or San Francisco... you're still in the wrong place. If you asked me the exact location and I just kept saying, "Meet me at Walmart," you'd have to decide that either (a) I don't know, or (b) I don't care whether you meet me at Walmart or not.

Vision is like that. If you don't make clear to people where you want to go, don't be surprised when they go any old way. As with Walmart, they might even hit a target that *looks like* what you want to achieve... but quickly, you'll discover that it's still the wrong one. You are accountable for articulating the vision.

You decide what has to happen, where you want to go, what you want to accomplish. You should do this for yourself personally, before you ever attempt it for your business. If you don't have a vision for your life because you're trying to avoid pain... you won't fix your business by changing prices, buying new software, or updating benefits. First, get ready for change—and that means forming a clear picture of who and what you want to become.

So begin with yourself. Vision works the same way as change: since owners are the "heartbeat" of their business, the company can only adapt itself to an improved leader. No scenario exists where you can skip personal vision for your life while creating vision for the company. Do you want to be in better physical shape? You need a vision of what it would look, feel, and perform like to be in the best shape of your life. Do you want to have a happier marriage? You need a vision of your marriage firing on all cylinders.

Before you get carried away, I'm going to give you an important sequence to follow. A lot of owners concentrate their visionary writing on who they want to become... without being honest about where they currently are. That's wishful thinking. In your first step, understand where you truly are, because some visions have start times and shelf lives relative to factors outside your control, such as age or physical limitations. If you're already in your fifties, you're not going to play professional sports like NFL football or NBA basketball. If you want a house full of kids and you're in your late fifties, depending on your spouse, you should probably consider adoption.

When I consult, one of my favorite questions to ask leaders is, "Tell me about yourself. Who are you?"

Usually I get partial answers to this from people telling me who they *want* to be. They might say, "I like to travel," but when I ask them follow-up questions about their last trip, they reveal they haven't traveled in eight years! That's not someone who loves to travel! Do you see in that answer how they focused on what they want to become without being honest about where they currently are?

If you want to create a vision you can achieve, you can't skip this part. Be honest and say, "I would prefer to travel, but I've been so bogged down by my business problems that I canceled my last three planned trips." Otherwise, it's like trying to throw a football across Lake Michigan. You can throw it, and it'll fly a couple of dozen yards... but it'll end up in the water.

Don't lie to yourself or pick stuff out of a hat just to say you have a vision! Be honest about where you are, why you think your problems started, and what you'd like to see change.

You could start by saying, "I'm a business owner who can do a lot of things right... but I'm having trouble in [name the areas—health, marriage, faith, parenting, etc]. For a future goal, I'd like to overcome those deficits, and become a [name it—fitness buff, world-class husband, strong believer, powerhouse parent]."

Now we're talking. If you get honest about your current state, you can more accurately determine whether you have a realistic vision. Remember: you are the captain of the ship. Your company will *never* change if you don't. Before you can effectively lead your team through transformation, you have to know what needs to happen deep down in your own character and heart.

You need to **invest in yourself** more than your business.

Do you think your business can resist following if you become a new and improved version of yourself? I've never witnessed a scenario where someone hit the gym, took care of their body, took care of themselves mentally, worked hard on loving their family, and then failed in business. I've *never* seen it happen.

On the other hand, if you skip working on yourself and rush to create a vision for your business… you might make some headway, but you'll only succeed to a certain level. You'll feel unfulfilled, and you'll aim for lesser rewards, like money or clout. You might end up at a Walmart, but it'll be the wrong one.

Another important part of casting vision is serving as the #1 optimist in your organization. When employees have low morale, you can see it in their faces. You (and only you) have the greatest power to influence and raise employee morale. Inspiration and motivation come from the top, from the pacesetter in the company, and if you work on becoming the kind of leader people want to follow, they will (generally) follow along. You must become the chief cheerleader for your company. If anyone rises up against you, take it as a clue about whether that person should really work there. No matter how difficult circumstances might feel in the moment… deeper pessimism won't help *anyone*. Especially you.

Refinement

As I progressed through my transformation, I encountered "plateaus." In weight loss journeys, plateaus are when you get stuck at a particular number on the scale, and your body stubbornly resists further fat loss. You might have dropped fifty pounds in the first six months of your journey, but now losing just five pounds seems impossible.

In the world of personal and professional growth, you'll find a similar resistance once you reach certain levels. From my mechanical background, I understand there is little difference between a Z28 Chevrolet Camaro sports car and Ford's least expensive car—the Fiesta. The Camaro uses a much larger, more powerful engine. But by the principles of design, its engine is simply larger and processes fuel faster. It creates a more powerful explosion when the fuel gets mixed with oxygen and sparks from its plugs, propelling the Camaro forward at a much greater speed than a Fiesta. Other than that, the design principles are the same. So you could go from a Fiesta to a Camaro as easily as going from, say, 250 pounds down to two hundred.

But if you took a Camaro and tried to scale it into the performance of a Ferrari... that's more challenging. The engines are designed differently, in addition to the Ferrari's precision and much lighter body. Even if you think a Camaro has more in common with a Ferrari than with a Fiesta... it doesn't. The Camaro could be compared with a leader who makes several leaps forward on the pathway of growth, but either misses the mark or stalls when they reach the need for Ferrari-level performance.

Going from the Camaro to the Ferrari is like trying to drop from two hundred pounds to 195 after you just lost the first fifty pounds. But those five measly pounds mean the difference between "fat storage" mode versus "fat burning" mode. Refinement is like the invisible border between "good" and "great," as Jim Collins put it.

No leader can pass certain stages without help, and you'll know when you hit it because you'll "max out" on your current success. It would be nice if you could just put your company on autopilot and check out... but that's not how it works. Your company will decline—slowly, at first. If you leave it long enough, that decline will pick up speed. Eventually, it will unravel completely. When I reach the limits of skill, aptitude, or the returns on my time begin to diminish, I hire outside, expert eyes to take me to the next level. If you've reached that level, reach out to someone who can help you. I've got some resources that can help at my website, deansvarc.com.

You've Got Personality

On the "DISC" Personality Assessment, I score as a very high "D," which stands for "dominant." I talk directly and clearly, and sometimes I *seem* upset because I don't smile while I'm thinking. I might appear angry, but I'm not... I'm just thinking hard.

I can also sound like an FBI interrogator because I don't ask questions and settle for surface answers. I might ask, "Why did that happen?" and follow up with more questions when I don't understand the response. "Explain to me... why did you do it that way?" I keep drilling until I get down to the core problem. (Remember—the hardest thing for leaders to do is to discover the real problem!) When people aren't used to that level of detailed questioning, it makes them uncomfortable.

I think very fast. "D" personalities think and decide quickly. I'm often unaware that I'm doing it. But over the years, enough people have told me, "Slow down. I'm still on Step One, and you're on Step Six," that

I've taught myself to slow down. Some of my employees confess to being afraid that they'll fail me because they can't keep up. They're not used to a leader who comes up with solutions and executes at top speed.

If you're ready for change, you can be straightforward with yourself and your company about what kind of person you are. I don't want everyone to be like me; I just want to solve problems. To me, mistakes and failure are simply how we learn, so we can improve. The only thing I can't tolerate is if you refuse to learn from mistakes or fix problems.

For people who are "non-Ds," I've got hope for you. But depending on your readiness to change and the condition of your business, you may need a "D" on staff or alongside you for a while. The B.A.S.I.C.S blueprint is hard to implement if you're mild-mannered, easily distracted, or quiet and reserved. You can't use your personality as an excuse forever, especially if your business is in trouble or you want it to grow. You have to communicate effectively if you want your company to change, and sometimes it involves being assertive and uncompromising.

There's also something to be said for "training" the parts of your personality that are weaker. I have seen leaders who score strong in the "I," "S" or "C" categories become more open, persuasive, and direct. You can learn ways to speak and achieve the same results a "D" would without being inauthentic or risking relationships. So don't feel the need to change who you are… but you shouldn't stay the way you are, either.

By the way, I too have worked on my non-dominant traits. I've worked to be a better listener (like an "S"), more detail-oriented (like a "C"), and more personable and fun-loving (like an "I"). Any kind of leader can change.

QUICK RECAP

The next signs you're ready for change show up in the ways you speak and act. You're ready for change if:

- You can take **immediate action** to fight stress, depression, and anxiety
- You're committed to find the **real problem** in any situation
- You're focused on **facts** rather than your **opinion**
- You're comfortable **standing alone** to make unpopular, difficult decisions
- You're ready to make changes to **how you speak**—to yourself, and to others
- You're committed to a **daily routine** of healthy, growth-oriented habits
- You accept that you're accountable for **casting vision** for yourself and your business
- You expect plateaus and roadblocks, and you seek outside eyes to help with **refinement**
- You're comfortable talking candidly about your **personality**, and you're eager to understand how others' personalities are different from yours

In the next chapter, we'll dispel some myths about change, and you'll learn how people should experience a new and improved version of you.

Chapter Three

Are YOU Ready for Change?
Part 3

"Leadership is the problem; leadership is the solution."
Bedros Keuilian

When I consult for business owners and managers, it takes a few rounds to persuade them that they already have most of what they need for change. Here's an example of what I mean.

Some of your employees previously worked for employers or cultures that devalued them. In some cases, abusive tyrant bosses verbally berated them, or they worked among cultures that thrived on rumors, whispers, and backstabbing. Other employees got left in the dark, plain and simple. The culture or leadership was silent when it came to appreciating a worker's strengths or talents. If any of these describe you, stop it—right now.

When leaders treat people this way, they become completely ignorant of the strengths, talents, and assets already at their command. They turn a blind eye to the trust and commitment they can create or nourish. A leader may talk a big game about building trust with customers... but I can tell how they feel about their capacity for change by how they treat their employees. It becomes particularly obvious if I confront them about how they behave, and they respond with indifference or become argumentative.

A leader who doesn't know, or doesn't want to acknowledge, what they already have will struggle to grasp that change is possible.

Other leaders have the same obstacle but from the opposite approach. They treat their people well, but they assume too much of the burden because they feel awkward about challenging their employees. If you're that person, struggling along in your company, feeling discouraged because it's all on you to be smart or work hard enough... this is for you. Trust me—you have everything you need. If anything, you may have a few things to rethink or get rid of to be ready for change.

I'll start with the top three roadblocks to success: **intelligence**, **laziness**, and **ego**.

Intelligence, Laziness, and Ego

Do you remember the examples of employees backing up a truck and hitting a wall or tearing off a door? They don't do it because of a failure of their intellect, or so little common sense that they can't tie their shoelaces. These are able-bodied, intelligent, working adults who lead lives and raise families. They're hard workers with marketable skills. They communicate in full sentences, they can read and write, they pay bills, and they enjoy hobbies and pastimes. There's no way they're *that* dumb.

The same is true for you, as the leader of your company. Are there parts of your business where you're inexperienced, illiterate, or know just enough to be dangerous? Of course. That doesn't make you *dumb* anymore than it makes Jeff Bezos or Elon Musk dumb for not understanding parts of their companies. So right away, we can dispose of **intelligence** as the reason your company's struggling. A person with an IQ that low wouldn't be able to read this book, either... so, rest assured, you have all the brain power you need. Out of all potential leaders, fewer than one tenth of one percent qualify for low IQ to seriously affect them.

A larger percentage (30-40 percent) run up against **laziness**. They know what they should do; they just don't want to do it. If you're the captain of the ship, you have a decision to make. If you continue to be lazy, it will affect others besides you. You'll hire people and fail to direct them appropriately, and their lack of performance will undermine the success of the entire operation.

I can spot laziness easily, but people have difficulty acknowledging it. Who wants to stand up in a room full of business peers and say, "Hey, everyone! I'm lazy!"? In fact, most leaders believe the opposite; they assure me of how they work sixty- to eighty-hour weeks all the time. But what difference does it make if you work sixty to eighty hours a week *on the wrong things*? If you need to make more sales, but you spend all your time maintaining equipment, you could work all 168 hours in a week and not make a dent. What counteracts laziness is *doing the right things*, not hours worked.

"Discipline weighs ounces; regrets weigh tons."
Jim Rohn

If your current way works, why on earth are you reading this book? If you have the best possible life and business, you're wasting your time; dump the book, and keep doing what you're doing.

Since it's not working, however... let's try another way.

The third (and biggest) roadblock to success is **ego**. I want to emphasize here—we're not talking about being *egotistical*. Most leaders I meet are people whose egos come across as needing to *prove* themselves. They're not braggarts who walk around wearing t-shirts that say "Look how great I am." It's more subtle; they behave as though they're qualified to be their own brain surgeons. They never ask good questions. They're determined to figure things out on their own. They've got all the answers, just like the example I mentioned in Chapter 1 who say, "Yeah, we already tried that."

Another form of ego in business is "analysis paralysis," and this comes up occasionally with engineer personalities. It's a form of egotism because you analyze a topic to death, but you never ask for advice or seek mentoring. You trust only in your own ability to understand a topic, including topics where you have zero experience, interest, or context. Ultimately, you can't move forward because you're "still trying to understand." That's a bad idea.

The greatest antidote to egotism is **you**, as the core of your business. You have to *know who you are*. Remember where we talked about vision, in Chapter 2, and the difference between knowing who you are versus who you want to be? Part of this means knowing and acknowledging your weaknesses, shortcomings, failures, and current circumstances. Unless you acknowledge that your strategy doesn't work, you over-analyze or want to prove yourself… and you won't ask for advice or help.

Skip the deep internal work required in Chapters 1-2, and it will taint everything you do. You'll try the same strategy over and over, and never really succeed. You'll hire one manager or employee after another, and they'll either quit or get fired. Then you'll try to fix surface issues—you'll hire a new marketing firm or a high-priced consultant. At some point, is it possible that *you* are the problem rather than the employees? The only common denominator in all these relationships and outcomes is <u>you</u>.

Complaints and Emotions

William Shakespeare once said, "Heavy is the head that wears the crown."

Do you remember the part from Chapter 2 about being a "chess player" to handle anxiety? Chess also provides other useful analogies for leadership.

The "king" piece in chess doesn't have any real power. His moves are extremely slow, limited to one square at a time. He can't really kill any of the opponent's pieces. This is why he's surrounded by a lethal queen, bishops, knights, and rooks, as well as pawns he can sacrifice.

Yet, by killing your opponent's king, you win the game. Isn't that interesting? To become good at chess, you must think several steps ahead of your opponent. As the "king" in your business, you must anticipate the consequences of saying the wrong thing or making the wrong move. You must strive to remain in control and avoid behaving more like the queen, who moves anywhere she wishes along the board, killing opponents indiscriminately.

There's a story from long ago of a medieval court servant who said, "I would love to be the king and sit on the throne." Overhearing this, his king agreed and said, "I can arrange that. Why don't you come back tomorrow, and you can sit on the throne?"

Delighted, the servant went home and looked forward with anticipation to ruling the kingdom. He arose the next morning, went to the palace, and made his way to the throne room. When he arrived, the throne was empty. The king stood next to it, beckoning the servant to take his seat. "Go ahead," he said with a smile. "Sit down." As the king had promised, the servant was about to get his chance to rule.

But just then, the servant noticed a large, extremely sharp sword suspended directly above the throne, hanging by a horsehair. The tip of it dangled over the head of the person who sat on the throne. One false move, and that sword would drop directly into the top of the servant's skull.

All of a sudden, the servant felt less enthusiastic about being king. Despite all the wealth and power he could acquire, the constant threat of imminent death overshadowed any potential happiness. The king smiled, and gave the servant leave. He'd made his point. To be the king is to accept the blame for what goes wrong in the kingdom and to restrain yourself from what the lower-ranking people feel free to say or do. Here's a modern translation of how Shakespeare put it in his play, *Henry V*:

Blame the king! Let's blame the king for what happens to our lives, our souls, our debts, our sad wives, our children, and our sins! I have to be responsible for all of it.

What a difficult situation it is being powerful, being talked about by every fool who can't understand anything except his own hardship.

What wonderful calm do kings have to give up that other men who have a private life enjoy? And what do kings have that people with private lives don't have too?

I love that line, but let's face it—you shouldn't say things like this openly, in front of your employees. They look to you to be resilient and optimistic, to rise above finger-pointing and blame. If you resort to whining or bemoaning your position, you open the floodgates of chaos. You start feeding chaos to management, and they in turn pass it down to the entry-level workers. You must be the rock of your organization.

As for complaints… you must also not complain "down." You're the captain of the ship, and the captain is accountable for everything, including the words he allows to escape his lips. If you're going to complain anywhere, do it away from your team, in the presence of a confidante or close friend who has the ability to sit quietly, keep your confidence, and offer reflections and feedback. In other words, "complain up."

Do not complain to those who report to you or your management team. Your employees can complain "up" all they want to… but you must keep your cool, control emotions, show optimism, and model resilience. I also recommend you find *peers*—owner groups, masterminds, and so forth. Don't do this with a spouse or children. You need feedback from people familiar with the unique challenges you face.

The same goes for your emotions. You have to play your cards close to the chest, because you can never be sure how the other person (or people) will receive it if you openly express how you feel. Some people might have grown up in a home with lots of yelling and screaming. If you do it to them, they might take it personally, or they might be so used to it that they respond with indifference. Others grow up in quiet homes where intense expressions of emotion are simply "not done," and they'll start looking elsewhere to avoid your tantrums. Still others come from codependent backgrounds, and they'll heap shame and guilt on themselves because you're in a bad mood.

You must not lose control in the presence of your employees. Don't be depressed about the past or anxious about the future. Your company looks to you, above all, for stability and direction. If you descend into yelling and screaming, pointing fingers and blaming people, you'll expose yourself as unfit to lead.

A king is only a king because **people believe** he's a king.

One time, I really lost my cool. I've never yelled at an employee in public, but I did it once in private. It was a bad idea.

We have strict no-cell phone policies at all of my companies. They're a huge distraction and safety issue. But one day, I saw one of the senior guys, a man named Doug, talking on his cell phone in the middle of the factory floor. When he finished his call, I called him into my office.

"Doug," I asked, "what's going on? You're not supposed to be on your cell phone."

"My car broke down last night," he said, "and I'm just trying to call the tow truck."

"But it's not break time," I said. "It's not lunch time. What are you doing? We're trying to establish rules here, and you're standing in the middle of the shop where everyone can see you. Couldn't you come to me and ask for a few minutes to step into an office and make the call so everyone else knows I've allowed it?"

"Well," he replied, "it was just a quick two- or three-minute call."

"You're not getting it, Doug," I said, and my temperature began to rise as we went back and forth about four more times. Finally, I blew up. I'd been under a lot of pressure, and this was the last straw. I raised my voice as loud as it could go. You could hear me through the walls.

I later apologized to Doug. Eventually, I sold the company. We're friends to this day… and I'll never do that again.

Read, Listen, and Learn

Aside from books you should read, I recommend you treat the people who work in your company as *living, breathing stories*. Let me explain what I mean.

Remember how most leaders can't find the real problems in their business? There's a parallel for employees. Most employees don't know how to communicate their real problems, either. Sometimes they don't know what their problems are... but, in my experience, it's more likely that they know what's really bugging them, and they're afraid to tell you. Maybe they expect you would respond with something cold-blooded, like "Who cares? Get back to work." Or maybe they've worked for a company that told them to keep their personal and work lives separate.

Here's what I know: over 90 percent of the time, when employees come to me with a problem, the issue they describe is *never* the real issue. They might come into my office and say, "Dean, Tony's being so difficult. I've told him over and over how to use the machines, and he just won't listen." No sooner do they say this than my radar goes up. I know instantly that it's unlikely that Tony is the real problem.

The first step in effective listening is to "mirror" what people say to you with sincerity. I'll stop what I'm doing, look people in the eye, and calmly respond, "I'm sorry to hear you feel that Tony's being difficult. That's got to be frustrating when you show someone over and over how to use the machines, and they don't listen." By doing this, you help people feel seen, heard, and understood. Through your body language, tone of voice, and choice of words, you *connect first* with the other person.

Once you've established a sincere connection, now you can start to pick apart what they tell you by asking, "Do we have a process in place for this situation?" This question is useful because if one of my companies lacks a necessary process, we need to create one. But even if we don't have a process, it rarely ends there—if I hear what I'm trained to listen for.

So let's say the employee responds, "Well, no, we don't have a process... but I've told him three times!"

"Okay," I reply. "It sounds like the problem is you've had to tell him three times because we don't have a process for this. Am I right?"

At this point, if the problem truly *is* a lack of process... we fix the problem, create a process, and move forward. But judging by how these things usually go, they usually want to say more. They might look down at the floor and despondently say, "Well, I guess so. Okay." Or they might protest, "But I've also had to deal with Bob failing to get his work done on time, and Sally's been late the last four days straight!" If any of these things happen... I know it's not process-related. Something deeper is at work.

I stop and ask, "What's going on here? It sounds like there's more to this than just a lack of a solid process."

That's when I learn the real answers: the employee's dog died. They lost a grandparent. Divorce is on the table. Debt collectors are hounding them. They're getting evicted from their apartment. Just like you, employees can never fully separate their personal and professional lives. They bring these issues to work with them as well. But most managers, co-workers, and society in general teach people to avoid talking about them. Any decent boss with an awareness of situations like these would empathize and try their best to be supportive and compassionate. But most decent bosses don't dig that deep.

You can be a decent boss, but if you want to be an *exceptional* boss, you must work to understand the *real* problems rather than the one the employee throws up in front of you. You have to read between the lines of what employees tell you and listen to the invisible *stories* of their lives—the stories they're afraid to tell you, unless you create safety and demonstrate that you care more about them than the bottom line.

Another way this works is to ask people about their unspoken expectations. Sometimes, they want you to get involved in their issues; other times, they just want a listening ear so they can get stuff off their chests. Have you heard of the husband whose wife "just wants to vent," and wants him to listen to her instead of trying to solve her problems? Employees, male and female, often run on similar programming.

So I'll stop them early and say, "I hear you're having a problem with Tony. Do you want me to get involved?"

Typically, the answer goes, "No, I just wanted to tell you what was going on."

"Okay," I'll say. "So, what can I do to help?"

"Well, nothing for right now. I just wanted to tell you what was going on."

That's how you listen effectively. As I've bought and sold all these companies, I've tried it on everyone—employees, supervisors, customers, suppliers, negotiators, attorneys, and shareholders. It never fails.

Along the way, I discovered something even better than effective listening. I believe leaders should empower employees by teaching them how to think critically through these issues for themselves. Imagine how much less stressful it is on everyone if an employee can stop, self-evaluate, recognize their deeply-held motivations, and self-correct without help from anyone! You know you've become an exceptional boss when an employee can handle their issues... like a boss.

Work "In" or Work "On"

With every company I purchase, I start with the Brute Force period of working "in" the business. I need to move quickly to break bottlenecks, eliminate outdated processes, reset the layout, and evaluate roles. In a short amount of time, I have to clearly communicate expectations, create policies, and establish order. I believe in training employees correctly the first time so I don't have to keep doing it over and over. Every owner sometimes has to work *in* their business.

Do you work **in** your business? You might be the senior technician, do some accounting, make phone calls/sales, run operations, or interview and hire new employees. Whatever the specifics, here's the trade-off: the more you work *in* your business, the quicker your business disappears if you die or become incapacitated. It depends on you showing up every day, doing some or all of the grunt work. That's one way to run a company, but it's not the only way.

By contrast, working **on** your business means you cast the vision, set the goals, develop the team, and double-train employees so the company can perform even if you're no longer there. If you work *on* your business, you have more time to act like the owner and architect, not just a worker. You have fewer (or no) deliverables. Your employees handle fulfillment, operations, sales, and finances. Preferably, you train them well enough that you can recognize easily when they don't need your help because they can fix issues on their own. In turn, this allows your business to scale, run efficiently, and grow sustainably.

If you want to work in your business, be my guest. But be prepared for the downside: most owners simply don't have the time or bandwidth to do both. I certainly don't! Once I've spent those first few months exposing my teams to how I talk, how I say/do things, and what I expect from them… they're able to work independently. My job is to train them rather than do the work itself. Throughout the process, I transition myself from working *in* the business to working *on* the business. I eventually have no deliverables.

Remember, from Chapter 1: if you want to move beyond your current circumstances, you have to live differently from how you live now. In the same way, if you want your business to become greater and more prosperous than it currently is, *you can't keep doing what you've always done.*

Specifically... you have to do less work *in* your business, and more work *on* it. To do that, get comfortable with delegating authority, responsibilities, and tasks. Many business owners are afraid to let go of the controls and levers in their business. Ironically, this keeps them from growing and succeeding.

Your employees will never care about your business like you do. They're not as skilled as you. They're not as fast as you. They can't do what you do. They don't stay late like you do. I know it feels risky and uncomfortable, but here's what I've found: as long as you can accept (and expect) **60-70 percent** from them, it will work. It will be much more effective than you doing 100 percent of the work. As John D. Rockefeller said:

"I would rather earn one percent from 100 people's efforts than 100 percent from my own efforts."

Let's break down that math.

Your company earns $1 million in revenue from installing an electrical system in a commercial building. If you have one hundred employees, that means their work earns $10,000 per employee to the company. One percent of $10,000 is $100, so as the owner you earn $10,000... for doing *none* of the work. You earned *ten thousand dollars* by simply waking up in the morning. The work itself takes several weeks, eight-to-ten hours a day, and if you pay your average worker $30 per hour, that means they catch up to you in earnings after a month on the job... and more than two hundred hours of labor. (These numbers are just for example purposes.)

Work ON

One Percent from 100 People's Efforts

100 employees x $10,000 revenue per employee = $1,000,000

$1,000,000 x 1% to you = $10,000 earned

— vs —

Work IN

Earn $30 per hour

333 hours x $30 per hour = $10,000 earned

In other words, if you do some of the work, you might earn a fraction of what you're actually worth. But if you pay someone $30 an hour to do the work, and you spend those same hours working on things only you can do… you earn 100 percent of what you're worth. To a general contractor who wants to finish a construction project, an electrical subcontractor like you is worth a lot. You offer prepackaged knowledge, tools, parts, and labor. That general contractor doesn't want to do all that work themselves.

So the cost of delegation is nothing when compared with the value that you get back from it, especially when you go from hiring generalists to hiring specialists. Believe it or not, there are people out there who are more skilled at your specialty than you are. There are plumbers, electricians, manufacturers, and managers who are gifted in the same kind of work as you.

Elon Musk is a big believer in hiring employees who understand science and technology better than he does. Do you want to argue against the outcomes his companies produced? Of course, specialists cost 20-30 percent more than generalists... but their performance is 200% better. Today, we have digital payment systems, fully electric vehicles, internet you can use in the middle of the Sahara Desert, and rockets that can *land* on launchpads, as well as take off from them.

I can tell when my employees are ready to take responsibility and operate my companies without me. It's when I notice them making the same kind of decisions I make and getting the same results from them. It's when I ask them to come up with solutions, suggestions, and final decisions—and they provide them, execute on them, and succeed faster than I could. If they get it right nine times out of ten... I've won. When you see your team excel because they're empowered to make decisions and take action, you've won.

Facing Challenges

Remember the panicked moment in my office, when my first company was down to its last $10,000? I wasn't the first owner to get caught in a storm. It happens to everybody, including the most successful owners I've ever talked to. All of them have lost everything (or almost everything), multiple times. But looking back, you know what I'm grateful for today? I'm grateful for *everything I learned* from it, which I would never have learned if the business hadn't come so close to failure. Success teaches you nothing, but failure teaches you everything. You can only learn from pain.

One of my companies used to manufacture components for firearms. If you know anything about the gun industry in America, you know that it rises and falls with current cultural and political events. For example, when one party holds the presidency, gun sales skyrocket; when the other party holds it, they shrink down to almost nothing, statistically. When there's a school shooting, gun sales surge in fear of sweeping legislation to take them away.

I pay enough attention to news and politics to know gun control is a big issue. But several years ago, I failed to anticipate how a changing of the guard would affect sales for one of the parts we made. One president left, another entered office, and all of a sudden, demand for our product went through the floor! I remember hoping and praying at the time that it was just a "temporary" setback, but there was no getting around it. People simply weren't buying as many guns and ammunition as they had been, and nothing I could do would change that.

How I failed to see it coming remains a mystery, but I know this: the success I enjoyed during the previous administration gave me *zero* warning! It didn't teach me a damn thing. The company survived the massive loss, but it taught me an important lesson: **challenges will come**, and how we respond to them makes all the difference. We must not give up just because we don't currently see the results we want. Right when you feel like giving up the most, you must press even harder—because the hard times are when everyone else gives up, too.

> The worst part about success is that it **doesn't teach you anything.**

Know the Value of Your Time

When it comes to valuing their own time, most leaders step over dollars to pick up pennies. I have struggled in the past with this one, myself. It is *so* easy to undervalue your time, and it shows when you waste it.

You can put a financial number on your time based on simple ideas like a per-hour rate or annual salary. But it won't reflect the true value of your time unless you factor in what you're *capable* of earning in the same period of time. For example, let's say you work forty hours a week in your business and pay yourself $150,000 per year. But in your spare moments, you invest in real estate, stocks, or other businesses as a venture partner. If you can calculate your compensation from that work and combine it with what you earn from your business, *now* you're getting closer to what your time is truly worth.

Here's the rub: most leaders do *worse* than diminish the value of their time. They're so busy working *in* their business, doing jobs they should no longer be doing, that they turn their hourly rate into a net negative.

Let's think through that scenario: you earn $150k per year, but if you combine it with what you earn from investing, you earn closer to $350,000. Now, you spend at least four hours per day attending to bookkeeping, sales calls, and serving customers. Maybe you own a plumbing business, and you're still out there fixing sinks and toilets. You pay your employees between $25-35 per hour for those jobs. If you just stick with your $150k compensation, that works out to an hourly rate of $72 for a forty-hour work week. Do you see how you're cutting your value in half?

$150,000 per year = $72/hr

Fixing sinks and toilets = $35/hr

Seventy-two dollars per hour is more than double what your employees earn. And that means you have no business doing it.

Now let's do the math when you factor in your investments or perhaps some independent consulting and speaking. Now you earn close to $350,000 per year, which works out to an hourly rate of $168. So if you're fixing toilets in the morning, rushing home to get changed, and then heading to a speaking engagement that afternoon... you're working for *80 percent* less per hour than the value of your time.

$350,000 per year = $168/hr

Fixing sinks and toilets = $35/hr

Maybe it's time to hang up the overalls and let the team turn the wrenches. You're leaving a lot of money on the table. I know my hourly rate at the time of writing. This is why, once we pass the Brute Force and Analyze phases, I tell my employees, "I have no deliverables. I don't answer phones, sign checks, or develop enterprise resource planning (ERP) systems." You know why? *Because I lose money doing them.*

The only projects I work on are projects
no one else can do.

Antennae Up, Head Down, and Where You Spend Your Time

Skilled chess masters play silently for a reason. If they excitedly tell opponents and audiences how they plan to win, they guarantee themselves a loss.

The only people who should know intricate details of your plans are mentors and confidantes, particularly because they can see your blind spots. But if you run off excitedly telling employees, spouses, children, friends, and anyone else who will listen about your plans… your probability of succeeding drops through the floor. Sure, you'll get a brief high from endorphins and dopamine, but you've become the proverbial leader who failed to count the cost of what he plans to build. Keep your head down and your plans quiet, and work away at them deliberately.

Don't tell people what you plan to do.
Just do it, and let them react to it.

Along this same thread, you must learn to **open up your senses** as you go through the day. If you commute to and from your office, that's the time to push "play" on an educational podcast or audiobook instead of a song or an afternoon talk show. If your activities take you into someone else's business, attune your mind to where they could improve and make note of changes you would make if given the chance. Notice their sales process, their levels of customer service, whether they offer you additional products/services, and how well they train their employees.

Pay attention to your surroundings wherever you go, and keep the Five Whys ready for the right moment. I excel at identifying what's wrong in a business within moments of entering. I notice the location, entrances and exits, condition of equipment, and friendliness and efficiency of staff. Sometimes, I even get into conversations with management or ownership if they're there, and it leads to incredible connections because I'm curious about why they do things the way they do them.

You're judged by the company you keep. You rise and fall on the strength and sharpness of who you spend your time with outside of work. As I went through my transformation, my friends changed as well. Until I began to succeed, it seemed like my friends supported me. But once I actually *did it*, they suddenly became "concerned" for me. All of a sudden, they had one warning after another, and they were the biggest experts on everything that could go wrong! It took me some time to realize that this "concern" sprung mainly from the fact that I was doing things they couldn't dream of doing... and succeeding at them.

Once upon a time, my then-wife and I bought a beautiful home in a brand-new neighborhood. She worked on a master's degree in the evenings, which left me with more free time than usual. So I decided to build a deck for the back yard. The home came with a small concrete pad step from the back door. We didn't like it, so I ripped that out and replaced it with a massive 1,500 square foot deck—complete with a built-in hot tub and large screenroom. The homes were built close together so that several of the neighbors could see what I was doing, and once it got dark I set up floodlights and worked into the night.

After a while, a few of the men in the adjacent houses came up to me and said, "Hey, Dean, would you mind taking it easy?"

At first, I was alarmed. I thought they were complaining because I was working at night, drilling and sawing. "I'm sorry," I began. "Is it too noisy at night? I know you guys have kids. I hope I'm not keeping them awake."

"No, it's not that," they said.

I was puzzled. "Well, why do you want me to slow down?"

"Well, you know," they said, "our wives see you out there working at night, and now they're asking us to build decks for our houses."

This is a prime example of being surrounded by people who feel threatened watching you succeed or grow, while they stay the way they are. They will try to hold you back.

Maybe you think, "Well, that's in a residential neighborhood. Things are different in business."

Not in the business world I live in! When I won Manufacturer of the Year in 2019, I stood out from a bunch of family-owned manufacturers, often where second- or third-generation owners still ran things the way their parents or grandparents did. Some of them still ran things under the *control* of their parents, which they resented. But I only reported to myself, which gave me the freedom to innovate or reform how my companies ran. When I attended a meeting with several of these generational owners, I discovered quickly that they weren't very welcoming, eager to talk to or befriend me. At the time, I didn't understand why they seemed ... defensive. Later, the leaders of the association who gave me the award told me–the kids of the owners were jealous. They envied the freedoms I enjoyed and changes I made that they themselves were not allowed to do.

I then realized: if you plan to improve yourself, don't be surprised to attract naysayers. You make them feel and look bad. I finished that deck in my backyard, and I never got a single visit from any of those men to see how it turned out. I won Manufacturer of the Year, but all I got from my peers was token, insincere acknowledgment. So, if the people around you *stop supporting you* once you accomplish something... it's time to find some new friends.

Eagles fly alone for a reason. If you're going to have friends, aim to be in groups where you are one of the least accomplished, experienced, or successful people in the room. You want to contribute and learn from the people around you, but if you're the most accomplished person in the room, you forfeit the opportunity to learn.

Know the Value of Failure

Do you know what it "costs" you to fail? You've probably heard the saying, "F.A.I.L. stands for 'First Attempt In Learning.'" It's true. You go to college or trade school to learn so you can succeed. Failure is the same thing. So let's look at failure from the standpoint of long-term financial gain.

I'll give an example: my lowest-level employees make what we call "fifty-dollar mistakes." Whenever they fail at something, we lose a minimum of $50. If you factor in their hourly rate, benefits, and attach a fraction of operating costs divided among all personnel... the lowest-paid employees usually cost closer to $50 per hour. So if they make a mistake, it usually takes at least sixty minutes to recover from it.

Sometimes, it involves cleaning up a mess, and it always includes the review process—the Five Whys.

If you run a company earning $2-3 million in revenue, perhaps $50 here and there doesn't sound so bad. You can afford to make a certain amount of mistakes on that level. I made enough $50 mistakes early in my career that I don't make them anymore. But as the owner, mistakes are far more costly. When I make a mistake today, it's a six-digit dollar value to the company. One year, I lost over $200,000 because of some risks I took that failed to pan out. Remember the chess example? The king moves very slowly, one square at a time. His moves carry tremendous consequences, and sometimes they fail, no matter how well he plans.

How do you think I felt when I calculated that I'd lost that much money? If you said, "Not good," I'm happy to disappoint you. It was one of the best things that's ever happened to me. I gained insight and experience I'd never have learned if everything turned out perfectly. The way I see it, I paid over $200,000 for the kind of education you simply can't get anywhere else.

This is why it's so important that we reclaim the word "failure" from our culture's short-sighted understanding. To the average person, failure is A/B, black-and-white: either you win, or you lose. I disagree! Thomas Edison, who invented the lightbulb, is famous for failing in his first 1,000 attempts to create it. How did Edison comment on those failures? He said, "I have not failed 1,000 times. I have successfully discovered 1,000 ways it will not work." Thanks to Edison's persistence, today we enjoy well-lit homes, streets, buildings, and cities around the clock, worldwide. I can't imagine life without electricity... Thank goodness Edison failed.

Look at Elon Musk's decision, after SpaceX crashed its third rocket attempt. Musk could have abandoned the cause at that point. On paper, it was the only rational choice; they didn't have enough cash to risk a fourth launch. The crash reverberated across Musk's empire, threatening to put Tesla out of business as well. If they attempted one more launch, (a) they would need to scrounge up enough cash to do it, and (b) if it failed, it would definitely put them out of business. How many digits do you think fit into *that* decision if it failed?

Today, of course, we know that Musk took an enormous risk, and it paid off. But the only way he got there was by taking several *other* enormous risks in the first place, most of which failed. The point of this is to understand how much financial impact your mistakes have… but also to show you that you can make them and still survive. You can make them and still enjoy huge success.

The most practical advice I have for failing is to *practice gratitude—* immediately—when it happens. Failure is a positive, not a negative. You can always learn from it, whereas success feels good but teaches you nothing. Our culture says that if you fail, you're a loser… but I say that if you fail, you're a winner. You found the right way *not* to do something, just like Edison.

If you were a young man looking for a romantic relationship, and somebody told you that you would find a good woman if you got rejected by the first nineteen you asked, then that twentieth woman is the only one you need to worry about. If that were me, I'd get on the phone right away and ask nineteen women out as fast as I could, because I know that the twentieth woman would say "Yes."

> Failure is a win, because every failure
> represents **one step closer** to winning.

Turn off the noise of other people's opinions about your failure. They talk poorly about you because if they talked about themselves... no one would listen.

QUICK RECAP

Some leaders believe that change costs enormous amounts of money or requires "cleaning house" and a complete company retrofit. Not true! You're ready for change if you understand that you already have everything you need. Most change requires *getting rid* of things you no longer need or shouldn't have to begin with.

You're ready for change if:

- You understand that the biggest impediment to meaningful change is **ego**, versus intelligence or laziness

- You're resolved to **control your emotions** at all costs, and *never* complain to anyone below your station

- You're committed to a **routine** of fitness, self-education, and eliminating distractions

- You accept that the people you lead are living, breathing **stories**, where you must observe, read, and listen so you can understand them

- You're determined to **work on** your business and delegate as much as possible, so that you only do what only you can do

- You accept that challenges will come, and each one gives you an opportunity to learn and discover **what you can do differently** in the future

- You exercise **discretion** with sharing your plans and goals, you're **indifferent** to criticism from naysayers, and you're **intentional** about being the "dumbest" person in rooms where you spend your time

- You **embrace failure** and understand the "value" of mistakes, even big ones, as stepping stones that move you one step closer to your goals.

In the next few chapters, we're going to switch to the readiness of your *company* for change. As you ought to see by now, change starts with you. But it doesn't end with you, so now it's time to get your employees ready, too.

Chapter Four

Is Your Company Ready for Change?
Part 1

"Culture eats strategy for breakfast."
Peter Drucker

F or every company I've purchased, it takes at least four weeks for the entire team to learn:

"WWDD?"
("What Would Dean Do?")

WWDD? is a dialect of American English. It's an interesting language because it contains several words and phrases I do *not* want to hear, particularly if someone says them in response to my Five Whys. Just like regular English has words and phrases considered offensive and rude, WWDD? has them, too. But in WWDD?-speaking companies, we do a much better job of wiping them from our vocabulary. The most powerful expression of a company's culture is in its language.

I pick up on poor cultures quickly because I know what to look and listen for. Sometimes, the language is verbal, but more often than not, it's behavioral. I once took over a machining shop where employee behavior around quitting time made the existing culture painfully obvious. About twenty minutes before closing time, all the machines shut off. The employees gathered around the time clock and began to socialize.

This was a dead giveaway, but I know better than to judge without asking questions. So I walked up to the employees and said, "Hey! What's going on here? We've got at least twenty minutes left in the workday."

The second giveaway: they all looked around sheepishly at each other. Everybody knew this was unacceptable, but nobody wanted to own it. So they kept silent.

I asked, "Do you guys do this every day?" But they remained silent, as if they'd been pulled over by the cops. This kind of thing never begins with a twenty minute gap before quitting time. They probably started years ago, at first with five minutes, progressed to ten, then fifteen. But if I allowed it to continue, they'd soon be shutting down an hour or more before the end of the workday. It's how human nature works.

So the next day, I called a company-wide meeting. I didn't condemn anyone for what had happened, but I needed them to understand who they were dealing with. The previous owners lacked the courage to confront this behavior, and I could see that if I didn't say anything, the problem would get worse.

Sloppy cultures run by poor leaders
tolerate **bad behavior** from employees.

And why do they tolerate it? I'm sorry to say, but they do it because *they just don't care that much*. It's not worth it for them to care. They have base motivations, like money. They see their company as a piggy bank, and they could care less about employee morale or work ethic. It goes right back to Chapter 1: "Are you ready for change?" Too often, the answer is "No."

At another of my companies, I told the general manager, one day, "Hey, I'd like to reward the staff with some gift cards. What do you think I should get them? Subway? McDonald's?"

"McDonald's," he said, with such certainty that I got curious.

"Why McDonald's?" I said.

"Well," he replied, "I know a lot of the ladies go there to get coffee every day."

For a few moments, I moved on to the next subject in our discussion. But something in my brain wouldn't let go of his comment about the ladies going to McDonald's every day to get coffee. "Gary," I told him, "hold on just a minute. Can we go back to the coffee thing real quick?"

He nodded.

"The ladies are bringing coffee from McDonald's every day, right?"

"Yes," he said.

"Now, this is a huge factory," I continued. "We're the size of a Walmart (80,000 square feet). I don't understand—for how much money they make per hour, I'm surprised they would go to McDonald's. Why don't they just drink the coffee here?"

A few seconds of silence followed before Gary told me: *they didn't have a coffee maker*. Not one! In an 80,000-square foot, Walmart-sized manufacturing warehouse, there wasn't a *single* coffee maker.

"Gary," I said, "how is it possible we don't have a coffee maker?"

"Well," he said, "previous management decided it was too expensive."

I have no idea how I prevented my head from exploding. Maybe it's worth mentioning that when I took over this business, the previous owner had $2.5 MILLION sitting in the business bank account! How could it be "too expensive" to provide coffee for your employees? I was so shocked by this answer that I got online, found eight people selling commercial-grade coffee makers, and messaged them saying, "I want to buy your coffee maker *right now*." The first one got back to me quickly, and I personally drove to pick it up, along with a bunch of filters, creamers, sugar, paper cups and stirrers, *that day*.

The next day, we announced to the whole company that we had coffee. You could hear them in the back of the room saying "At last!" and "Finally!"

Broken cultures lack accountability. One way this shows up is that if something's broken, it usually *stays* broken—especially if it doesn't directly affect the owner. The employees know the leadership doesn't care, so rather than bring it up… they adapt to the reality, often to absurd degrees. Inefficiency goes up, profitability and morale go down, and nobody wins.

At another company I bought, the operations coordinator was in charge of replacing broken or damaged equipment. We had one large refrigerator in the break room where all the employees could store lunches and drinks for the day. It broke down one day, and the coordinator came to me to ask what she should do.

I told her, "Just go buy a new one, and have it delivered. Can you take care of it today?"

She nodded yes.

Eight days later, in an unrelated meeting with the production manager, he said, "Hey, Dean, just one thing—we could really use a fridge in the break room."

"What?" I said. "I just had a fridge put in! What's wrong with it? Did it break already?"

"No," he replied. "We never got a fridge."

It had been eight days. The employees went *eight days* without a fridge! So I called the operations coordinator, the lady who was supposed to get the new fridge, to find out what happened.

She told me she'd held off on buying the fridge because she thought she could get a better deal. The total cost for the first fridge she looked at was $250. As I kept peeling away at her answers, I discovered that she'd adapted to the previous owners. They were cheapskates, at least when it came to taking care of employees.

I could have burst into flames. I jumped back online (after hours), found the first person willing to sell me a fridge, and the general manager and I took the company box truck, drove out to the seller, hauled a fridge down two flights of stairs, brought it back to the plant, and set it up. The next morning, I held a public meeting during the first break. I apologized to the staff that they had to go a full week without a fridge and took accountability for the untimely resolution. (*Apparently somebody thought $250 was too much to spend on them.*) When issues like this appear, it's either a "process" or a "people" problem. This was a people problem. A short time later, we parted ways with that coordinator.

When I apologized to the staff about the fridge, I emphasized that *I*, Dean Svarc, was accountable for the failure. (The operations coordinator was *responsible* for getting the new fridge, but I was accountable for it.) The biggest sign of a strong company culture is when **leadership is accountable**. I never blamed that operations lady for being stingy with buying equipment for the employees. She *learned* to do that from the previous ownership. They were absentee owners who thought skimping on employees would save money and increase profits.

Openness and Transparency

Some company cultures are secretive and controlling. One business I bought had an owner, a lawyer, and an accountant as their ruling "trio." The owner turned out to be extraordinarily difficult and unreasonable. As I visited the factory several times, I noticed that those three disliked my habit of speaking to employees and managers one-on-one without them present.

A key part of the Analyze and Culture steps in this book is talking to individual people… alone. You don't have to be in the process of purchasing a company to do this. I'm a fan of asking real questions and getting real answers. To do that, you have to get the owners and senior managers out of the room so employees feel less concerned about repercussions from leadership.

At any rate, the accountant at this company was a guy we'll call David who was in charge of HR and payroll. He and the general manager accompanied me on the factory floor as I walked around and talked to people… but David stayed on my coattails! It didn't take long to figure out that the owner sent him to monitor all of the conversations, and he tried to hurry me by telling me that he needed to leave soon to pick up his kids or something like that.

We stopped at one point and David began to look at his phone, perhaps six feet away from where I stood talking to Gary, the production manager. I lowered my volume and said to Gary, almost whispering, "I want you to go somewhere in this building, and move very quickly. I don't care where you go, just walk very fast." Gary did so, and I took off right along with him. By the time David realized we'd left, we were more than thirty feet away.

As we walked, I said to Gary, "Why is David riding my coattails?"

"Because he's afraid of what I'm going to say to you," Gary replied.

"Oh," I said. "What are you going to say to me?"

"I'm going to tell you the truth," he said.

That was all I needed to know. Gary and I have had a great relationship ever since, and he's been a star employee for me since I bought the company. He never hesitated when I told him to walk away quickly from David, and he later told me how both the owner and David disliked him. They hadn't wanted to focus on solving problems; they just wanted problems to go away so they could make money.

The employees at my box company felt alienated from the previous owners because of behaviors like this. Today, that same company looks forward to days when I show up to review our successful changes and celebrate the growth of the business. It's also a time they know, "If you want to talk to Dean directly, his door is open, and now is the time." While that's true—my door is always open and I emphasize healthful interaction and fixing problems, it's surprising how rarely they pull me aside to complain or bring up a problem. But if they do, they know—their jobs are never at risk.

Abuse and Assumptions

After I bought that company, I formed a strong relationship with an employee named Ron who'd worked there for over thirty years. Ron's story goes to show you what people sometimes put up with... because the previous owners treated him very poorly, and so did several of his co-workers. Despite this, Ron worked for three decades at a company full of people who thought he was dumb, and told him so.

It turned out that not only was Ron a smart man, but no one ever put his talents to good use. At the time I took over, he worked in a role where the best he could do was average because no one ever looked closely to see where his true talent lay. He grew comfortable enough with me that he shared how the previous owner would walk out on the factory floor and get into confrontations where he screamed at people.

When you mix a lack of appreciation and an abusive environment with disinterest in people's talents, you should expect a lousy balance sheet. By digging a little deeper, I discovered that Ron had incredible talent. *Management* acted in ignorance. At first, they seemed to perceive him correctly; because of how he'd been treated, he did struggle to perform at his job.

But after a few months of working together, Ron improved dramatically. He developed the ability to juggle multiple tasks at once, without making mistakes. He's an absolute rock star in his job. When we gave out awards a year later, Ron won "Most Improved." The previous leaders didn't want to take the time to get to know Ron. They just wanted to fill a seat and make a buck. That's as bad as you can get, when it comes to running a business. It involves a whole lot of **assumptions**.

Assumptions are everywhere in poor company cultures. It could be something as simple as when I ask, "How much is the bill for gas at the company?" Inevitably, the responses begin with three phrases, all of which tell me that nobody knows anything about anything:

- "I think it's…"
- "I feel it's…"
- "So-and-so told me it's…"

The problem is that people speak as if their assumptions are facts, and management then makes decisions based on assumptions presented as facts. As a leader, you don't have the luxury of "assuming" based on feelings, vague thoughts, or hearsay. But neither should you create a space where people feel afraid or threatened while they learn. Remember Chapter 2: your role is to ask, "What are the *facts*?" But to avoid being mistaken for my predecessors, I will add, "There are no wrong answers besides guessing or making it up. If you don't know, just say, 'I don't know, but I'll find out.'"

In WWDD?, when I ask someone how much we pay for gas, there are only two possible answers:

- "It's X amount."
  or
- "I don't know, but I'll find out."

If you can give me either of those answers, you're speaking the WWDD? language. (If you can quickly produce a copy of the bill to show me the exact amount, you speak it fluently.)

The good news is that for every company I've bought, ninety percent or more of the employees are willing to adapt to new communication styles, particularly if they're an improvement over old ways. An even higher percentage are willing to adapt to a non-abusive environment! After the first four weeks, my staff shows clear signs of "catching on" with how they communicate. They stop using phrases like "I feel like" or "So-and-so told me," and they remember that their boss is only interested in facts. They feel safe enough to say the words "I don't know," because they understand that I'm asking questions to fix the problem, not lay the blame.

You can't put your hands on abstract ideas or possibilities. You can't confirm rumors or speculation. If you have a history with the people who work in your company, it might take a while for them to get used to different ways of communicating than they're used to. That's okay, because you can't start here in Chapter 5 anyway. Your team can only adapt positively to a new, improved version of you. You have to go through the transformation, as the nucleus of your business. If you get Chapters 1-4 correct, this will work. Skip them, and it won't.

So Let It Be Written

WWDD? also has subtle rules in its written form. At every company I own, the employees know:

If it's not documented, it didn't happen.

You can imagine the frustration when someone from your purchasing team says, "Mr. So-and-So over at XYZ Supply said we can pay in installments over six months, and we don't have to pay for another two weeks."

It sounds great. But then, two weeks later, Mr. So-and-So demands immediate, in-full payment and threatens to cut off the supplies if we don't pay right away.

You turn to the employee who told you about the original agreement. "What happened?" you ask. "I thought you said we didn't have to pay for two weeks, and we could do installments."

"Well," the employee says, "he talked to his boss, and his boss said 'Absolutely not.'"

Predictably, neither your employee nor the vendor's sales representative can produce any documentation of the agreement. In WWDD? we consider this "offensive" and it has no place in any of my companies. During the Brute Force phase, I go into overdrive training my employees to keep written, accurate records of everything.

If you and your company have been negligent about documentation, I have good news. It will take time to reorient your team to keeping detailed records of everything. You may have to take a slight dip in productivity while they learn. But we solve what we write down—especially when we're properly trained to check things off our to-do lists every day.

If you plan to use something similar to WWDD? as a language in your business, you *must* train management to reject phrases that begin with "I think it's…" or "I feel like it's…" Imagine you invoiced a customer for a major installation job worth tens of thousands of dollars,. Months go by, they don't pay, and they tell you, "But I *feel* like I paid it." Would you care at all about what they feel? Of course not. So don't tolerate these vague, mysterious words from *anyone*, including yourself. You lost the luxury of vagueness and mystery when you signed up to be the captain of the ship.

You **must** train your team to your expectations.

Chances are, if your company doesn't speak WWDD? (yet), they've been trained to communicate poorly, or not at all. No one ever taught them to focus on facts, documentation, or meaningful questions. They've instead lived on drama, make-believe, and fairy dust—and unless you step in, no one has plans to teach them any different. The company belongs to you, which means, in the beginning, only *you* can set and enforce expectations.

Don't just document the necessities. Keep track of wins and successes! I make a habit of photographing everything, and recording time-lapsed video footage. At the annual Christmas parties, I have an editor put together a video to recap everything we accomplished during the year. Once the music kicks in and people see these "memorials" to their work, their reactions are amazing. They feel included and important in something bigger than themselves. Some employees tell me they look forward to these videos all year long.

The Forbidden Phrase

The six worst words in the English language are "We've always done it this way." Someone saying them is the quickest way to agitate me.

At one company I purchased, the office administrator kept records of hours worked using two sheets of paper—one white, the other yellow. Aside from the color of the paper, the sheets were identical. The staff filled out the yellow sheets every day to record their time on each job and working hours. Using that information, you could determine whether or not the company made a profit on the jobs they did.

During the Brute Force and Analyze phases, I walked the floor regularly. I noticed the administrator would walk around and collect the sheets every day. One day, I stopped her to ask about them. "Tell me about these white and yellow sheets," I said.

"Oh," she said, "these are to help us figure out if we make money on the jobs we do. We give them to the employees to fill out how many hours and days they spend working on their jobs. Then we collect them and run the math to see if we profited from the work."

So far, so good. "Okay," I said. "What about the white sheets?"

"Those are backups, in case they forget to fill out the yellow sheets," she said.

I raised my eyebrow. "So let me get this straight. If they don't fill out the yellow sheets correctly, you refer to the white sheets."

She nodded. In my head, I was thinking, "If they forget to fill out the yellow sheets… how do they remember to fill out the white ones?" But that was just the beginning of the story.

"Go on," I said. "Do you take the data from the white sheets and put it into a database somewhere?"

"Oh, no," she said. "I collect all the white sheets, staple them together, and put them in a box next to my desk."

"What percentage of the time do you refer back to the white sheets?"

She said, "Almost never."

"So, they get entered into a database later?"

"No," she replied. "When the box fills up, I throw them out."

Read that again carefully.

- They created two different sets of sheets to track exactly the same data.
- The employees spent twice as much time as they would by just filling out one sheet.
- The administrator collected all the sheets.
- She piled half of them up in a box.
- She never referred back to them.
- Then she threw them away.
- And the company paid for all the paper and payroll, just for the privilege of doing it!

That's a true story. You can't make this stuff up! Three seconds after she told me that, I canceled the white sheets. I said, "Announce to the team that we're killing the white sheets immediately." When she did, the workers let out a huge cheer. They hated filling out the white sheets. It was double the effort and for no reason or return.

If you notice, that administrator didn't utter the forbidden phrase out loud with her mouth. She didn't need to; her answers spoke volumes. Rarely do people actually say "We've always done it this way" out loud. You don't need to hear it… you can see it by how they behave, and by whether or not they're curious about why they do things the way they do them.

At that same company, I discovered another example of the forbidden phrase: they only took customer orders via fax machine.

Are you old enough to remember when the fax machine became popular in the business world? We've long since moved on from that technology. So when I saw the fax machine, I asked the staff, "Hey… what's the deal with the fax machine?"

"Well," they said, "that's the only way we get orders. We deal with all these small businesses, and all they do is fax. They don't do e-mail."

"They don't do e-mail?!" I thought to myself. "That's absurd! How can they only do orders via fax… in 2015?!"

So I got on the phone to our top five customers and asked them, "Do you guys *really* insist on using fax machines to place orders?"

"Oh, no," they told me.

"We have a server. It converts everything that comes on fax into email, and the only reason we fax is because of you guys."

My head exploded again. That was the end of the fax machine. We emailed all of our customers and let them know we'd accept orders electronically. I personally removed the fax machine from the office and placed it where it belonged—in the dumpster out back.

Bad Employees

Make no mistake: you are accountable for everyone and everything in your company, but your employees are still *responsible* for themselves and their behavior. Start treating them that way, and you stay on the positive side of accountability. Some employees just won't respond to good leadership, aren't open to training, and that makes the solution simple: **terminate them**.

One guy I fired worked the graveyard shift at our company. He got hired because his dad was the production manager. He probably assumed I'd never visit the plant at 2:00 AM, so he brought along his guitar and started practicing chords during his shift.

He should have learned how to play that country song, "Take This Job and Shove It," especially when I walked in at 2:00 AM one day and found him playing. I asked, "What are you doing?"

"The machine's running," he said, trying to play it cool.

"So?" I said. "You have nothing to check? Nothing to do? Your machine runs for four minutes... how can you sit there and play guitar? You should check your last set of parts. That takes at least two to three minutes."

"No," he said, "I checked my parts."

I could have fallen over backwards. "Are you missing the point?" I asked him.

Then he decided to try sarcasm. "Well, playing my guitar at night is one of the only reasons I'm staying here!"

I lowered my voice. "Then I guess you don't have any other reason to stay here." I fired him on the spot.

Some people are attracted to bad cultures. That night employee certainly seemed to like them. That was how the previous owner and management rolled; they allowed stuff like this and never checked on it.

Then there was the time a holdover employee in one of my companies got hold of the admin password for our servers. At nighttime, he'd try to get VPN access to our servers from the outside where he would download our data. It was a new experience for me calling the FBI to report someone stealing proprietary data.

This same employee also thought it would be a good idea to give me a sob story about his parents getting sick so he could take time to go out of state and help them. I agreed immediately, and I gave him two weeks.

A few days later I got a call from a nearby competitor. Their manager said to me, "Hey, there's a guy named So-and-So working here."

"Working there now?!" I said, raising an eyebrow.

"Yes," he said.

"He's on family leave from us," I said. "He told me he had a family emergency."

"That's not what he told us," the manager replied. "He started work with us two days ago."

My soon-to-be-former-employee was testing out another company to see if he liked them better. I suspect he ended up not liking either of them because he got fired from both. You can't make this stuff up!

Bad employee stories always take me back to Brent, the general manager at the CNC manufacturing shop. The guy I spent hours meeting, training, and providing direction—without micromanaging. The guy who cost us about $250,000 by increasing expenses artificially and scheduling unnecessary overtime, which eventually left us with just $10,000 in our account. (According to another employee who asked him about it, Brent shrugged his shoulders and said, "Dean will figure it out eventually").

I should have fired Brent within three days, and instead I waited three years. I paid a huge price in terms of time, money, and anguish. He was a key man in the company, and I was concerned with what would happen with the company culture if I kicked him out. When I finally fired him, I had to take over running the shop. We later discovered he had a ton of complaints from the customers, to whom he'd over-promised and under-delivered, as well as from the employees, who were afraid to talk about him.

Don't forget about the message you send to all your *other* employees —the ones who show up on time, work hard, put in the effort, and don't complain. If you tolerate a bad employee, your behavior sends a message to the rest of the staff that they're wasting their energy trying to be good.

After I fired Brent, the next three months were the highest shipping volume months we'd seen in over a decade. That gave me the confidence to fire *anyone*; I've never had a problem firing top leaders since then. I'm thankful I got the experience of dealing with Brent and how difficult he was. I can fire anyone now.

If you've got toxic, negative, lazy, or entitled employees... no matter how high they rank on the hierarchy—terminate those people. They're killing your company from the inside. Today, I'm very clear with senior management at every company I purchase: I have *zero* qualms about firing people.

Who Does What?

Let me share some more offensive phrases in WWDD?:

> *"Janet and Joe both handle XYZ task."*
> *"He works here, but we don't know what he does."*

Nope! That doesn't fly with me. Shared roles and phantom jobs are prohibited at my companies, because when a mistake happens, we need to know who's responsible so we can fix it. When we spend money on an employee, we need to know whether we're earning money as a result. Do you have roles handled by two people? That has got to go, *right away*. When we discuss the Brute Force and Analyze phases, you'll see what I mean... but for now, here's what you need to know: you have to define what your people do and who does what.

You need detailed job descriptions and a clear organizational chart with responsibilities.

At one company I bought, we had a holdover employee that they brought back on my first full day as the new owner. He'd been laid off and hadn't worked there for three months prior. The previous manager had no idea what he did, and they kept zero documentation on his job description or employment history.

I was puzzled. "Why did you bring him back on my first day here?" I asked them.

"Oh, we thought you might want to meet him," they said. "He works for the company."

"What does he do?" I asked.

"Well," they said, "he used to do shipping."

"What's he do now?"

"I don't know."

You can't make this stuff up! The fact that he'd been laid off for the previous ninety days didn't matter to the previous owners at all. They just wanted to be rid of the problem without the awkwardness of firing him, so they handed it off to me. We spent the next two weeks evaluating to see if there was an alternative role he could perform, but we couldn't find one.

The next thing you know, he turned around and sued me for age discrimination. He claimed I fired him because he was too old!

So there's up-front work to do if you don't have clear definitions and assignments in your company.

Who's In Charge?

Another difference in WWDD? culture is decision-making. If you call all the shots in your company, you're doing it wrong.

If you insist on working *in* your business, you'll have to do this, but you shouldn't do it at the expense of working *on* your business. You must empower your team to make decisions in your absence, and take the risk that, many times, they actually know better than you what to do.

At my companies, I show key leaders how to make decisions without me. The rule in the beginning is that at least three people must be involved. The intent of this is to empower the company to run without me, and I've done it enough times to know that if you show people the right way to make a call, they'll do it the right way. Eventually, one employee can make the decision.

You only need to have worked a teenager's job at a household name like McDonald's, Walmart, or Petco to know—their CEOs can't make the millions of daily decisions employees make. They can't even make most of the decisions of their executive teams and vice presidents. The best they can do is try to document and reproduce their decision-making style throughout the organization. You need to do that, too.

Speed and Quality

When it comes to getting a quality product out the door and into customers' hands as quickly as possible, I use the **90 Percent Rule**. This rule states that unless you're dealing with quality, safety, HR, or accounting, the final 10 percent of your effort almost always falls prey to the law of diminishing returns.

There's a point past which
"more" doesn't necessarily equal **"better."**

Your company is ready for change if you can set a "90 percent" tone. This is where you embrace the idea that "'Done' is better than 'Perfect.'" Keep in mind, part of your goal is to grow and expand your business. That only happens when you increase the amount of customers who trust you to deliver what they want without taking forever to do it. You can't afford to waste time perfecting everything you do.

If you spend ten hours on an assignment, does that somehow make it "ten hours better"? I once asked an admin to design a mouse pad for our computers. I gave her a basic design and told her, "Copy and paste, and add a few things on top." It took her *six hours* to get the project done. If your team takes this long on simple assignments, you likely have problems elsewhere, like culture.

You need quality in your product or service, but here's the problem: most companies get carried away on quality for things that don't require it. Speed usually fixes 90 percent of what goes on in any given company. Laser focus for quality should be on the "sweet spot"---the one that generates sales.

Harley-Davidson is a great example of a company that works very hard on the quality of its top-selling product—and believe it or not, that product is their *brand*, more than their motorcycles. Mechanically, Harleys are not the highest quality bikes when compared with brands like Honda or Kawasaki. (Harley owners sometimes joke that the letters "HD" stand for "Hundred Dollars"—as in, "Another hundred dollars to fix another broken part.") Those competing brands outperform and outlast Harleys in every measurable direction. But Harley knows their audience very well, and when it comes to connecting with their customers' aspirations, no brand of motorcycles comes close to the bond they've built. Wisely, Harley invests its most money and meticulous work into its brand, and it works!

Speed counts in a competitive marketplace. My 50 percent is better than most people's 100, so if we get to 90 percent, I feel extremely confident. But one surefire way to decrease speed is to over-emphasize quality in the wrong places. Make sure your quality is very high where it's critical, but don't sweat all the other details. If you make toilets, for example, you don't need to worry about making the underside of the toilet shiny. For most aspects of your business, you can only make things "so good" before you sacrifice time and energy for no return. Even brands that manufacture aircraft, such as Boeing or Lockheed, know to focus on quality and precision where it counts—hydraulics, controls, actuators, and so forth. But for seat cushions, in-flight entertainment, and airline food… they compromise. (*Even the engine covers fall off sometimes!*)

Ultimately, speed and quality come back to our core question to you as the leader: **Are you ready for change**? If you're focused on a perfect score in areas that don't matter, or if you're too relaxed about areas that do… your employees will follow your example.

Another kind of leader feels they need 100 percent in *everything*. This is equally counterproductive to success. Your team won't be able to meet your expectations. I don't look for perfect scores in my companies, because (a) I know it's unrealistic, and (b) leaders are *never* the people to achieve 100 percent in quality. If perfection shows up anywhere, it's usually with an individual employee or a handful of people who take tremendous pride in their work.

That's good news for you. It makes your job simple: find that 100 percent person who is a good fit for your company. In the meantime, you can legitimately settle for 60-80 percent, which is what you'll get from most decent employees.

QUICK RECAP

Changing your company only begins when you've truly changed yourself. But once you're on the track of personal growth, employees pick up on your attitude and example. Your company is ready for change if:

- You've set the table with a vision of cultural **openness** and **transparency**
- You're firmly against **neglecting** employees and operating on **assumptions**
- You understand that you can't build or scale a business without proper **documentation**
- You recognize that doing things the way you've always done them is a recipe for failure
- You're prepared to fire **bad employees** … *now*
- You're unwilling to entertain **dual roles** or **phantom employees**
- You're sick of making decisions alone, and you want to **delegate** authority
- You believe in scoring **90 percent** on non-critical tasks as fast as possible, and only seeking higher scores on the things that really matter

In the next chapter, we'll get down to brass tacks with creating an inspiring and productive workplace so you can motivate your employees to row in the same direction toward the "promised land" of your vision.

Chapter Five

Is Your Company Ready for Change?
Part 2

*"If the ladder is not leaning against the right wall,
every step we take just gets us to the wrong place, faster."*
Stephen Covey

W e're almost at the B.A.S.I.C.S of change, but your company still needs more work before it's truly ready.

You can strike a new tone, improve the culture, document everything, review employees, terminate bad employees, spell out job descriptions, and work on quality where it counts. But your employees also need a smooth runway to execute their roles day-to-day, especially if they're used to faulty systems, inefficient methods, or lousy incentives. That's what this chapter is about.

Work Smarter, Not Harder

One of the worst inefficiencies I ever saw happened at a box company I bought. An employee there spent part of his day in front of a five-foot stack of 36x36-inch "chipboard," which is a thick form of cardboard. Chunk by chunk, through ten pallets each weighing about 5,000 pounds, he would flip them over from one side to the other to get them ready to put into a machine. It was insane! I got exhausted just watching him do it. Eventually I walked over to the production manager and asked him, "What is that guy doing?"

"Well," he said, "he has to flip each stack over because one side is white, and the other side's brown. The machine only accepts it white-side up."

"How many of these does he do?" I asked.

"He can usually get the first pallet done in about half an hour," he said. "The second one, maybe 45 minutes... the third one, another hour. After that, he needs a break."

"So why don't we just have the factory flip it?" I continued.

"I don't think they do that," he said.

"So how long have we done it this way?"

"Over thirty-five years."

Thirty-five years. I felt like that monk from the Sixties who set himself on fire protesting war. I had the operations manager call the factory and ask, "Can you guys flip these stacks when you send them to us?"

"Oh, sure, no problem," they said.

"Any extra charge?"

"No, no charge."

Ever since then, the factory flips the chipboard stacks for us. It saves us *at least five full hours* of hard physical labor every day. On a good day, that employee might have got through five or six pallets; today, we can work through *fifty* pallets a day. All because we called up and asked the factory to do the work with their machines instead of having our employees do it.

Sometimes, the factory makes a mistake and still sends us pallets with the chipboard brownside-up. So I bought a piece of equipment that flips the pallets. Do you want to know how fast it flips them? *Ten seconds.* When I bought that flipper, I didn't yet know that we had as many as 135 pallets throughout the building that needed flipping. We got through all 135 of them in record time and still continued to use it. Take advantage of the age we live in, and let machines do the work they're capable of doing.

Your company might not be ready for change, especially at the management level, if you haven't yet trained them to **work smarter, not harder**. In this chipboard scenario, the employees simply accepted the shipments of the product the way they came, and they never thought about how it would change their lives if the factory flipped them before delivery. The workers didn't question it. The managers didn't question it. The previous owners didn't, either.

People are too passive about work, especially when their company cultures are dysfunctional. It's better than being *opposed* to better ways of doing things, for sure. But leadership fails to come up with solutions or empower workers to do it for themselves... so they just take things at face-value. No one was trained to think; they were trained to execute, and avoid making mistakes. That's the wrong way to do it. There was high turnover in that chipboard role, because the work was so physically demanding. Do you see how just one phone call solved a problem that lasted more than three decades? As the leader, you need to work smarter, not harder… and teach your team (especially management) to follow your example.

Needlessly Complicated

That same box company occupied 80,000 square feet of a 90,000 square foot facility. A plumbing company rented the remaining 10,000 square feet. There were nine separate units at 10,000 square feet apiece. Unfortunately, the way the building was set up, we couldn't access the receiving bays directly, where suppliers delivered most of our finished goods. They arrived in a separate building across the lot, which we normally used for storage. We'd move our goods there for future use, and then pull them back when we received new orders. Our main building had too much clutter, unused machines, and no racking system to accommodate the goods.

We co-leased that receiving area to the tune of $6,500 per month. The previous management had two employees assigned to pick up the finished goods. They would drive a box truck forty-to-fifty feet to the receiving bays, load the goods onto the truck with one of our forklifts (which sat there idle for the rest of the day), and then drive forty-to-fifty feet back and unload them. Just a handful of two-to-three pallets took over two hours of work, and they went back and forth three-to-four times a day. This was as crazy as anything I've ever seen, and it also went on for thirty years.

This is an example of ownership and management making (or keeping) things **needlessly complicated**.

I quickly researched the cost and space we needed to install industrial pallet shelves inside our existing warehouse. If we could set up those shelves, we could access our finished goods directly from inside our existing 80,000 square foot warehouse. We could eliminate the daily routine for those two employees and return them back to their jobs. We could bring the extra forklift back to work inside our plant. Best of all, we purchased the shelves at a cost of $5,800 per month for one year—$700/month less than leasing the inefficient receiving area.

If you make or leave roadblocks like this for your employees, your company's not ready for change. The business had two guys spending 50 percent of their workdays *not doing* their real jobs. They had a forklift sitting there doing *nothing* for most of the day. There was unnecessary wear and tear on the box truck's engine by using it for fifty-foot drives and not much else. All it took was an hour or so of simple research and a few phone calls, and we increased productivity and reduced waste by tens of thousands of dollars every month.

The box company also had several "holes"—places where manufacturers put equipment and machinery they no longer use. Sometimes, these holes create huge, unnecessary obstacles to get where you need to go. Elsewhere, it simply means more clutter and disorganization: machines scattered randomly throughout the building, a die cutter next to a gluer (next to another die cutter) doing nothing, and no one knows how (or why) they got there. I call this "completely unacceptable."

During the Brute Force phase at the CNC machining company, I made holes one of my top priority fixes. We put all the mills in one area, the lathes in another, and so forth. We get rid of every obsolete piece of machinery we can. This frees up a ton of space to put in new equipment as we purchase it. When we moved that company into a brand-new, state-of-the-art, 70,000-square foot facility, everybody knew the layout. There were no "holes."

Counterproductive Workspace

At the box company, even after moving and reorganizing the equipment, something else still wasn't right. It was almost like the place was designed to *prevent* people from being productive.

The box company's shipping office was at the opposite end of the building from the shipping bays! The shipping manager wasted countless hours and money walking to and from one end of the building to the other just to use a computer, complete paperwork, and print labels. I'm sure he got a great step count every day, but *what a waste*! We built a small, 12x14 foot office with a ceiling, lights, glass windows, a couple of desks, and a computer. Now our shipping manager stays near the office all day and never leaves until quitting time.

Your company is not ready for change if you neglect or tolerate a **counterproductive workspace**.

At another of my companies, the employees would do this by carrying buckets of water and coolant to fill the machines once a day. Like cars, manufacturing machines need fluids and water to run efficiently. Staff drained them each month and emptied the buckets into a large container in the back of the plant.

So we connected spigots to each machine. Now, instead of lugging those buckets back and forth, the employees could turn on a tap and refill the machines with the fluids they need, on the spot. It cost maybe $1000 or so to set that system up, but the return was huge; productivity skyrocketed because the workers didn't have to stop and bring fluids for the machinery.

The machines at my machining company have fixtures that attach to the machine depending on the job. The company kept all these fixtures on shelves or in carts, completely disorganized. Nobody knew where anything was, and I watched employees spend as much as an hour and forty-five minutes looking for the fixtures. We reorganized this and used a computer program to tell the staff exactly where to find the fixture they needed. It reduced search time from about an hour on average… to mere *seconds*.

Shortly before I took over, my box company bought a $1.2 million die cutter. This machine is the size of a school bus. It was meant to replace two older die cutters, but when I showed up to start work, nobody was using it.

"What's the deal with the new die cutter?" I asked. "We just bought it last year, didn't we? Why isn't it running now?"

"Well," they said, "we kind of… don't use it."

"Why?" I asked. "Why do you not use our $1.2 million die cutter that cuts 9,000 sheets per hour, when these old ones only cut between 500 and 5,000 sheets an hour?"

"Well," they said, "we're afraid we'll break it."

"What do you mean?" I asked.

"We're afraid to run it. We're afraid we're going to break it."

"Ka-boom!" went my head again. I knew what they meant by that one-dimensional answer: they had been trained, but didn't have the confidence or support of the previous owner, who spent over a million dollars to buy the machinery. The staff, whom they never trained to use it, was afraid of getting blamed or fired if they tried to use it and it broke. The real issue was *culture*, more than training.

"So the choice is to not run it at all?" I said. "Listen! You have my full permission to break that machine. I will take full accountability for it."

They began to use the die cutter, and I have good news: it continues to work perfectly to this day. Nobody ever broke it, but we *did* break the counterproductive environment left by the previous owners. Today, we have a professional operator on staff who runs it like a champ, and productivity has never been higher.

Constant Interruption

Owners and management are accountable to run a tight ship for employees, so your door should always be open. But if people keep coming through the door every few minutes and you can't get anything done without being interrupted... you aren't ready for change.

The box company had this problem. Issues would come up, and employees kept walking into the office to ask questions. Eventually, I questioned why this kept happening. The employees told me there were issues with paperwork, incorrect quantities, logistical hurdles, and so forth. So I called a meeting the next day.

I told them, "Going forward, your default go-to for questions and problems is the production manager."

Then I held up a handful of tags. "Do you all see these tags I'm holding up?" They nodded.

"From now on, if you come to the production manager with an issue, I want you to fill one of these out. I don't care how simple it is, even if it's a typo or misspelling on an order form. I want to know about it."

I continued, "Now, if the production manager can't solve your problem, he'll send you into the office. If you come into the office, I want you to have one of these tags with you. I need to know which job

---

ISSUES SLIP FORM
EMPLOYEE TO COMPLETE 4 SECTIONS BELOW:

Team Member: _____
(1) Department: _____
(2) Job Number: _____ Part Number: _____
(3) Issue Experiencing: _____
_____
_____

it is, who's the operator, and what's the issue. Nobody comes into the office without a tag."

The staff complied with my instructions. In the meantime, we started holding "corrective action" meetings once a week among management. Soon, the origins of these problems grew more clear: one category might have a single tag, while others would have seven or eight. The first "recurring" complaint we noticed was when materials arrived too late. So we changed our process to ensure we had materials on hand sooner in the cycle. We also created a spreadsheet to track issues the staff brought to our attention, as well as how and when we resolved them.

Like magic, 95 percent of our problems disappeared, along with employee complaints, in a single month. The management team learned that every time you notice duplicating or recurring problems, you have to document them right away, and solve them as quickly as you can. Otherwise, you will run into them repeatedly without ever truly solving them.

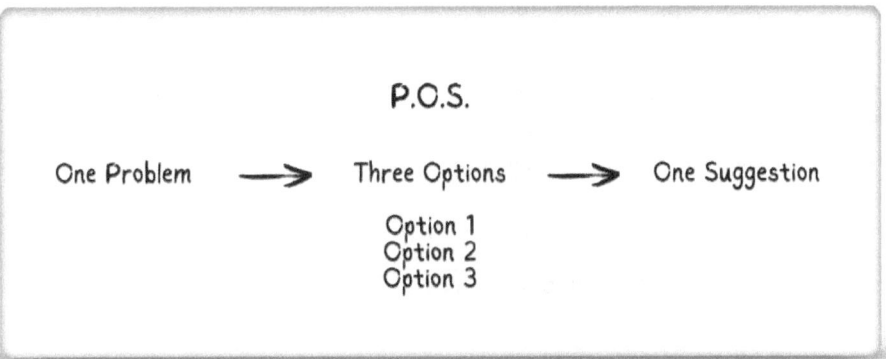

In my companies, we follow a process called "**P.O.S.**" (**P**roblem, **O**ptions, **S**uggestion… *yes, I know what else it stands for*) to cut down on interruptions is empowering your employees—something most employers feel too nervous to do. For me, it's like a breath of fresh air.

I tell my staff, "Before you bring a problem to me, I need no more than half a page that shows me (a) the Problem, (b) three possible Options, and (c) a Suggestion from the employees." You'll be amazed how often they already know the solution to the problems they bring to you. If you just give them the chance, you can reduce several hours of distraction into a ten-second decision:

"Of these three solutions, which one do you favor or think will work?"

"Option C."

"Great! Let's do it. Let me know how it turns out or if you need any support."

Conflict Resolution

Your company isn't ready for change if you don't **handle conflict well** —even less so if you lack the skill to train your employees to handle it themselves.

Some people picture shouting matches or fistfights when I say the word "conflict," but it's much broader than that. Any time two or more people look at the same thing and see it differently, you have conflict. Conflict can go unspoken. It can be stifled. But it's there, and your job as a leader includes (a) being aware that conflict exists and (b) being prepared to call it out, navigate it, and resolve it effectively.

Learn to ask the question:
"What could you have done differently?"

There's no such thing as a scenario where people have "zero choice" over how they behave or respond. None. Remember this when conflict breaks out, because unless it happens right in front of you, the challenge is to hear both sides of a story *and not take either side* because you don't have all the facts. Nor are you likely to get them right away; sometimes, you never do.

One day, a verbal scuffle broke out between a veteran employee and a newer, younger employee at one of my companies. I arrived at the office in the middle of the day, and the general manager told me what happened. They'd already tried to resolve the issue, but it wasn't improving, and they wanted some guidance. So we assembled the management team and brought the employees together to see if we could solve the problem.

Neither would budge. The veteran, an older man, was a "Back in my day, sonny" type of guy. He was used to doing things the way he learned to do them, and he wasn't interested in any other approach. The younger employee, meanwhile, was still learning, interested in trying different methods, and much more concerned about how he felt emotionally when the conflict escalated. Both were fully convinced they'd done nothing wrong and it was the other's fault.

So I took them aside separately, one by one. To the veteran, I said, "I hear what you're saying. Now, first of all, you know that the whole 'this is how we used to do it' thing died the day I showed up. I don't care how we used to do it. This is how we're doing it now."

He nodded.

I continued, "Here's what I suggest. I don't know if you're wrong or whether you plan to apologize. But could you have handled anything better or worse, in that scenario?"

"Nothing," he said bluntly.

"Nothing at all?" I asked. "There's not *one* thing you could have said or done differently? Nothing where you could admit, 'I probably shouldn't have said that'?"

"Well, okay," he finally said. "Maybe I was a little over the top."

"Okay," I said. "So here's something you could do to extend an olive branch. When we go back in that room, you could say, 'Hey, I probably could have handled that better.' I'm not asking you to apologize; I just want you to acknowledge that it could have gone better. I'm not demanding you do it… but think about it."

Then the younger employee came in. For him, it was all about feelings and emotion: "I feel like this" and "I feel that." I told him, "I hear you, and your feelings are valid. They really are. But if you can't describe in simple terms what bothered you, there's no way he's going to understand, and there's no way I can fix it. I need you to explain to me in a way that I can understand."

He began to talk, but quickly diverted to telling me more about his feelings, so I stopped him. I said, "I understand how you feel, but you're still not answering my question. I don't know how to fix the problem, because I don't know what the problem is."

More back and forth occurred until I said, "Is it possible you're upset more because of how you feel versus the reality of what happened?"

Finally, he admitted, "Yes, I see what you mean. Yes, it is possible."

So I coached him through a similar routine; when we resolved the situation, there was no need to apologize or admit that he was wrong. He only needed to acknowledge that he'd got carried away by his feelings, and that would be enough.

We brought both employees into the room together. The veteran took the initiative and admitted he could have handled the situation better. The young guy admitted that he'd got carried away by his emotions. Before you could look around, they both went back to work… and eventually became friends!

Conflict, when handled appropriately, plants the seeds for better cooperation and stronger bonds. It's neither wrong nor unusual for people to have different perspectives, so why do we treat it that way?

We should treat conflict as an opportunity to find ways to work together. But most leaders go back to the Band-Aid™ section in Chapter 1: they *separate* the two employees, and hope the conflict will go away! In this scenario, neither employee would have been challenged to rise above their current levels. They'd never have discovered what they were capable of doing. Their conflict would have kept getting worse.

Remember: if you want the kind of change that leads to lasting success, you have to find the *real* problem, not just the surface one. It's likely there are other issues in employees' personal lives that fuel their quarrels—the reverse of how a man stressed at work brings it home. If you put stressed employees working together for eight hours a day, there's a chance they'll take it out on each other. So you must resolve the conflict, which means the two parties need to come together and work out a solution. Separation is the last thing you should do.

Don't forget… some conflicts don't get resolved in a single session. You always have the option of sending employees home for the day. This is good if you're less comfortable with confrontation than I am. But at some point, if employees refuse to reconcile, you have to warn them that they're endangering their jobs. Personally, I put the employees together and say, "You're going to work together until I can see you've resolved it. I'm trying to help, but if you won't work with me, be aware that one of you is going to go home without a job."

Cultures of Conflict

Some companies bring conflict right to your doorstep; it's in their cultural DNA. Remember my union gearbox company? On my first day as director of operations, the union leader came to me and said, "Just so you know, we're nine out of nine."

I didn't know what he meant, so I asked him to explain.

"Well," he said, "we've had nine grievances with the company, and we've won all nine."

A "grievance" is when a union disputes disciplinary actions from an employer; they fight back when an employee gets fired, or written up for being late, and so forth. At this company, management hated the union, and the union hated management. But I was determined to have zero grievances while I ran operations. So I began to meet one-on-one with all the union leaders by myself. It soon led to meetings with their entire leadership team where I asked their advice on how to handle employee issues and disciplinary situations.

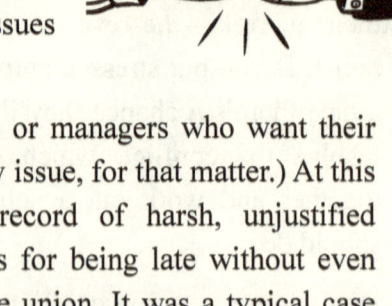

Union leaders aren't used to employers or managers who want their advice on employee discipline (or on any issue, for that matter.) At this company, management had a track record of harsh, unjustified punishments. They wrote up employees for being late without even talking to them or discussing it with the union. It was a typical case where leaders focused only on the bottom line. The fact that I was willing to seek the union's advice and input spoke volumes, and it disarmed their ordinary, suspicious stance toward management.

One employee, whom I'll call "Jim," kept showing up late and got brought into my office one day, along with the union representatives. "Jim," I said to him, "you're not showing up on time. What's going on?" At first, he tried to deflect me with a cheap excuse, but that didn't slow me down. I took him through the Five Whys and tried to understand his problem as deeply as I could.

It turned out that he was tired most of the time from a combination of his job and raising a young family. "What can I do to help you get here on time?" I asked him.

Afterward, the union president (I'll call him "Chuck") came into my office and said, "As long as I've been in the union, I've never heard *any* operations manager, president, or leader ask an employee, 'What can I do to help you?' Not once." Sadly, it's not surprising. Most employers (including those at the gearbox company) would attack the employee by saying, "Fix this or I'm gonna write you up," which adds stress to the employee and forces the union to fight back and file a grievance.

But in all my time as director of operations, we never had *one* union grievance. I never let things rise to that level. Sometimes, you can be as conflict-avoidant as you want, and conflict will come looking for you anyway. Even in those situations, you'd be surprised what kind of cooperation you can inspire. Quietly one day, Chuck told me, "I like you, 80 percent."

"I'll take 80 percent!" I laughed.

"I can't say '100 percent,' he said with a grin, "or else the other unions will think we're in bed with management."

A (Non-)Family Affair

If you want your company to be like a "family," you're not ready for change.

I go against the grain of referring to any of my companies as "family" or "like a family." You know why? Because families mistreat each other, whereas professionals don't. If people mistreat each other at my companies, we deal with it. We don't excuse it by saying, "Oh, that's just Uncle John," or "Oh, ya know, it's Aunt Sally doing what she does." No! If Uncle John or Aunt Sally behaved toward their co-workers like they do to their family, what do you think would happen? They might get an opportunity to fix it, but eventually they'd get reprimanded and terminated! You don't get to choose the family you're born into, but you definitely get to choose your co-workers.

The idea of a business being a "family" is the biggest joke I've ever heard. It's like when people compare their marriage with a business contract. It doesn't make sense; one is a lifelong commitment you make, whether or not it works out perfectly. The other is an agreement that can be broken, as soon as one side no longer needs or wants it to continue. If you want it to be a "family," your business is not ready for change. Don't expect from professionals what you expect from family. It's unrealistic and unfair.

Of course, this doesn't mean you walk around treating people like robots with no emotion whatsoever. I always say, "We're professionals who treat each other with respect, and if we happen to laugh and enjoy being around each other in the process, that's even better." Professionals who care about each other are, in some ways, as good or better than family. Think of soldiers fighting in a war zone or a championship sports team. The winning mindset common to these groups is commitment to one another while *in pursuit of a shared goal*. Remember how family doesn't understand your goals and vision as a business leader? If your family doesn't get it, there's not much you can do about it. But fellow professionals can get it—if you teach them! The best way to pull your team members into your vision is to find out how it aligns with what's important to them.

Learn What's Important

You can employ basic and advanced levels of showing people that you care about them. Every time we hire a contracting company to renovate or build new sites, I make a regular habit of buying lunch or donuts for their entire crew. I'll take time and spend money to take owners, executives, and management to lunch and build relationships with them. Each "touch" gives me one more opportunity to meet people, gather useful information, and be a "hands-on" leader who knows his company (or companies) at a detailed, intimate level. Caring for your employees' basic physical needs like this goes a long way.

For more advanced care, think about it in more complex ways. Most owners and managers don't know what employees want, or care about... but they imagine they do! I've heard things like, "Oh, I know all their family members, the kids' names, and their ages." *So what*?! What if they don't care about that? What if your employee's eyes roll every time you send his kids a birthday card because what he really wants is cross-training to move into management?

Other leaders act like money is the answer to everything. "We pay them, don't we?" they ask, incredulous. Sure you do, but so did WorldCom, Lehman Brothers, Jordan Belfort, and Martin Shkreli. So do all the companies that go out of business and lay people off, even the most well-meaning ones. Paying salaries means you pay salaries; it doesn't make you knowledgeable about what matters to your employees.

Your company is not ready for change if you don't know **what motivates your people** to work hard and succeed. You'll know by how they react indifferently to your "generosity." One Christmas, I spent a pile of money on iPads and generic tech gifts for employees... and they appreciated it, but they could tell I hadn't put much thought into it. The next year, I resolved to give personalized gifts to each person, and we spent the interim learning what our staff cared about in detail. It made a world of difference.

Caring about what matters to your employees changes everything. Few owners and managers ever do it... which is why they stay stuck in the cycle. It's funny; you'd be amazed what you can discover when you take time to ask. I'm talking about going to them, one-by-one if your company is small enough, and finding out what they value. (If you lead a very large company where you have thousands of employees, surveys work great for this.)

I do this with all of my employees. I sit them down for a meeting and say, "Tell me about yourself. I'd like to get to know you better and learn about what's important to you. I'll start… I enjoy snowmobiling in the winter. What's something you enjoy doing?"

If you notice, I lead the conversation by sharing some information about myself to get the ball rolling. *Don't skip that step*, because their defenses might go up if you jump straight to trying to get information out of them. But once they start talking, listen carefully. Take notes, if you need to. Like any other group of people, employees love to talk about themselves, their passions and interests. They will tell you a lot of useful information you can leverage… not only for things like gifts, but also to encourage and help them get closer to what they want in their careers.

As sales guru Zig Ziglar said, "You can have everything in life you want if you will just help enough other people get what they want." That's the secret: make the time, and take the time.

QUICK RECAP

Changing your company takes empathy and sincere attention to detail at the ground level. To prepare your staff for change, you have to try your best to see their employment and daily duties with you *through their eyes*. Your company is ready for change if:

- You're obsessed with **working smarter, not harder**, and want the same for your team
- You hate it when things are **needlessly complicated**, and you're hungry to improve efficiency and simplicity
- You can accept where you've created or maintained a **counterproductive workspace**
- You're tired of **constant interruption** and want your employees to think for themselves
- You're prepared for **conflict resolution** and see disagreements as opportunities

- You're unafraid of **cultures of conflict,** and you're inspired to reduce or eliminate tensions
- You recognize that **business is not "family"** and you don't want to pretend otherwise
- You know and care deeply about **what's important to your team**, not just yourself

No more delays. Let's get to the B.A.S.I.C.S Follow me.

SVARC

B.A.S.I.C.S.
BLUEPRINT

**A Turnaround Framework
for Business Recovery**

 ## BRUTE FORCE
Break Bottlenecks, Eliminate Outdated
Processes, Reset Layout and Roles

 ## ANALYZE
Deep-dive Into Departmental Problems,
Systems, and Inefficiencies. Prioritize
by Impact.

 ## STRUCTURE
Document Core Processes
and Assign Clear Responsibilities

 ## IMPROVE
Modify Policies and Procedures Based
on What's Essential vs. Outdated

 ## CULTURE
Instill Accountability, Urgency,
and Continuous Improvement

 ## SUSTAIN
Secure Success, Seek Significance, and
Review Where You Stand in the
Daily Operations of Your Company

Part Two: The B.A.S.I.C.S

Chapter Six

Brute Force
Break Bottlenecks, Eliminate Outdated Processes, Reset Layout and Roles

"The training is nothing! The will is everything!"
- Liam Neeson, as Ra's Al Gul in "Batman Begins"

Brute Force is the first phase we go through at each company I purchase. Every one of those companies has baggage left over from the old guard. They have stalled functions (bottlenecks), outdated processes, poor physical layout, double-assignment roles, and/or phantom employees. I have yet to manage or take over a company with a virtuous, high-trust culture; up-to-date and efficient processes; a well-organized physical environment; and everyone understands and works, responsibly and intensely, in well-defined roles. If you've read this far, your company is probably in similar straits.

When I talk about Brute Force, don't picture turning into a tyrant or a dictator. Aim to be an authoritative leader, restoring order and efficiency to an upside-down corner of the world. By the time I sit at my desk on Day One, I've already spent time researching, planning, observing, and interviewing. I don't spend the first day asking the employees, "What should we do?" or "Who's in charge around here?" I carry a clipboard with half a dozen pages of tasks outlined, assigned, and ready to deploy. I've got an organizational chart, so I know who everyone is and what they do. If I have to be firm, then I do it... but most of the time, most people simply follow my lead. Remember—an average of 85 percent of employees will begin adapting themselves to meaningful change almost immediately.

Kari, one of the managers at the box company, told me she was thrilled when Brute Force began. From her experience with the previous owners, she was used to "sometimes" meeting and discussing new ideas with management... without ever implementing them. She put it this way:

> You came into the company with a ton of changes, and we bulldozed through a lot of areas where it was overdue and necessary. But you still took in people's insights along the way. I was excited, because I'm passionate about technology, and to see us move several decades into the future was very fulfilling for me. I feel more empowered.

If you remember the section on personalities, and if you're anything other than a "D" on the DISC Assessment, this phase is a good time to have someone like me at your side. Yes, I'm assertive, but the main reason to have a strong "D" in your ranks during Brute Force is because *the business needs help*. There isn't enough time to build consensus, ease people into things, or spend hours analyzing and calculating data to predict every possible outcome. It's time for fast, consistent, determined action to reverse damage and bring order to chaos. "D" personalities excel at action-taking. In the back of the book, you'll find my contact information. Reach out to me and schedule some time to meet.

Brute Force, Your Team Members, & Goals

You can't build a strong team and lead them to the promised land without admitting that the current lineup needs work. I'm not saying you need to fire everyone... that would be suicidal! But you have a good chance *some* people will self-select out of the new direction. Anytime you work hard to improve yourself, somebody somewhere gets offended. Take it to the bank.

Remember what we talked about in Chapter 3, about the company you keep? You rise and fall on the people who surround you, outside of work. My old friends supported me as long as I only *talked* about launching my first business. Once I did it, things changed. Next thing you know, they had one "warning" or "concern" after another and tons of experience to share. They didn't actually care about my welfare; they turned more negative over time because I did things they couldn't imagine doing. It made them feel bad about themselves.

During Brute Force, you should expect similar outcomes from similar people. Look for the sudden attitude switches among your staff. You will always discover at least one squeaky wheel or naysayer who doesn't want to go along with your plan. Don't make the mistake I made with Brent, my toxic general manager. Expect resistance, and tell people up front: "We're going a different direction. I hope it's a good fit for everyone, but I recognize that some people might not like it. All I'm asking for is the same thing we already agree to as employer and employee: If I ask you, 'Move the lathe,' move it. If I ask you to move it again, it's because I've learned new information I didn't know before—so move it again."

The Quick and the Dead

Brute Force is about going for the lowest-hanging fruit and fixing problems that require the least discussion or analysis. If you've got a corner of your building with file cabinets full of twenty years of paperwork or old equipment that should have been thrown out thirty years ago… just get rid of it. Brute Force is a phase of making quick decisions with significant impact in rapid succession. With enough planning up front, you can make a lot of these changes on Day One.

Other Brute Force decisions are the opposite of "slash and burn." One of my companies had an old truck in the parking lot that hadn't run or been used for nine years. My operations manager and I walked outside, fiddled around with it for an hour or so, and got it running. We ended up using it. Another company had eleven dock doors on one side of the building with a bunch of idle semi-trailers backed up to them. We hired a company to move them to the other side and open up the access to the docks.

Manufacturing companies often have equipment "mismashed." They put it wherever they have empty space. Over time, as they keep adding to the pile, it gets ridiculous: your shop stays full of equipment you don't use, piled up in the center of the building… while the stuff you use daily ends up outside or in hard-to-reach places. My CNC machining company had some of its machines on one side of the building and all the tooling for those machines on the other… so employees spent hours every day walking back and forth to get the tools and return them. Organize your shop so your equipment and tools are all close to one another for efficiency.

Goals

"Tease" or hint toward your vision and goals during Brute Force. Don't get super-specific, but remember: most people are trained by society *not* to visualize or imagine their future. It's your job as the leader to turn that around and make your team believe they can achieve something together.

Brute Force is more than a phase in a corrective process.
It's a huge step on a pathway toward a brighter future.

If you don't yet believe this, go back and spend more time in Part One of this book, because you're not yet ready for change. But if you feel a deep conviction burning you up on the inside, you should be telling your staff things like:

- "We're burning the ships. There's no going back."
- "We'll never be the same again—in a lot of really good ways."
- "This *has* to happen. We don't have a choice. This is our destiny."
- "We're already a Fortune 100 Company. We just don't know it yet."

You say these things with deadly seriousness and a straight face, because you believe them. You've smashed the blockages in your mind, but your employees aren't there yet. That's why it's so important to show up with a full, prepared list of tasks and objectives early on and connect what you ask of them to the vision. Tell them how their daily actions affect the long-range vision, and reinforce that along the way. Show them how you do it, tell them they can do it, and encourage them as they learn. As John Maxwell says,

"A leader is someone who knows the way,
goes the way, and shows the way."

With all that in mind, set reasonable expectations for how long this will take. Another popular saying in the business world goes: "We overestimate what we can achieve in one year, and underestimate what we can achieve in five years."

You have ideas—big ideas. Maybe you see your company growing, scaling, and becoming a household name. Good! Ambition is good—but don't get fixated on perfect timelines or imagine you have the perfect environment and circumstances to win big inside of a single year. Driven people (like me) who put forth a ton of effort tend to get overly optimistic: "If I do the work, things happen... so if I just outwork everyone else as fast as I can for a year, I'll get to the finish line first!" Don't rely on drive and enthusiasm alone, and don't forget how many variables can impede your progress!

Most owners and managers burn out after the first year, for exactly this reason. They overestimate what they can accomplish, and when the results fail to materialize, they lose their enthusiasm. Instead, think about it this way: even if you move through the B.A.S.I.C.S. phases in less time, ninety percent of leaders give up after the first year, as you can see:

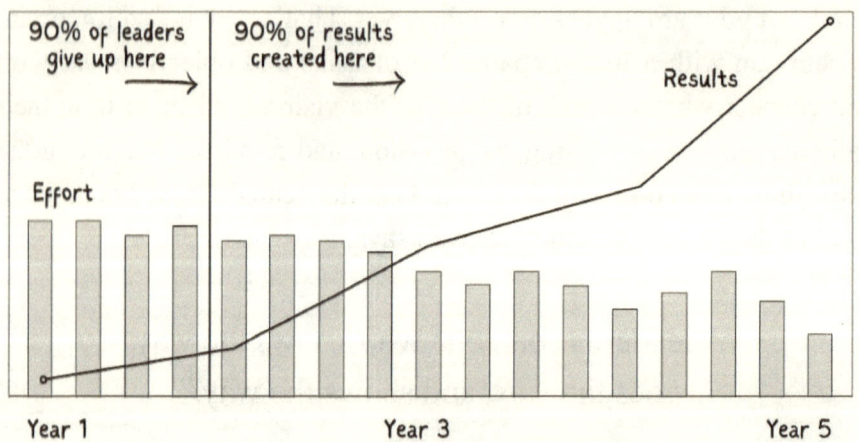

They want to reach in Year One what they should expect to reach in Year Three (or beyond, in some cases). If you outlast the first-year quitters, that means you're already part of an elite group—the 10

percent still standing. But remember: **it won't look like you're winning just yet**.

In fact, by Year Three, you should expect to give yourself a pat on the back... *for laying a solid foundation*. You might still have work to do on your Culture and Sustain phases, at this point. Some companies take that long to go through the B.A.S.I.C.S properly. In the next chapter, I'll tell you about my company that still dealt with Brute Force issues eight months in! It will take endurance, grit, and constant communication with your team (a) to remind yourself and (b) to let them know that this is no "fly-by-night" fix.

By Year Three, if you stick with it and work through all the issues until they resolve, it's reasonable to expect a windfall for your hard work. You've changed who you are, and you continue to evolve... and, now, you have a changed company to show for it—a company that can become ten times bigger than it originally was. You can exceed your wildest dreams if you commit to three years of hard work with the right mentor (me), goals, and direction.

In the meantime? Share short-term, quick-win goals with your staff for the next thirty-, sixty-, ninety-, 180-, and 365-day chunks:

> *"We're going to get thirty new customers in the next three months."*

> *"By end of year, we'll have systems and processes for all job descriptions."*

> *"Six months from now, we're going to buy three new company trucks."*

If you're a smaller company, these goals are much more reasonable and attainable than telling your team, "We're gonna be a hundred million dollar company by this time next year." There's a lower probability that will happen.

Fire Fast

Pay attention to how relationships develop between you and your employees. Many years ago, before my personal and professional transformation, I moved very slowly through self-improvement and change. From several directions, I felt more pressure against what I wanted to do. I had a wife and children, a group of friends, extended family, co-workers, and employees. I heard a lot of opinions and perspectives—too many for me to make headway without upsetting people. I sensed the weighty challenge of planning my future. Because of this, I felt more hesitant about another important part of business: firing people.

When I took over my machining company, one of the "Three Amigo" bad employees I failed to fire was Charlie, the quality manager. I was nervous about firing him because I knew I couldn't easily replace that role, but like the general manager, Brent, and the administrator, Kelly... Charlie refused to adapt. I spent a long time trying to work with him before I finally pulled the trigger. (He later wrote a two-page apology and asked for his job back... but his reasons focused on how that would benefit him, not the company. So I declined to rehire him.)

Nowadays, especially during Brute Force, I'm much more skilled and fast at firing people who don't want to get on board. I'm better at hiring people who appreciate what we're doing and want to be part of it. Most importantly, I communicate the vision and direction consistently, and I tie it to the daily rhythms in the company so people can decide if they want to keep going.

Practically, this means you should pay attention and try to gauge people's reactions when you hint at the goals and vision for the future. If people get inspired and grab the bull by the horns, great! But watch for people who react with indifference, cynicism, or opposition. You've heard my horror stories about the managers I've had to fire who fought against or sabotaged my reforms. At some point, you should stop trying to spend time or energy persuading or winning them over; you haven't got the time to spare. Just show them the door.

Brute Force and Knowledge

In Brute Force, what you don't know *will* hurt you. You're attempting to smash bottlenecks, eliminate outdated processes, reset your layout, and define/assign roles—ideally, depending on your company's size, within months.

You know how the media covers a new U.S. president's "First 100 Days"? I want to show you a parallel. You're leading your team in a direction different from the one they're used to, which means you have a lot of persuading to do. So you'd better come prepared with a thorough understanding of what needs to happen and a full list of tasks to get the ball rolling. Knowledge is power, especially during Brute Force. Soak up all the knowledge you can before you take your first ride in the saddle.

Know Your Tasks

Restore order to chaos.

That's your #1 priority. On Day One of Brute Force, I have a pile of **weekly task sheets** for each and every employee. It's not "busy work"; I base these tasks on an **issue log** I keep as I work through buying the company. Typically that content ends up on my whiteboard, which I organize into individual tasks for each department. If you already own your company, then spend four to six weeks compiling these issues before you start Brute Force. Clear your schedule, hold your calls, get off the service calls, and dig for one thing: *issues.* Get as much detail and insight as possible. Knowledge is power.

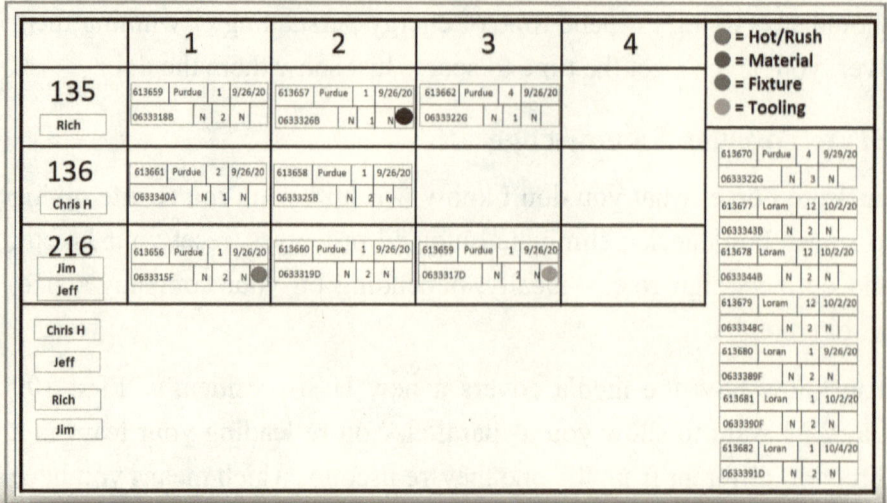

One of my actual whiteboards with jobs by manufacturing function

The larger your company, the more you must delegate. Your job is to describe what you want to happen to management at a high level. We're not talking about creating a task sheet for sweeping the floor or cleaning toilets. Let the managers collaborate to create their own spreadsheet with tasks, assignments, and due dates. This helps you avoid micro-managing your team. Don't forget the 90 Percent Rule; you'll fine-tune specifics and nuanced processes during the Analyze phase. For now, delegate the quick changes to your senior leaders and turn them loose.

For task sheets, create a template document so you can change the names and details, but keep the rest consistent. Include spaces for due dates, priorities, and special notes. (If you have an admin who can do this, delegate the data entry and review/fine-tune it yourself.) Now, go back to your whiteboard and record all the high-level tasks, assignees, and due dates. Bingo—you can now track on a weekly basis what you expect your employees to do. You can forecast when projects will be complete and verify that they've fulfilled what you asked them to do.

Before you leave on Friday evening, take a photo of your whiteboard with your phone. On Sunday night, sit down and revisit your progress. Then plan out next week's phases and goals. This continues after Brute Force and becomes a year-round, permanent weekly practice–initially for you, and (eventually) your management team.

Knowledge: Family and Friends

I talk a lot about family-owned companies and their problems, as well as the dangers of hiring friends. But it's okay to admit: you might need some direct support from family or friends during Brute Force. If your financial situation takes time to improve, inexpensive or free support are lifesavers. Some people are capable of working together even if they're related or best buddies. If you have people you can lean on in your personal network, take an inventory of what they do so you can approach them about working together.

One example is hiring ambitious younger relatives or your friends' adult children. Young adults need to gain experience to make themselves attractive to employers. If they're willing to work for you short-term in exchange for real-life experience or a low wage… you can sidestep hiring and/or firing full-time adult employees. Also, in this day and age, let's face it—kids who grew up on the digital grid often know way more about technology than you do. So if your nephew's great at designing websites or coding, give him a shot. If your friend's granddaughter needs an admin job for the summer, hire her. You'll be surprised how much they can help you.

I owe a debt I can never repay to Justin, my friend of forty+ years, who faithfully showed up and helped me set up IT systems at every company I've ever owned, often without asking for anything in return. We've been friends since we were kids, and in our teens, we worked on car and computer projects together. Both of us are strong leaders, and I've benefited from Justin's willingness to question and challenge my ideas from a tech standpoint. I love getting to work with people mature enough to walk the long road of relationship together. Justin is an example of someone I've leaned on for help over the years, and plays an instrumental role supporting my companies.

I've known plenty of people, however, who weren't so lucky. Some dumped their unlucky streak onto me. (Remember the guy who refused to fire his brother-in-law?) Family is permanent. If you hire a lousy employee, you can fire them and go your separate ways. They might even steal from you, but you don't pay the same price as you would if your child or a relative did the same. But family lasts forever, and you can't replace valuable friendships. If you decide to work with family or friends:

Put everything in writing, and only work with people who can handle personal and professional relationships simultaneously.

Know Your Issues/Fixes

In addition to the issue log I bring on Day One, I also come prepared with a **company issue log,** and direct the team to report *everything*. The details you need vary from business to business, but I believe every issue log needs the following fundamental data:

- Original date of reporting the issue
- Name of the person who reported it
- Name of the person who recorded it
- Description of the issue
- Impact the issue has, directly and/or indirectly throughout the business
- Suggested resolution
- A column for the outcome, with comments from the manager who closed the issue
- A status column
- A priority ranking
- A special notes column

Project & Issue Dashboard

	Job #	Customer	Part #	Dept	Issue	Result	Corrective Action (TBD)	Owner	Ass. Dat	Due Dat	Comp. Da	Pri	Status	Notes
8	41469 & 41468	John Doe Co	12 oz. and 6 oz. fudge	Office	Jobs were sent out with the wrong part numbers (flavors were flipped)	Caught by label department when labels were being checked in.	XX to double check all jobs that go out to shop to ensure they are correct.	Kari	8/5/25	8/5/25		Critical	Open	XX updated jobs after they were brought to attention. Insured case labels would properly print as well.
9	41695	Mike Doe Co	1824797 (#4)	Shipping	Shipping paperwork had 500 pieces, but 600 pieces were shipped	Customer received incorrect paperwork and had to be adjusted in M1		Travis	9/11/25	10/1/25		Important	Open	
10		John Doe Co	Sharkgrip	Office	Shipping paperwork was marked as PPO&ADD and had Frt info Attached - Customer should not have been billed freight	Customer questioned freight charge	Tom instructed Atlas to pay short	Kari	9/16/25	10/1/25		Important	Open	
11		Mike Doe Co	1825518	Office	PO was not correct to note dray strip for film	Gary is scuffing film to be able to glue	Dry strip needs to be noted on the PO and a Layout sent in the future	Tom	9/15/25	10/1/25		Important	Open	
12	41692	John Doe Co	29215018	Shop	Job Traveler was in office w/o sleeve or magnet - ready to file without any production.	Job due to be released but nothing completed.	pulled partial stock and rushed the remainder - ran with next job (41740)	Travis	9/24/25	10/1/25		Important	Open	
13	41687 & 41680	Mike Doe Co	Purlns	Shop	No sample print with job traveler	Had to come to office to retrieve	Found copy in print room	Alex	9/25/25	10/1/25		Important	Open	
14	41740 & 41692	John Doe Co	29215018		Partial ready to ship - held for complete order(see line13 above). Completed shipped off 41740 instead of 41692	Wrong PO referenced		Lynell	9/30/2025	10/1/25		Important	Open	
					Customer Rejected 60 pieces due to adhering issue item is	Customer requesting to check adhering	Per TP: Production to "spot check" 20 pieces in each							

Current Issues Log   Project   Discussions   Requests   Parts   Supplies   AutoFill

Remember from Chapter 5 how my box company employees kept approaching management to ask questions? Use this as excellent time to nip that problem in the bud. As I said to my employees that day, tell your team: "From now on, I don't care how small the issue is. I want to know about it. I want you to stop what you're doing, jot it down, and get it in our log as soon as you possibly can." (*Remember, this will get better over time; eventually, you will have very few issues to resolve.*)

Similarly, you need to start a **weekly review with management** of every issue the team logs, especially for repeating and recurring problems. These meetings should divide their time between solving critical or immediate issues, discussion, assigning responsibility, and oversight for "important, not urgent" ones.

I learned this from my days as a machinist, when we used "CARs" (corrective action reports) to prevent problems from duplicating.

What keeps showing up never gets fixed.
What gets fixed stops showing up.

You can fix **employee movement** quickly and early during Brute Force. As I walked the floor at one of my companies, I noticed employees shuffling back and forth throughout the day, carrying tools. I stopped one of them and asked, "Hey... I see you walk back and forth every day, and when you come back, you're usually carrying tools. What are you looking for? A tool or a part?"

He replied, "I usually grab these tools for this machine, here, or that machine, there."

"Okay," I said. "But then a few minutes later, I see you coming back across the floor again. Is that because you're putting the tools back?"

He nodded yes, and my head exploded again.

You can't make this stuff up! They wasted at least four minutes, several times a day, walking back and forth across an 80,000-square foot floor because they lacked tools. To make matters worse, they would also stop and talk to their co-workers along the way. Before you could find the "Stopwatch" app on your phone, they'd waste ten minutes per trip walking and chatting with their co-workers and searching for tools. Can you imagine how much time and energy got wasted when several of them did it every day?

There were twenty-seven machines at this company. *That same day*, we went to the local hardware store and bought twenty-seven toolboxes, along with *every* single tool they could possibly want or need to do their jobs. I didn't even set a budget for the manager. I said, "Whatever they want, they can have."

Fix stuff like this right away. I don't know about you, but I want my employees to spend every last working minute of their day on the most important things they do. If I allow our plant to run like an industrial version of the Chicago Marathon, that's not going to happen.

Fix the broken stuff, right away. It should be obvious, but it isn't. Go through your entire shop—equipment, vehicles, whatever—find broken stuff, and fix it, fast. At one company, the machinery looked so jerry-rigged, it wasn't even funny. The machines had women's hair ties, duct tape, zip ties, pieces of wood, cardboard, and manufactured buttons attached to them. That's fine for a day or two, if you're waiting on replacement parts or fixing it temporarily. But to leave it like that is absurd! Make an itemized list of these issues, prioritize them, and get them fixed or replaced. *Do not defer maintenance.* If you take care of your shop, the employees will take care of it, too. But if you leave everything looking jerry-rigged, your employees will get the hint—you don't care about quality or the company... or them.

Then comes the hard part: **fire bad employees**. If you're not used to firing, it will feel scary the first time you do it, but I promise you—it gets easier.

One of my worst Brute Force firings came from a machining company I bought. The old owner retired at age seventy-two, and I came in at age thirty-eight to replace him. This didn't sit well with three of the key employees—the production manager, the quality manager, and the admin. (Remember the lady with the white and yellow time sheets?) They were core staff, fairly high up the chain. They knew all the employees, existing procedures, and the company rules, written or unwritten.

The admin was the second-worst of the three. She tried to sabotage me from the beginning, and subtly. One day, she ordered several custom twelve-foot solid bars of solid aluminum—a product we *never* use in that size. These things are way too big for anything we make, they weigh more than a car, and they look like the pillars in front of a mansion. The vendor received the order and sensed something wasn't right. They called her to make sure: "Are you sure you want to order these?"

She disregarded the warning and proceeded with the order, and she didn't notify me or any other manager. A few weeks later, the pillars arrived. "Those can't be for us," I said, when I saw how big they were. "They're way too big. We don't even have forklifts that can lift them."

(Most of the products we make at this company are small enough to hold with your hands.)

I called the manufacturing company. "I'm sorry, Dean," they said, "but you guys ordered this, and we checked to make sure when we received the request. They're custom, so we can't take them back." The total cost of the order was *$48,000*, and *we couldn't use one inch of it* for anything. Shocked, I confronted the admin. "How could you order this?" I asked her. "What happened?"

When we finally got to the bottom of it, she'd proceeded with the order… because of a typo. A *typo*! Someone had filled out the order form incorrectly. It was missing *a quotation mark to signify inches versus feet!* She had worked for the company for twenty-two years; she knew every piece of material we'd ever ordered, and she knew we didn't use stuff like this. It was a deliberate, passive-aggressive work of sabotage.

We couldn't sell those aluminum bars to anyone. We couldn't even give them away! I called every metal company I could find and offered them for ten cents—no takers. We had to sit them in the back lot and leave them there. Finally, we found a way to recycle them, just to get back the extra space in the lot.

We also "recycled" that admin, along with the quality and production managers.

Brute Force and Your Finances

When I take over companies, profitability-per-product is a moving target. If you're trying to rescue your company, however, you should have an idea of what products/services make money for you versus which ones don't. Whether you get paid per-hour or per-job, don't mistake this as the time to "step over dollars to pick up pennies." You have to do the analysis quickly to figure out where your profit margins come from.

When it comes to finding your sources of profit, you'll face two major obstacles: tasks **inside** and **outside** your wheelhouse. The first is situational, while the second is a no-no.

For factors *inside* your wheelhouse, this means "greater" versus "lesser" margins. If you own a hardware store that makes a 43 percent profit on lumber and 3 percent chump change on brass fittings, it's obvious: maximize your lumber sales so you can build a bigger financial cushion. You may need to remove or discontinue unprofitable products and services and make more room for items and tasks that truly generate profit for your company.

For elements *outside* your wheelhouse, just say "No." Specifically, we're talking about things you *can* do... but should not do. Let's start with the obvious: if you bake cookies, you shouldn't offer diesel engine repair. Most people can wrap their heads around that. What's less obvious is whether you should bake cakes *as well as* cookies. Baking cookies and cakes are similar skills... but you only make money baking cookies. Only bake cakes if you know for sure that your customers demand them.

One of my companies tried to please one of our best customers by manufacturing products that, technically, we *could* make with our existing equipment. It put greater wear and tear on our machines, and making them was time-consuming and challenging to complete. Eventually, we had to admit we simply didn't have the right machine for the job. That's an example of something *outside* the wheelhouse. We should have said, "No."

Imagine an electrical contractor who's great at wiring commercial buildings, and his customer asks, "Could you help me with the electrical wiring in my fleet of cars?" Pause and think about it: on one level, electricity is electricity, right? Positive, negative, ground wires, alternating and direct currents, etcetera. But electricity in cars plays by different rules than in commercial buildings. Should this contractor take the job? No! It's more trouble than it's worth, especially if his business is already in trouble.

Improving your financial situation during Brute Force comes back to knowing the value of your time, like we discussed in Chapter 3. In this case, you have to learn the value of your *company's* time. Just like your individual time as an owner or manager, you have to ask: "Where is my company's time best spent?" If your company makes its money from baking cookies… then double down on baking cookies.

How to Implement Brute Force

Think back to Chapter 2: whatever stress is on your mind, write it down. Whether you're going through a divorce, your best friend turned on you, life hasn't turned out the way you wanted, you've got some kind of disease—**write it down**. Get it off your chest and out in front of you on paper so you can take action.

We're going to re-use that principle here. You need a convenient way to document issues, notes, thoughts, reminders, and to-dos. Some people use the Notes app on their phone, others carry a pocket notebook… *find the one that works for you* so you immediately jot concerns down when they appear. Most of the thoughts, ideas, and tasks we come up with appear in our heads at random. Get a physical method to capture them so you don't say, "I'll have to remember that." Trust me… you won't remember it.

For me, it's the **whiteboard**. At every company I own, I buy a giant ten-foot whiteboard where I list every company department, and I jot down every issue that comes up for each one. After a couple of weeks of Brute Force, it's covered in ink… but now the issues are out in front of me so I can look at them more intelligently and prioritize. I can see which tasks need immediate attention and figure out the sequence to tackle them. It turns me into a problem-solving machine because I move through issues methodically. Plus, the staff sees the whiteboard as well, and it makes an impression on them. They can see—Dean is tracking *everything*.

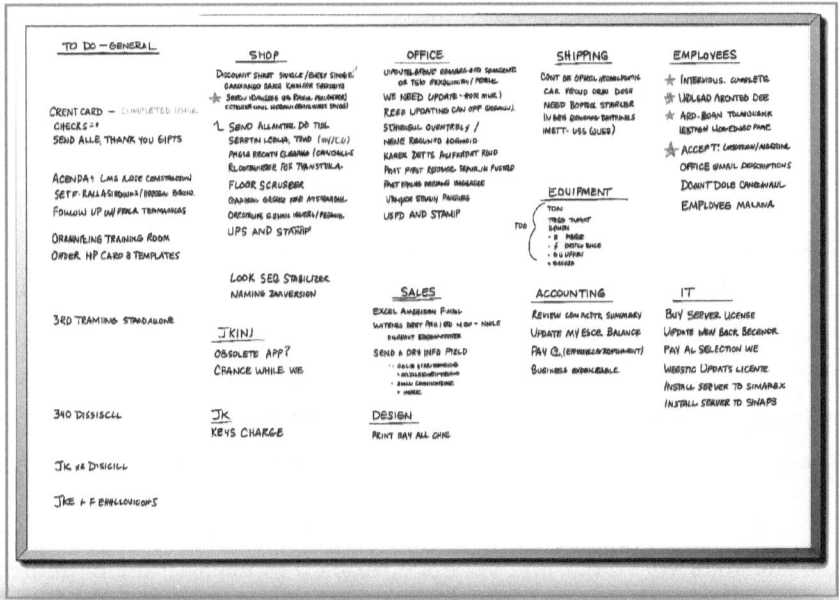

Get the noise out of your head and onto paper or a whiteboard. Empty your inner "bucket" so you can focus on the business. Take time to sit with management, and find out from them what the *worst* problems are. Walk the floor and take your employees aside to find out what they see. Keep it all written down and, preferably, visible.

K.I.S.S - Keep It Simple, Stupid

Change is hard. When we talk about keeping things "simple," remember the difference between the words "simple" and "easy." This is not *easy*.

> "There are no easy answers.
> But there are *simple* answers."
> President Ronald Reagan

People who struggle to change on the inside find it even more difficult to make major outside changes. That's why we spent the first four chapters of this book detailing how much change *you* need to go through before you can change a company. But even if you're ready and your company appears ready, you will run up against people who don't handle it well. You have to keep it as simple as possible, and even when you do that, some people still won't get it.

I once encountered someone like this while buying a new car for my wife. I passed by two dealerships that literally sat side-by-side in the same lot, and I noticed they both had the vehicle she wanted—a KIA Sorrento SX. The years and mileages were the same, and they were both in great condition. So I went to the first dealership and told the salesman, "Look, I just have forty-five minutes… would you be able to sell me this car for this price?"

This salesman was older and very accustomed to his script. He ignored my question and launched into his shtick about the dealership, particularly the long-term benefits of working with them. (I lived more than two hours away.) After about five minutes, I stopped him and repeated my question… but he wouldn't adapt to it. He kept on reciting his script, and chewed up all forty-five minutes I gave him without ever discussing the price. Eventually, I left.

I walked into the dealership next door. Out came a much younger salesman, and I put the same question to him: "Could you sell me this car for this price?"

He ran inside, grabbed the keys for the car, and told me to give it a test drive while he went inside and played "good cop, bad cop" with his sales manager. Forty-five minutes later, we inked the deal. My wife got a new car, that young salesman got a sale for the day, and I walked away with a story to share for my book. The moral of the story? Change isn't easy… but it is *simple*.

```
K.EEP
I.T
S.IMPLE
S.TUPID
```

K.I.S.S (Keep It Simple, Stupid) is nothing new. For an owner or manager taking a company through Brute Force, it's your best friend. I used to work for companies that wrote elaborate procedures or processes to fix issues. Your employees don't need an elaborate manual to clean the restrooms! If it's hard for you to write, it'll be hard for them to execute. Do not create complex processes. In a case like this, make a simple one-page visual using bullets and phrases (not sentences).

I've been guilty of this in the past. One day, a mentor showed up while I was writing one of my super-complex procedures. When I showed him, he said, "You know what? Just K.I.S.S."

I'd never heard the expression before, so I asked what it meant.

"Keep It Simple, Stupid," he said.

> "The most valuable of all talents is…
> never using two words when one will do."
> President Thomas Jefferson

"Keep It Simple, Stupid" is not an attack on your intelligence. It's a way of saying, "Don't make things 'stupid-hard.'" Don't make them complex for their own sake. There are leaders who try to get everything 100 percent right, and then they write the most convoluted, complex instructions to cover every possible scenario. I'm the opposite; in the beginning I sometimes have to stop my employees mid-sentence and ask them to tell me everything they just elaborated *in one to two sentences.* If my own two eyes glaze over when people tell me complex stories… I shouldn't expect anything different from others if I do the same thing to them.

The problem with perfectionism is the law of diminishing returns. Remember my unionized gearbox company? They had 397 different training courses for their employees. (That's not a made-up number; they actually had that many.) Each course was (on average) twenty pages long. Some were a hundred pages long! When you get that complex and detailed, it's easier to create new curriculum than to improve existing content. Nobody could finish or digest it all, because it was "TMI"—"too much information." TMI is the opposite of K.I.S.S.

Simplicity doesn't mean you're reckless or irresponsible, either. If I tell you to write up simple bullets using short phrases, it might sound like I'm telling you to be vague or lax with your staff. No! I'm telling you the exact opposite: activate your brain, take all your detailed knowledge, and distill it into simple, direct instructions any employee can follow. If that sounds like a challenge, it *is*. As Steve Jobs famously said,

---

"Simple can be harder than complex:
you have to work hard to get your
thinking clean, to make it simple.
But it's worth it in the end,
because once you get there
you can move mountains."

The most difficult part about K.I.S.S. is **understanding hierarchy**. I mean this: "Understand who you're talking to and working with." Every company has a hierarchy, whether they admit it or not. You can have more formalized hierarchies, like an organizational chart or a rank structure like the military. But even if you operate much more loosely and informally... not everyone in your company shares your goals, dreams, habits, or desires. They fall elsewhere on the hierarchy than you do as the leader.

It falls on you to (a) understand the hierarchy in your company and (b) train management to understand it. I once made a mistake and took one of my production managers out to dinner at the kind of restaurant where I normally meet with other owners, clients, or mentors. My employee was a regular, blue-collar guy who preferred the local bar. He didn't like the restaurant, and he was uncomfortable throughout our entire time together.

Understanding hierarchy depends on your willingness to survey your people and learn what motivates them—without judging them. That's why the whole "flatscreen TVs, Beats headphones, and iPads as Christmas gifts" thing wasn't the hit it could have been, and why many corporate attempts to be "generous" go nowhere. The tech gifts weren't what the staff really wanted, so the following year I gathered and surveyed them, asking them to write down specifically what they'd like for gifts.

I was shocked when the results came back. Some asked for ice-making machines and blenders to make mixed alcoholic drinks. Others wanted a pizza maker or sporting goods. I couldn't believe they didn't want tech gadgets... but that's because *I* like tech gadgets! I made the same mistake most leaders make: *I failed to understand the hierarchy.* I projected myself onto my team and assumed without asking. If you want to keep things simple at your company... know the hierarchy. Know your audience. Not everyone wants to be you or self-improve the way you do. Not everyone wants to be king; in fact, most people prefer to be told what to do—*simply*. So… Keep It Simple, Stupid.

Sales

Some gurus out there say things like "Unless making sales is your biggest problem, more sales won't fix what's wrong with your business."

There's truth to that… but for small- or medium-sized businesses, I disagree. You're reading this book because you want your business to grow, and businesses that achieve significant growth need higher revenues, lower receivables, lower accounts payable, fine-tuned expenses, detailed forecasts, and increased profits. Most likely, your company would benefit from a few million dollars in additional revenue. It would certainly benefit from a clearer picture of its real financial health. No company I've taken over has suffered, stalled, or experienced zero change when we focused on improving sales as part of the strategy.

There was, however, one larger company takeover where I chose *not* to focus on sales until my eighth month in ownership—and I'll never make that mistake again!

The company had a lot of serious issues that required immediate attention during Brute Force, and they carried over into the Analyze and Structure phases. The culture was a mess. A lot of the equipment was obsolete, processes were slow, and the facility itself needed an upgrade. What should have taken six months lasted eight, and led to a four-month gap between achieving organizational efficiency and implementing our sales strategy.

Everything worked out in the end, but there's nothing more frustrating than when you figure out the real problem, develop a solution… and discover you can't implement it because the revenue's not there to support it! You can't short-change sales. If I had it to do again, I'd have hired some salespeople and trained them right away. Sales are the lifeblood of any business—especially a small business.

Facility

We're products of our environment. If your facility looks and feels like it hasn't been updated since the Bicentennial, don't be surprised that your staff moves at Bicentennial speed or your company earns Bicentennial revenues.

Your facility should be clean and serviceable, whether you admit customers onto the premises or not. Sweep up the dust on the floor, clean up the grease from the engines, and wipe down the dirt and grime on the machines. Once every couple of months at each of my companies, we stop production on a Friday afternoon in a single department and devote a couple of hours to cleaning and maintaining our workspace. We rotate departments monthly.

Bathrooms

One of my manufacturing companies had terrible bathrooms and employee areas. You might think it's odd, but one of the first things I look at when I buy a business is the state of their staff bathrooms. This company's bathrooms looked worn out and frozen in time. The sinks, toilets, fans, and mirrors in the bathrooms were obsolete, dirty, damaged, and corroded. The countertops had cigarette burn marks in them from the days when smoking was still allowed inside. The condition of these bathrooms spoke volumes about how much leadership cared.

Changing a company's culture is about more than words; it includes *actions* that show employees you're serious. I had those bathrooms replaced and upgraded as soon as I took over. I wanted the staff to know that change had begun immediately. You might read this and think, "What a waste of money, it doesn't change anything." But I say to you that companies with committed, hard-working employees who believe their boss cares about them perform better. I want to show my team that I pay attention to important details, and I care about things besides the bottom line. I want them to see that I care as much about the facilities and equipment they use as I do about my own.

The same goes for the employee break room. If it's shoddy, redo it. The cost is worth the return.

Furniture & Equipment

Small manufacturing companies don't think strategically about where they place their equipment. Remember the "holes" from the previous chapter? Holes are common because companies usually put new equipment wherever they can find or make room for it. Owners and managers rarely consider the process flow, which leaves the factory disorganized. Typically, this mess bleeds over into the office, where you find mismatched furniture and outdated decor.

Eventually, this leads to other problems… like employees walking from one end of the shop to another just to find the right tools or print shipping labels before walking all the way back to complete the actual shipping.

To fix this, you have to rethink the importance of **layout**. The office and the floor should reflect a professional environment and complement each other so that on a subliminal level, your employees sense your attention to detail. But before you can do any of that, you need to assess the current layout.

At every single one of my companies, I schedule a couple of "Maintenance Days" during Brute Force where we go (literally) through *every single machine* and document every problem with each one. It doesn't matter if it's only missing a screw—I want to know about it so I can fix it. We replace every missing screw and rubber grommet. We repair or replace every duct-taped mechanical problem so every machine functions correctly and has all the parts it needs to do its job. As we do this, we learn about how the machine gets used most often, which informs us about where to place it.

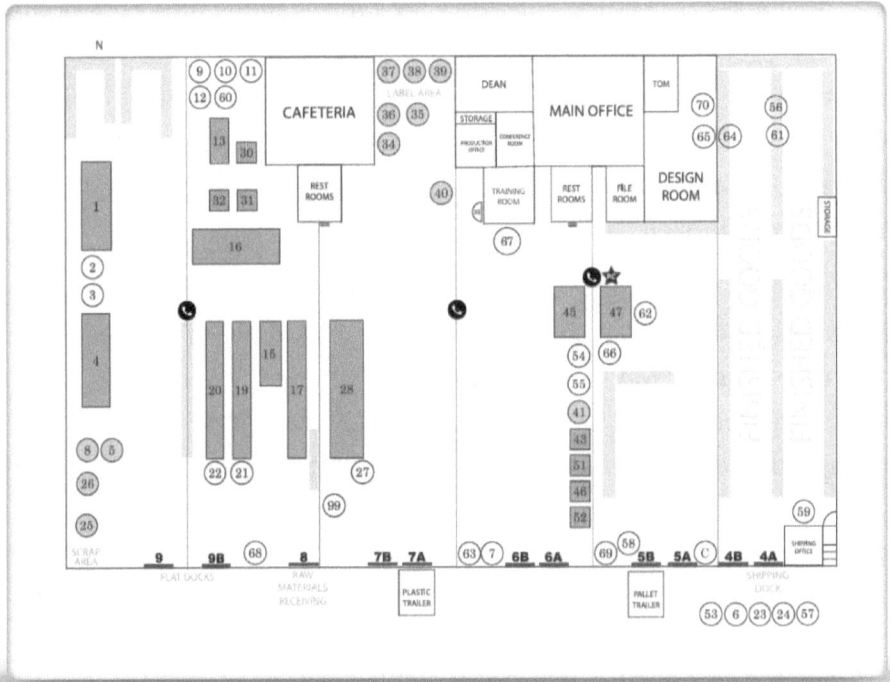

One of my actual layouts

We also look at the current state of the office and upgrade all the furniture throughout the facility. We spend the money to get matching, sharp-looking furniture. If you're on a budget, there are resale stores that sell office furniture. This gives the staff a new, clear contrast between what's working versus what's broken. It teaches them a new standard for the condition of the facility and equipment: I want it clean, serviceable, functioning, and pleasant to the eye and the touch. Why do this? The answer might surprise you:

If everything is broken, then *nothing* is broken.

Before I take over, employees don't bother to tell management when something breaks or stops working. They don't worry about making or leaving messes in the break room. They don't maintain the bathrooms or treat the furniture with respect. They're used to a cluttered environment, and cluttered environments lead to cluttered minds. When everything's broken, people assume, "This is how we do things," or "I told management, and they didn't do anything about it." Everything's broken... so *nothing* is broken.

This works the other way, too. If you provide employees an environment where everything works, they'll assume, "This is how we do things," and "Management listens." Vehicles, equipment, break rooms, restrooms, the shop floor, and the management offices are clean, stocked, and maintained. They're more likely to take action when something breaks... because it sticks out like a sore thumb in a place where everything works! They'll likely fill out a repair order for a machine that stops working. They'll more likely wipe down the bathroom counters and keep the break room counter free of trash.

A building we renovated for one of my companies had a cracking floor in the center of the building. We hired a contractor to lay down epoxy flooring, but when I saw the cracking, I told him to fix it before he laid down the epoxy. He proceeded to argue with me and insisted it would be fine. I pushed back because I knew that as soon as our forklifts began driving over the cracks, it would damage the epoxy. He wanted to take the easy route, and didn't really care if the floor cracked after he left. He was not happy to have to fix cracks, but I leaned on him to get it done because the condition of the facility matters. If you don't fix things when they break, don't be shocked when your employees don't fix them either.

Technology

You'd think, as we're now a quarter of the way through the twenty-first century, that business leaders understand how technology needs regular updates and upgrades. But for several of my companies, I encountered outdated computers, servers, email systems, software—you name it. I realized early on I'd have to do it at almost every company I purchased. One time, I even sent my son on an eight-hour drive (one way) to buy twenty-seven used corporate computers.

Technology has so many details and expiration dates that it's worth regular updates, no matter how well you maintain your current system. Once we installed new servers and laid out the new computers, our IT issues melted into nothing. It freed us up to introduce newer ERP systems, which put all our employees on the same technological footing. We also got rid of outdated IT contracts with monthly costs. As technology improves, it needs less and less traditional maintenance.

How You Know Brute Force is Working

The clearest sign Brute Force is working is company morale. If you follow through on the changes, morale usually improves right away. People begin to communicate better, alerting management when issues arise. Sales start to climb, and fulfillment cheerfully embraces the increase because you've supplied them with what they need and removed the obstacles that blocked them in the past. You should sense the company's overall "acceleration."

If you get a bad apple who brings morale down, address it—then fire them, *fast*. I've never had more than two employees at a time turn negative about Brute Force; it's always a tiny minority that's upset. But it only takes one or two people to poison the whole tree. Look for the person who repeatedly objects to the changes and uses sweeping phrases like "everyone says" or "everyone agrees." That usually means "One or two negative people say negative things and agree with each other; everyone else is minding their own business."

When morale goes up, you can tell because people work harder. They have more optimism and excitement to work. They smile more often and cooperate more easily. They say things that show they want to do better, and they think proactively, outside the box.

Good work, captain. You've stopped the bleeding, turned the ship around, and set it on a new course.

Now, it's time to **Analyze**—to dig deeper, get ahead of potential issues, and prepare the ship to perform at levels that once seemed impossible.

Chapter Seven

Analyze
Deep-dive Into Departmental Problems, Systems, and Inefficiencies. Prioritize by Impact.

"Most decisions are not binary, and there are usually better answers waiting to be found if you do the analysis and involve the right people."
Jamie Dimon, CEO, JP Morgan Chase

I enjoy the Analyze phase because it's 99 percent positive. You deal with most of the negative "sludge" in your company during Brute Force. But once you get to Analyze, you start playing chess—observing, recording, seeking to understand, and choosing the next right move.

Decisions you make during Analyze propel your company forward, sometimes by leaps and bounds. If you compare B.A.S.I.C.S. to building a house, Brute Force is like breaking ground… but Analyze is like when you pour the cement foundation. Here, we lay the first large, solid pieces of the puzzle. Buckle up for a thick chapter because, like real-life analysis, we have *loads* of detail to get through.

Analyze Team Members & Goals

During Brute Force, you collected data from your employees about their values and priorities. Analyze is the time to review what they shared with you and incorporate it as you incentivize them. By now you've probably discovered—money is not as universally important to them as you thought. Some employees are motivated by it, for sure… but the most common factor I've found is *recognition*.

When I say "recognition," don't jump straight to "trophies and certificates of appreciation." Awards ceremonies are great, but let's be honest—how often do you have them? Once or twice a year? Quarterly? We'll have a section on awards later (*yes, they are very important*), but what about the time in between ceremonies? Hundreds and hundreds of days go by each year where employees feel (at best) misunderstood, underappreciated, or both.

"Misunderstood" is how I describe Ron, one of my star employees. Management considered Ron as "not very smart" until I showed up. How could Ron be a bit slow one day and one of the most reliable men on the planet a few months later? How did he get that much smarter and work that much harder in such a short period of time? The answer ought to be obvious by now:

Workers don't need better brains;
they need better <u>leaders</u>.

As in, "leaders who appreciate and acknowledge employees, and who communicate that those employees are wanted and needed." When Ron felt the difference, he rose to the occasion. He paid more attention. He *wanted* to do better for the same reasons you and I would want to live up to the opinions and esteem of people who affirm and appreciate us.

Ron transformed his work life because, for once, he had a leader curious about his talents and abilities. I asked him, "Besides what you do now, do you want to do anything else here at the company?" Ron jumped at the chance to fill a different role where he had passion and talent. Overnight, he became a rock star. During the Brute Force phase, he pulled the production manager aside to say, "Gary, I've never worked harder in thirty-five years at this company... *and I've never been happier.*"

That's what I mean by "Analyze." I didn't do anything other than ask meaningful questions and leverage the responses. Ron gets the credit for being the superstar that he is. But I "analyzed" his role, just as you need to do for your employees. If you see someone striving to be their best, offer to test them with greater responsibilities or tasks that line up with their interests. Give them instructions and see how well they follow them. *Do it more than once*; ask throughout the year. Give your employees regular opportunities to showcase their skills. Sometimes, they may not jump at it right away because they're uncomfortable. But on the second or third pass, you'll be surprised.

I can't get over how, in most cases, employees rank recognition as their top priority in a work environment. Personally, Ron is a very easy-going guy. You don't get the sense that he is a highly-driven, overachieving personality. But once he had a sincere person calling out the best he could offer and complimenting his work in front of co-workers and peers... he became unstoppable. When we started, he would have flinched if I'd asked him to get a small number of tasks done in a short, fixed amount of time. But after six months, he can get a much larger number of tasks done in *less* time. We hung two beautiful plaques in the building and gave him two custom t-shirts as the Most Improved Employee of the year.

Positions

You put together a basic organizational chart during Brute Force. You know who everybody is, and you have a basic idea of what they do. Now you need to figure out the cost to the company of what they currently do and how much the company makes by employing them.

An employee's salary (at best) represents almost *half* of the true cost of hiring them. If you pay someone a $50,000 salary per year, in other words, their true cost is closer to $85k. So if you do the math and find out that the employee's role nets $110k per year to the company… now you can compare. A more attractive net might be $200k, where the employee's role is twice as valuable as what they cost. If they return 100 percent of your investment, you can compensate for mistakes they make or other deficiencies. But if they only net 10 percent over their cost… maybe it's time to look at additional responsibilities, a different role, or parting ways with them.

When you Analyze positions, you ascertain how employees contribute to revenue and profit. That's easier to do with salespeople who have obvious revenue targets to acquire more money for the organization. But even with non-sales staff, you can always figure out if the role they perform supports the business' income.

Let's say you hire an administrative assistant. You can ask, "How do they perform with accounts receivable and accounts payable? How are they doing with invoicing and collecting payment?" If they're way ahead on duties like this, you might ask whether they need to work full-time or if you should combine their current role with another one. If they've fallen behind, it's vice versa—look into whether you need to hire additional help, or see whether they might perform better in a different position.

If you analyze production workers and management, you ask if their performance fulfills your promise to customers: "Do they meet production quotas so our customers receive orders on time?" Or you could ask how the company would perform the role without them. For example, to determine the value of your production manager, you could flesh out how you'd handle it if they suddenly became unavailable. Who would manage the shop? Would it be you? If it is, remember Chapter 3: "Know the value of your time." Maybe you need to realign expectations with the production manager or set new performance targets to justify their employment. Think about this especially if it would ultimately cost you more to do the work yourself.

Goals

You showed up ready for action on Day One with task sheets. You took time to hint at the vision, goals, and direction for the company. Now, you need to put pen to paper and **explain the vision** in a way everyone in your company can see, hear, understand, and interact with.

Most owners and managers miss this opportunity by a country mile. They might talk about revenue targets, profit margins, cost savings, and so forth. Stop doing that! *Executives* are interested in company metrics... but to employees, those numbers don't mean anything! If you want to harness the strength of your workforce to reach a goal, you have to partner with them to help them get what *they* want. Talk to the employees about how achieving the vision makes possible the things they've shared with you, like recognition, flexible working hours, or more time off.

Remember from Chapter 2 how you can't cast a reasonable vision unless you've been honest about where you are? The Analyze step is where you do that—but to scale, in partnership with your team. Instead of picking numbers or ideals out of thin air, be frank and honest about the current situation, and then show your employees where you want to take the company: "Right now, we have to work six days a week, and I know several of you would like to have more

flexible schedules and time off. Here's how we can accomplish that."
Visuals make a great asset here, if you have them.

> ## Show the team how the business needs to improve... *so they can get what they want.*

For example, let's say you currently work six days a week, staying open on Saturdays to soak up as much revenue cushion as you can. Many of your employees, in your surveys or interviews, expressed a desire for a shorter work week or shorter work days. Out of forty employees, fifteen said they preferred to work four ten-hour days, while twelve others wanted Saturdays off. Here, you have the chance to offer them what they want and show what they must do to make their dream come true. The mere fact that you ask goes a long way, even if you can't necessarily agree to their preferences.

You set targets based on the numbers you need to make healthy margins and fund the company's growth. But you tell the team, "Hit these targets consistently for the next ninety days, and you'll get to go home two hours early on Fridays with pay. Hit them for 180 days, and you'll get a paid day off. Also, some of you are now going to work different schedules—some will be here Monday through Thursday, and others will cover Wednesday through Saturday." (*As a side note, most employees want overtime... but not excessive overtime.*)

Plan for how you want things to look in five years, translated into the *employees'* interests and concerns. Show them what kind of salary raises or benefits to expect if they do their part, but don't forget about all their non-monetary aspirations. For example, if some of your employees said they want to grow into management or executive roles, you could talk about expansion in your five-year plan. You could say, "If we double our revenues in three years, we'll start a second shift or location, and several of you will be up for roles in management and leadership."

As you gain the team's attention and enthusiasm, create a **roadmap** for the promised land. A project plan that includes high-level tasks, due dates, assignments, and key details each team member needs to cover. You can create several versions of them for a week, a month, one year, and five years. Distribute these plans to the employees. This lets them know you're serious and accountable for project success. Set times weekly, monthly, and annually to review the goals *with your team*, not just by yourself.

Communication

Turn up the volume and detail on your vision and goals. You hinted at it during Brute Force, but Analyze gives you the opportunity to assess how it resonates when you spell it out. Don't take your team through Brute Force and then proceed down the tracks with the goals still hidden in your head.

Most employees can self-explain actions you took during Brute Force; if you got rid of a bunch of old files or bad employees, that makes sense to almost anyone. During Analyze, however, you put the company under a microscope and start to examine things that don't *appear* to have any issues—even though they do. A leader who starts Analyze without explaining the vision and direction jeopardizes trust with employees. When workers don't know why the leader asks tons of questions or makes decisions about layout and equipment, they're predisposed to worry about their jobs. Remember—they *thought* they knew how to do their jobs correctly. Yet here you are, picking their methods apart with questions. If you do it without explaining, employees can only make so many good-faith assumptions before they turn toward the negative.

At least once a quarter, if not sooner, you should schedule a company-wide meeting to explain what you're doing. Also, in contrast to Brute Force, your communication should become more frequent, lengthier, and detailed. In the first ninety days, you needed to give maybe one up-front explanation: "The general manager has been terminated because we were not working together in the same direction to achieve the company goals." Okay, that makes sense and doesn't require a lot of further explanation.

But Analyze is different. Now you're questioning the *good* things employees do.

During Analyze, you *communicate* the vision and *build* on it.

You ask these questions to gain as deep of an understanding as you can as to why employees do what they do (or how they do it). You start to seek more input on your vision, mainly from the employees' answers. For example, if an employee describes a task they do with a resigned or cynical tone of voice, pay attention. Comment, "It sounds like you think there might be a better way to do it." If they feel safe enough to tell you how they feel it should be done, take note of their answer. Why? Because *you might be sitting on a goldmine*. They might know a more efficient method to get their task done! If they do and you implement their idea, that accomplishes two things: (a) it builds a sense of *ownership* in your employee, and (b) it gives you one less procedure to create.

Throughout Analyze, some of your employees will feel anxious. Beneath the surface, they'll wonder: "Are you checking out my job? Are you trying to find an excuse to fire me?" You must develop a consistent rhythm of reassurance and tell them, "I'm asking these questions to understand. Nothing you tell me will compromise or risk your position with the company. I want to solve problems and make work better for all of us."

As you go through Analyze, take the quarterly meetings as occasions to **celebrate** what the company achieved during Brute Force and going forward. Point out how systems, processes, and employee cohesion are improving. Show the team that because they worked so hard to eliminate waste, their productivity now trends upward. Show them how they're moving closer toward the goals they've shared with you, such as recognition or more time off.

Analyze What You *Think* You Know

Sometimes, completing Brute Force can make it *seem* like you've solved a problem—when you actually have more work to do. You move fast, strike hard, and push for the shortest number of days, and you see initial success... but then, issues slowly begin to resurface. Stay optimistic. You have the chance to dig deeper and discover more clues about the *real* problem.

One of my manufacturing companies appeared in excellent shape after Brute Force. We'd attacked our inefficiencies from Day One. I sat with each individual employee and manager as we documented the company's issues and hand-picked the most critical ones for priority. One day, well into the Structure phase, I walked the floor and noticed a whiteboard with a couple of jobs running late. I called a meeting with the production manager.

After some back and forth, I discovered the jobs often ran late because the office delayed the purchase orders, usually by two to three weeks (a major delay in our world). I went and spoke with the office staff, who told me that they frequently got too busy with other orders to complete the late ones. I suddenly realized I had more to learn about the company's quote-to-cash process and timeline than I'd assumed, though it seemed straightforward at the beginning.

A similar thing happened when one of my companies implemented a new Enterprise Resource Planning (ERP) system. I love these tools—they automate and systematize your entire operation. Of course, whenever you get a new one, you have to migrate a ton of data from your old system. We'd put hundreds of hours into preparing the merge, and I felt like we'd done a thorough job. All the analyses, spreadsheets, and tools got integrated with a few days to spare before the target launch date.

And then I found out the bad news: we could not electronically access some of the most critical invoice data.

We had intended to have a central "box" where you could retrieve invoices according to each customer. Due to a misunderstanding between staff, we failed to notice that every invoice had an individual number we had to enter for searchability... and now you could only search for invoices by date! Each date had tons of random customers with random pay dates. The setup made it impossible to reconcile... and to fix it, we had to back entirely out of everything we'd done and start again at the beginning!

So watch out for situations where you *think* you know something, but you don't... or you think you've covered something and you haven't. We knew our customers' names. We knew the dollar amounts, the services and products they bought... we knew all kinds of information about them. But when it came to tracking down invoices in a timely manner, as far as the new ERP system was concerned, we "knew nothing" without those invoice numbers.

Hiring

You got rid of some bad apples during Brute Force, but as you implement the rest of B.A.S.I.C.S, business should start to pick up some speed. You may need to hire—and for 99 percent of businesses, this takes more analysis and effort than they expect or want to put forward.

Most leaders I've talked to describe their process like this:

"I talk to applicants, I read their resumes, I see if I like them, ask them a few questions to see if they know what they're talking about... and then I give them a chance and see what happens."

NO! That doesn't tell you anything about the people you hire!

You need to go much deeper, and most of your questions should relate to an applicant's *personality*—NOT their skill set. Throw out everything you think you know about hiring, because it's almost all useless. Maybe you've heard people on the internet talk about "ideal client avatar," but have you ever figured out your ideal *employee*? Who is more important? Customers come and go, but employees last a long time. You and your staff will be around each other every day.

My companies give assessments that start off with simple questions and gradually get more difficult and complex. They ask psychological questions that prompt candidates to imagine themselves in certain scenarios to see how they respond. (*If you're in a hurry to hire a lot of help, hiring agencies can administer these tests to numerous candidates at the same time.*) We also have applicants fill out multiple-choice surveys to learn about their motives, priorities, and ambitions.

I don't care if someone tells me, "I've been a machinist for thirty years." That's nice... what if you've been doing it *wrong* for thirty years? What if someone says, "I've been doing plumbing for twenty years," but all they ever did was fix sinks and toilets? For certain jobs you need to quantify an applicant's level of competence, but I'm more interested in *how they think*. If I can get an idea of how someone thinks, I have better luck predicting how they'll do in the future with my company. If you "think" you can pull a fast one on me and talk your way into a job, I've got a difficult assessment with your name on it. We'll find out whether you *really* know plumbing at an advanced level, or if you spent the last decade just fixing sinks and toilets. But more to the point—we'll find out whether you think being honest is worthwhile. I don't want dishonest people in my companies.

Analyze Your Numbers

> When your business is brand-new,
> **money is your top priority**.
> *The same is true when it's in trouble.*

As an example, the Brute Force and Analyze phases leave the door open for involving family, friends, students, and other temporary workers. You have to find a way to earn as much money as possible while spending as little as you can. You need to get paid for every product you sell and service you render, and make sure that you take in every sale you possibly can. Hiring alternate sources of help is a great way to reduce expenses while you keep the company selling and servicing their customers.

But forget about getting help from low-cost labor. Most leaders have a much bigger, far more basic problem than finding temporary help.

Are you ready for the biggest problem with finances? Here it is:

> They're not tracking them.

That's it. I wish it were for better reasons, but a *lot* of businesses out there are broke because they fail to invoice, collect payment, follow up on their quotes and proposals, or pay attention to simple ratios, like revenue versus payroll. Do you remember my story of the company I took over with the broken website, where they literally had *thousands* of unanswered requests? That was not an isolated example. I've seen so many instances like it that I no longer give owners the benefit of the doubt. Once again, whether it's ego or laziness, they simply don't want to be bothered; they only want to make money. They're like kids demanding an allowance without doing their chores.

One of my companies had a nice Ford Fusion as a delivery car, and it needed an oil change. I wanted to meet the company that provided our vehicle maintenance, so I drove it to their shop personally, went to lunch, and returned afterward to collect the car. They told me the bill would be **$186**... for an oil change! I asked the guy, "What did you do? I only wanted an oil change. This is a Ford Fusion. It can't possibly cost $186."

"Well," the guy said, "that's what we've always charged the previous guy."

See what I mean?

Another company I took over—one literally going out of business—had $26,000 in accounts payable, and **$68,000** in accounts receivable, half of which was older than ninety days. *How do you go out of business with $68,000 in receivables?!* How can you have a net balance of $42,000 of money sitting there with your name on it, and you don't do anything to collect it? There weren't any disputes or refusals from customers, either. (*I know because we called all of them and collected the money.*) The only reason these accounts were left open was because *the company didn't follow up.*

The same thing is true for quotes and proposals. Do you know that your chances of earning new business go up by over 50 percent *simply by following up*? I know that like the back of my hand, and I'll confess right here in my own book—I used to get sloppy on this from time to time. I do a proposal for a client and send it, and then I get wrapped up in other things and forget about it. Keep track of your quotes and proposals and set reminders to follow up, like I do now!

Oh, and my company with the $68k in receivables... did I mention the owner's daughter was on staff? They paid her a full-time, forty-hour salary to work maybe thirty hours a week. So not only did they hit the snooze button on their $42,000 in receivables... they also kept paying their daughter's salary! Payroll was $15,000 per week, and instead of using those receivables to (a) pay off their payables, (b) purchase new materials, or (c) make payroll... they just continued to dig themselves into a deeper hole!

Most leaders don't even blink at what they charge for their products or services or at how much they pay to their vendors. For prices, they rely on competitors or casual marketplace opinions to understand what they should charge for their product or service. A majority of leaders could maybe tell you their gross annual revenue and their net income —and that's enough for them. They might have some idea of their operating costs. On a good day, they know if they're earning money, making payroll, and keeping the lights on, but that's where it stops. So long as they get to keep some of the profits, that's as much as they care about their margins.

Really, they ought to be called "absentee leaders," even if they work in the business every day! They get into some kind of "wishful thinking" la-la land where they assume numbers take care of themselves. They do zero analysis, and they get blindsided when it comes back to bite them.

The worst cases are the legacy-idealists who say noble things like, "I don't care about the profits; I want to build my company from within." It's a great idea... but if you can't fit your dreams neatly into a balance sheet, they need to wait. I get it; I love where I am today, where I can truly focus on building a legacy from within through the people I lead. *But I didn't start there.*

First, build to be **profitable**.
Then build from within.

Metrics

I'll share some key pieces you need to successfully complete the Analyze phase and move on to Structure:

Forecasts. Maybe you can tell me how much money you made last week, or even today. Can you tell me how much you expect to earn *next* week? Next month? Six months from now? Most people have no clue. For the Analyze phase, weekly forecasts are the starting point. If you worked six calls a day this week for your electrical business, you should be able to tell me how much revenue you expect to bring in over the next thirty days or whatever the terms of your invoice are. You should also be able to tell me what you expect to earn this week from work you did two to four weeks ago.

If you didn't work very much this month… next month is going to be hard.

"Well," you say, "I'll make it up next month."

I hope so, but… what happens if you don't? Have you made cuts to your forecasted *costs* since you can't project any revenue next month? The utility companies will still send their bills, vendors will still invoice you, and your employees will still expect their paychecks.

Low sales = cut hours

I know it's uncomfortable to tell your employees that they should expect reduced hours or layoffs. It's awkward and embarrassing, particularly if you're the reason the money isn't there in the first place. But if you've been running your finances on fairy dust and emotion, admit it—*you're the reason* your employees get fewer hours and lower paychecks. Few business leaders truly understand finances, and even fewer seek help or educate themselves until it's too late. (That's how I ended up in that head-spinning moment in my office with the controller telling me I had only $10,000 and my wife sobbing.)

Basic (Minimum) Operating Costs. Note how I used the word "minimum." That's because people often think they owe or have to pay more than they actually do. During Brute Force and Analyze, your priority is to know the absolute lowest number you need to stay in business.

Here's a basic number you'd think owners and managers would understand: *paying too much*. Why would you pay $500 a month for a two-yard dumpster when you can get exactly the same thing for $75 a month?! Why would you pay $600 a month for five company cell phones when I can find exactly the same deal for $130 a month? This is not like calling up DirecTV or the cable company and haggling on the phone… all I do is an extra ten minutes of research!

You want something even more obvious? How about *paying too little*? You step over dollars to pick up pennies when you get stuck in this mindset: "I don't pay $12 for that item… *I spend $10.99*." Look, if you're ordering 10,000 items in bulk, fine. But I have to remind myself all the time: if it's below a certain number, don't even mess with it. If it's a certain dollar amount or less, I don't bother to return the item; I just throw it away. My time is way too valuable to sit there on a customer service line or dig through some complicated website to return something. With some items, I ask, "Should I even spend my time *ordering* this?" Unless it's a significant cost requiring my specialized knowledge, I'm better off hiring someone at $20 an hour to order it for me.

Another number you need to know is the *last possible due date*. When's the last time you got a bill that wasn't due for another twenty-five days and you paid it right away? If they give you thirty to forty-five days to pay, you're not breaking the law, violating the contract, or making yourself look bad if you pay on Day 44! Most businesses don't train their staff to wait until right before the due date to pay. Learn to ask for terms that give you plenty of breathing room! I will sometimes ask for sixty days or more, if the vendor is open to it.

For example, let's say you manufacture small engines for lawn equipment, like grass mowers. A customer places an order for five hundred new engines. You take some of their money down, and afterward, you have two months to satisfy your customer and collect the rest. Then you turn around to your vendors and place orders for gaskets, valves, carburetors, and so forth. They require some money down, too, but they offer thirty days on the invoice plus a seven-day grace period. If you ask them for forty-five days instead, you close the gap on the time between paying for their materials versus getting paid for your production. You see how that works?

If you pay the full bill from your vendor the same day you receive it, you might feel good about yourself: "I pay what I owe, the moment I owe it!" But seven weeks later when you've done all the work and your customer's still waiting until the last day to pay you… you won't feel so good about yourself. Especially if your business is already in trouble. Running a tight financial ship in business is an equation in itself:

> When money's coming in, make it go fast.
> When money's going out, make it go slow.

Weekly Sales and Fulfillment Numbers. How much did you sell and how much did you ship *this week*? How much do you project to sell and ship next week? How do this week's figures (and next week's projections) compare with the previous year at the same time?

Successful companies build binders of past performance. Past performance may not be a guarantee of future results, but you can guarantee that having *no* record of past performance leads to greater confusion. Let's say one year, you have an incredible two weeks between Father's Day and the 4th of July. You pull in six months' worth of ordinary revenue in two weeks, and everybody's excited.

At the end of the year, you write your business plan for the following year, and you anticipate that the last two weeks of June will be huge. Then Father's Day Weekend comes along, and you get... crickets. Nothing. The two weeks come and go, and you feel down. What changed? Where did you go wrong?

If you have last year's performance documented, you can go back and look at what led up to that amazing two-week period. You can trace where the sales came from, who made them, what the circumstances were, etcetera. Maybe it was a pandemic and you benefited from panic shoppers... or maybe you changed strategies, and the new plan directed your sales team to different activities than what they do this year.

Categorization. Some company expenses are more straightforward than others, especially from a tax perspective. There's a difference between buying a new machine versus buying lunch for the staff. But if you don't categorize them correctly, you can be taxed on things where you shouldn't have to pay tax, or you can at least deduct depreciation. *Capital expenditures* are large, essential expenses that help the organization sustain or grow, and you can write them off over several years with depreciation.

The Role of the Controller

My first experience with a professional controller was with the guy who told me my business had $10,000 left in the bank. I had a CPA/ MBA wife and an accountant on staff. Most companies have a bookkeeper, and if they're big enough, they might also have a chief financial officer (CFO). All of these roles are good and necessary for a company. Accountants and bookkeepers crunch numbers and file taxes, and a CFO looks at the company's overall finances and develops an (external) strategic plan for the future. But most accountants and bookkeepers do what you, the leader, tell them to do. Very few offer advice about how to manage the money within.

Controllers, on the other hand, are (typically) financial veterans who can analyze and help you understand your company's *internal* financial health. They can spot errors and waste, and tell you what you should be doing with your money. In construction, controllers would be more like architects, while accountants would be like contractors. Controllers oversee the accounting operations of a company, including managing staff. They focus on the broader financial picture and strategy within your organization. They help design the "structure" money flows through.

Remember my story of the firearms business, where we lost a ton of money because the White House changed hands? You can't oversee election outcomes, so if you want to be smart about money, focus on things actually under your control. Once I hired a controller, we improved at anticipating sales fluctuations because we could identify where shortages popped up and investigate them. If we knew sales would be down, we could adjust production, schedules, and marketing strategies. Our accountant could tell us what *had happened* (sales were down), but the controller could tell us *what would happen* (a sales slump was coming) before we had a problem on our hands.

A good controller will tell you if it's the right time to make a large purchase, like a $50,000 company truck. You're still the leader of the company, and you can do as you please... but the controller will tell you if it's the right or wrong time and circumstance. When I hired that controller, I grew in my ability to make smarter decisions more often. I learned the value of forecasting, and how to understand metrics that illuminated our potential for growth. I could see where we needed to increase sales, how much profit we earned on each item we sold, and how to close the gap between paying and getting paid.

"Know thyself."
Socrates

Despite all this, be prepared to *train your controller*. Just because they know a lot about money doesn't mean they know a lot about *you*. This goes back to knowing and understanding yourself from Chapters 1 and 2. A controller can tell you all kinds of things about the money in your organization… but those numbers may not mean anything to you until you know which ones really matter. Remember the section about Personalities in Chapter 2? "D" personalities, like me, care about a much shorter list than most "C" personalities. So if you're a "C," your meetings with your controller will probably be the highlight of your day—but you'll still need to sort through what you need/want to know, versus information for its own sake.

Others might wonder, "What *do* I need to know?" You might be unfamiliar with even the essential weekly numbers every manager should know. So start with this list:

- **Gross Revenue:** Total income from goods/services sold before expenses.
- **Gross Profit:** Revenue minus the cost of goods sold (COGS).
- **Expenses**: Total operating costs per week: payroll, insurance, fuel, maintenance, utilities, supplies, taxes. Make sure you get fixed and variable expenses itemized, and have your controller factor recurring costs into production, providing services, and hiring employees. All of those functions require recurring costs like telephone, internet, electricity, water, HVAC, etc.

- **Net Profit**: What's left after you subtract all expenses from revenue.

- **Cash Flow**: The total amount of money that flows in and out of a business over a given period. Just because you have a big month in revenue doesn't mean you're "rich." If you lose fifty cents on the dollar in overhead... sure, you're doing better than normal. Your controller should be able to give you a realistic idea of your cash position.

- **Accounts Receivable:** Money owed to your business by customers, or unpaid invoices.

- **Accounts Payable:** Money your business owes to suppliers or vendors.

- **Inventory Levels:** Amount of goods on hand to sell or use.

- **Customer Retention:** Number or percentage of existing customers who return.

- **Customer Acquisition:** Number of new customers gained during the week.

- **New Orders:** Number of confirmed purchases or service bookings received during the week.

- **Cost of Labor**: This is NOT how much employees get paid per hour! This means their *total* overhead, including salary, benefits, their portion of the total operating costs (per employee, which frequently includes *other* employees being paid to work on the same projects), plus general operating expenses like fuel, insurance, equipment, and supplies.

- **Break-Even**: the absolute minimum sales figures your company needs to break even

- **90 Day Snapshot**: you need to know your sales from last month, your projection for the current month, and projection for next month... and whether it lines up with your business plan for the year? What will your bank account look like three, six, twelve months from now?

- **Margins**: Represents the profitability as a percentage of the selling price. Do you make money on jobs or not? If you don't make money, why?

- **Capital Expenditures**: significant expenses in the near future because of normal wear and tear. If you currently have three trucks, all beat to death and preparing to die in the next year and a half, now is the time to put the money aside so you can replace them.

- **Efficiencies**: equipment, staff, and supplies that enhance and accelerate your speed and quality of delivery. Back in the 1990s, for example, computers became "efficiencies" that nearly every business under the sun needed.

How to Implement the Analyze Phase

Your three major umbrella subjects for Analyze are **people**, **knowledge**, and **numbers**.

But which one should you work on first? Which one needs the most attention? What if all three are in serious trouble? It pays to have a solid grasp of the *impact* and *priority* of each one, so B.A.S.I.C.S. doesn't backfire.

Many leaders in tough straits jump to the conclusion that sales is the answer to everything. I'm cautious about backtracking on that, because higher sales always help to some degree. But I've owned plenty of businesses where if I'd focused *only* on improving sales, it would have dug a deeper hole. Remember—with my first company, the controller never criticized the company's gross revenue. The products sold very well! Greater sales definitely helped… but only after I did the hard work of personal transformation, firing the toxic general manager, and reforming the company culture.

If your company is inefficient, wasteful, or disorganized, more sales will add to the confusion and difficulty. You'll burn bridges and ruin your reputation with customers and prospects. You'll take away vital resources for Analyze and the remaining phases. So when you implement Analyze, here's the key phrase: **prioritize for impact**. Obviously, your company must continue selling and increasing sales to survive and grow. But if it can't yet handle massive growth, your next priority is to build a bridge to a future where it can. "Impact" equals (for the time being) the foundation you lay, not record profits or expansion.

In project management, a lot of people like the term "Critical Path," which measures time. Remember the "big rocks" analogy? Critical Path adds the element of time and asks,

> *"What are the longest lead times for each large task that depends on a previous large task to reach a worthwhile end cause?"*

Put simpler, it's like a contractor asking, "Which parts of building the house take the longest to build or assemble, so we can get those done first?" If framing, drywalling, and painting take the longest... then you prioritize those three tasks ahead of everything else.

Here's the problem with Critical Path: *what if the house catches fire?* Circumstances dictate a lot more about our projects than we'd prefer. Even if it's just a small fire confined to one corner of the house, you'd better put down those other tasks, find the nearest hose or fire extinguisher, and put the fire out before it spreads. You won't stop that problem by hanging drywall! After several years of experience in project management, I prefer to use "Critical Priority" to describe my approach because it takes the variables and unknowns into account and forces you to at least consider them upfront.

When we moved the CNC machining company to its new facility, I clashed with the foreman at the general contracting firm I'd hired to renovate the building. He didn't understand Critical Priority. (*More accurately, he didn't care.*) I helped to design the facility from the ground up and we spared no expense—epoxy floors, sixty tons of air conditioning, LED lighting, brand new power, you name it.

The foreman didn't know how to handle the project. He paid no attention to any details I told him, nor did he write down one word of what I wanted. I asked him several times throughout the process, "Are you going to remember all this?" and he'd casually say, "Yeah, I got everything covered." He was useless; the only thing he was good at was getting coffee… and I don't drink coffee.

At one point, it got ugly. I had a requirement that every wall be insulated because we have temperature-controlled rooms and "clean rooms" for our products. He ignored my request. They framed the walls and then drywalled them without adding the insulation. I could tell because typically, when you add insulation, you see little flakes or particles along the floors. So I pulled out one electrical socket and looked behind the walls, and sure enough—no insulation. I checked a second outlet and got the same result. I was so pissed off that I took a hammer and punched a hole between every stud, in each piece of drywall they'd put up and told them, "I put those holes there so you can see that there's no insulation."

They replaced the drywall for free. They didn't even call me out for damaging over one hundred sheets of it.

Then came the day where the building was ready to be painted. I pulled the foreman aside and told him four key requirements that needed to happen before the painters came. Of course, he didn't write down a single one, and the painters came and painted right over the issues I mentioned. When I came back the next day and saw that they weren't done, I confronted the foreman.

"Oh, no problem," he said, "we'll just tear it out, redo, and repaint it."

That was the last straw, and I fired him on the spot. I also called his boss, the owner of the company, and took over the project myself. After I took over, I hired my own contractors to finish the job. We completed it two months early, and $70,000 under budget. (Had I continued to rely on that foreman, it would have finished two months late and $170,000 over budget.)

Just like my facility, your company needs to work according to Critical Priority if you want it to succeed ahead of schedule and under budget.

Organize, Organize, Organize!

Remember the "Maintenance Days" from Brute Force? You inventoried each and every machine and piece of equipment and logged every fault or issue you could find. You instructed your team to set aside every old and obsolete item that hadn't been used in five or more years, and you tossed or recycled them. You have all the data and documentation you need for everything that's left; now it's time to **organize** your workspace.

You should have everything you need at this point to implement and, during the Analyze phase, *improve the flow*. Your goal is to "grease the skids" for production and ease of movement so your company's supply can meet customer demand as quickly as possible. Remember the 90 Percent Rule as you do this... we're aiming for *progress*, not perfection. I've completed enough Analyze phases to tell you that the layout will still need improvements later on!

The good news, however, is that the changes you make from here on out become much more subtle. In Brute Force, you simply piled up all the junk and got rid of it. You cut wasteful spending. You fired bad employees. There was simply more *junk*, and junk weighs you down. But during Analyze, your priorities shift, and you start to work with valuable people, resources, and supplies. Your key question should shift during Analyze from "How do we stop the bleeding?" to "How do we get the best results, or much closer to them, for our decisions and efforts?" Let me give you a few examples.

When I took over the box manufacturing company, I noticed a lot of chaos among the employees whenever the need arose for tooling. I'd see them here and there throughout the day, walking through different areas of the facility, stopping at each other's workstations, and searching (often in vain). I'd incline my ear and overhear them say things like, "Hey, do you know where I can find this tool?" or "Where do we keep the screws?"

This happened enough that I started pulling them aside to ask, "What are you looking for?" After talking to a few of them, I determined the problem: no common location or resource existed for them to find parts or components they needed for their jobs. Loosely, it's like working in a restaurant without a walk-in refrigerator for perishable goods like milk and cheese; every time you want them, you have to walk around the block to the local grocery or convenience store! As I documented the problem, I also kept track of time. In some cases, the employees would spend as much as *forty-five minutes* trying to find the most basic items.

This had to stop. We purchased and stocked a roll-around cart with basic tools, electrical components, plumbing supplies, screws, spare parts, wires, and other hardware. We rolled the cart onto the floor and told them, "From now on, come here to get whatever you need to do your job." After we made that change, you could find what you needed in *less than forty-five seconds*. You can imagine what that did for productivity!

When we evaluated our products according to profitability, we discovered two of our large, school bus-sized machines occupied a ton of space to crank out products that didn't make any money! So I outsourced some of the work and we got rid of the machines. All of a sudden, we had a ton of open space, which opened up flow on the factory floor. We concentrated more energy and effort on work and machines that actually turned a profit. We reduced the expenses and energy of operating and maintaining those two machines. This provides a good model of connecting employees, metrics, and knowledge to the right activities—the ones that keep your company growing and profitable.

Another example is from my CNC manufacturing company, where the employees had a similar issue with machine fixtures and tools. When owners and management neglect organization, they consign their teams to wasting hours of time and energy (*for which they then blame those same employees when profits dwindle*). I'd walk the floor and notice the employees checking different desks, drawers, or lifting up certain items to look for others. Others milled around worktables and tool chests, opening and closing cabinets, looking for tools.

The same went for our product inventory, raw materials, and finished goods. The previous owners simply didn't see the benefit in keeping them organized. Employees wandered the floor for hours looking for items. So we created designated spaces in the building for raw materials, in-process, finished goods, and long-term storage. Nothing helps people find what they need like simple, clear, organized storage areas.

When the employees couldn't find the fixtures they needed, they had to remake them. If the tool they needed wasn't available, they had to wait until they could borrow it from one of their co-workers. Those extra minutes spent searching and asking around quickly turned into *hours* of waste! So we built centralized, fully-stocked rooms for fixtures and tools, and we told them the same thing we told the staff: "From now on, you can find every fixture or tool you need in one of these two rooms."

Presto—hours of waste became hours of productivity, which led to boatloads of revenue. All it took was a little analysis from a leader who cared and knew what to look for.

Sales

The only thing more important than sales is money.

I don't want this book to be about sales because there are far too many sales books already. But I do want to emphasize some key details every leader should know. I don't care how determined you are to build a strong business with systems, processes, policies, streamlined production, efficiency, and so forth—you won't get far if your sales don't improve.

The problem with sales is that it's difficult to improve *overnight*. You have to work at it, over time. Most marketers will tell you that the efforts you put forth in January build up your conversions for April. That's fine if you're doing well, but if it's January now and your business is in trouble… you need sales in January. You might not have a business left by the time you get to April. Your employees, vendors, and suppliers don't want to wait until April to get paid for services or products they're providing now.

A lot of manufacturers learn this the hard way, even if they're generally successful. They rake in a million orders in a month but run out of money by paying for all the labor and materials up-front before they finally get paid—*if* they get paid! Sometimes, you do all this fulfillment work in advance only to have a customer turn around and say, "Oh, sorry! We have to cancel the order." Even if you charge a cancellation fee, it rarely covers the overhead you took on.

So when you take your sales process through the Analyze phase, you want to reduce or eliminate risks. Fluctuations and customer cancellations are the nature of the beast. The best ways to handle them are to **be prepared** to absorb them, and to **build a process** that improves your ratios of closing and winning customer loyalty. Nothing smooths out a bumpy road like higher sales and more money.

"Why Us?"

When was the last time you worked with a salesperson who asked you why you chose to work with them? It never happens! But to be fair, you might have just as much trouble answering the question as they would asking it. Most of my customers can't tell me (at first) why they want to buy from me. They don't even know *what* they want, never mind why they want it from me. If you ask a customer what they want, they'll say, "I want X." But if you learn to Analyze as you sell, you'll discover—"X" almost *never* marks the spot.

It would be nice if you could pull out the Five Whys on customers the same way you can with employees. But employees already have a working relationship with you, whereas many customers don't. So even if you sense an opening to ask them why they chose you, customers often start with vague answers, like "You guys do a good job." Most salespeople take that first answer and move on to their next agenda item.

The problem with answers like "You guys do a good job" is... *so do competitors.* Lots of people and companies work hard, show up on time, and deliver quality products and services. I've met enough of my competitors to know very few businesses do "a bad job." They might be mediocre or slightly above average... but statements like these from customers mean *nothing.* It's a polite and indirect way of saying,

"I feel positive about you." If a customer says that to you, you need to put on your detective hat and find out what they mean. They might like your:

- On time delivery
- Unique products
- Levels of service competitors don't provide

Or, guess what? *They might not be talking about any of those things.* Your competitors might do every single thing you do just as well, but what that customer really means is, "It feels different when you do it." So you should ask follow-up questions, like:

- "What do other companies do that you wish we did?"
- "What do we do that you don't see our competitors do?"
- "How do you feel when you use our product or when we perform this service?"
- "Do you feel like we take care of you or more like we help you take something off your list?"

At one of my companies, I extensively drilled customers and found they bought from us mainly because of one of the people on our customer service team, whom I'll call John. They absolutely *loved* dealing with John. He was charismatic, energetic, positive, and proactive. One by one, they all brought John up by name. So now, as the owner, my job was to understand what John said or did that everyone liked so much:

- "What is it about dealing with John that you like so much?"
- "How do you feel when you work with him? What does he say or do that makes it work for you?"
- "What has your experience been like with other companies where you wish they'd be more like John?"

Be prepared for all kinds of answers, not just positive ones. When I took over my tool company and surveyed my customers, I discovered their common thread was "You guys are the cheapest deal in town, we can't afford to go anywhere else!" That's a sign you need to improve your service and raise your prices! You need to earn customer loyalty. People don't stay loyal to cheap prices.

Understand the Customer

I once read a fascinating sales story in an article about a rich young guy and a salesman at a Lamborghini dealership. The young guy walked into the showroom and announced to the salesman, "I want to buy a Lamborghini."

At this point, the salesman could have gone into detail about a million different things: engine specs, horsepower, interiors, luxury add-ons, etcetera. What's not to love about Lamborghinis? They combine performance, style, and upscale imagery into one car. But today, after more than forty years in public recognition, *everybody* knows what Lamborghini's brand stands for—especially a rich, good-looking young man who actually wants to buy one.

So instead, the salesman said, "Sounds good. One thing, though— make sure you don't get the windows tinted."

The young man raised an eyebrow. "What? Why not?"

"Well," said the salesman, "you're a young guy, good-looking… you want to be seen in this car, especially when you pull up to a light or a stop. This car gets people's attention, so don't tint the windows or nobody will know who you are."

This story reminded me of something most salespeople fail to do— **understand the customer** more than you understand the product or service. Your customer will buy if they feel *understood*. It's not your job to persuade them of anything. That Lamborghini salesman understood his customer; people don't buy Lamborghinis because they have great fuel economy or safety features. They don't buy them because their Volkswagen beater is on its last legs. People buy Lamborghinis for very specific reasons, and the salesperson's role is to detect those reasons in how the customer speaks and behaves. That means that the *value* you truly sell lies in your ability to understand and relate to your customer.

Let me give you a more common example from how I sell the boxes we make at the box company. I borrow the example of the boxes Apple uses to sell their iPhones and other devices. Unless you've been hiding under a rock for the last two decades, you know how you feel when you open up Apple's packaging. It's smooth, scented, soft to the touch, with sharp corners and edges. The color never deviates from its pure, brilliant whiteness—except for the Apple symbol in a slightly darker shade of white. The package is vacuumed, so you can't open it quickly. In some ways, the box is more exciting than the contents!

Imagine what you can stir up in people's minds about boxes with examples like that. I don't need to talk about the materials we use or what dimensions are available. It's the experience the customer wants, so when they sell *their* products inside our boxes the customers will form a similar emotional attachment to the one they form with Apple's boxes.

Of course, all of this presumes a level of trust and confidence that, in some cases, you haven't yet built. For this reason, you can't forget about sales nuts and bolts, like going to your *existing or past customer base* first. You'll much more easily make or rekindle levels of trust with people who already do (or have done) business with you. You'll also more easily make $1000 by selling to a single customer rather than two or three, which is why you should always offer upsells *before* presenting the final product. If you give a customer a couple of options with more bells and whistles as the price goes up... the chances are, they'll choose the median product. So if you're selling a $750 product and you have between $50- and $500-worth of add-ons, you have a good chance the customer will even out at $250 and you'll gross $1000 from the sale.

Another sales nut-and-bolt is *shut up and listen*. Your customer should do 80 percent of the talking, and 90 percent of what comes out of your mouth should be *questions* aimed at understanding them. You've probably heard that people buy *value over price*, and most of the time, they'll express the value by talking about the price they paid. But not every satisfied customer brags about the lowest price. In fact, you don't want to hear your customers brag to their friends about how you gave them the cheapest deal they could find. It's far better to hear them say things like, "It cost me an arm and a leg… *and it was worth every penny*."

Demographics and Psychographics

This one's so simple, you'll love it. You've already done it with your employees.

Find your biggest customers,
and find out why they work with you.

Pay attention here—although I tell you to "find out" why they work with you, it generally won't do you much good to ask them directly: "Why do you work with me?" Instead, I suggest you find out *what's important to them*, just like we've talked about doing with your employees. If you share an interest, that's a clue—watch for those interests and passions to recur among other customers. They feel good about you for a reason, and it usually hides in plain sight. Find out what your customers enjoy doing in their spare time or where their interests lie. Do they like golf? Cars? Are they high-risk or low-risk people? Remember, this is Analyze, so when patterns emerge among your customers, make note of them. Something will bubble up more than once.

Most of my customers are middle-aged business owners who come in to work early and work their tails off so they can also leave earlier in the afternoon. They dress in business casual attire, and they tend to have hobbies or interests similar to mine—mechanics, cars, boats, recreational vehicles, and so forth. I've met a few during summer outings on my boat. I'll cruise around a large lake, stopping occasionally at one dock or another for lunch or fuel, and that's where these conversations strike up. I make sure to slip in a little detail about what I do.

Your sales team must know and understand your demographic and be able to hold conversations with your customers about their interests. There's a lot of chatter online about knowing your "avatar" customer, and it's a start... but I focus on interests and hobbies. I know how much I get a kick out of telling people about my adventures in boating or flying. If I enjoy talking about my passions and interests... there's a good chance they feel the same way if someone shows interest in theirs.

The Difference Between You and "Them"

Because of the internet, people undoubtedly have more consciousness of their buying decisions than they did thirty years ago. But that doesn't mean they truly have "knowledge" about a product or service. I've seen a funny coffee mug you can buy online for lawyers that says "Please don't confuse your Google search with my law degree," and I think that's true for many industries besides legal. I can't tell you how many people I've met who *think* they know something about manufacturing... when they don't!

To the general public, a box is a box. An engine's an engine. A house is a house, and a car's a car. Unless you can really educate them about the differences, people rely on their *perceptions* of your brand and social proof. Do you remember how I talked about the minor differences between a Ford Fiesta and a Chevrolet Camaro versus the Camaro against a Ferrari? The Camaro simply has a bigger Fiesta engine, better suspension, and a sleeker body design. Other than that, its components are essentially the same. But the Ferrari is truly on a level above both. How would your customers know that unless you educate them?

A similar thing happens if you're selling the Fiesta instead of the Ferrari. If your product is cheaper, how do you demonstrate to the customer that the quality is the same (or better)? Most salespeople jump ahead to this part—explaining the features and benefits—without understanding the customer or connecting with them at a visceral level. I only start to talk about the contrasts and comparisons to our competition once I've determined the customer feels seen, heard, and understood.

"I Don't Have the Money!"

Don't fall for this one, especially if your business is B2B like mine are. People who truly don't have money do one of two things: they either (a) avoid talking to you in the first place, or (b) find a way to get the money. This hinges on whether they think your product will solve their problem, and money is usually their problem—as in, "They need more money."

Customers who say "I don't have the money" usually mean they want something else (money itself) more than they want your product. In the B2B world, this is the perfect occasion to educate your customer on how your product or service will lead them to what they want. I take off my sales hat for a moment when people raise this objection and become curious about the financial health of their business. If our products improve revenue or efficiency and reduce waste or spending... wouldn't a customer want to know about that? Of course... but the problem is, they've lost sight of the big picture.

One of my favorite ways to deal with this is to say, "Okay... *if* you had the money, why would you purchase these boxes?"

They typically answer, "The boxes are great. I think they'd help sell more of our product."

"So you don't have the money," I continue, "but you do believe that if you bought these boxes, you'd sell more products."

The customer nods.

"So, let's suppose you had the money and you purchased the boxes. How much more of your product do you think you'd sell once you start using the boxes?"

"Maybe 10 percent more," they reply.

"Okay, so let's think now about your annual revenue. What's 10 percent of your total annual sales?"

"Well, we're doing $4.3 million per year... so 10 percent of that is $430,000."

By now, the wheels should begin to turn for a customer hesitating on a $35,000 order, which is (more or less) our average order value. Even if the customer only increased their sales by 1 percent, they'd still come out on top. A 10 percent increase would give them more than ten times the return on their investment!

"So you're telling me," I say to them playfully, "that you're going to save money by *not* spending $35,000... to avoid *earning* $430,000?" (*Pause for dramatic effect.*)

"Never mind," they chuckle. "Send me the invoice."

Current Revenue
$4.3M

Invest $35,000 | Revenue Increase

4.3M x 10% = $430,000 | + $395k
1128% R.O.I.

New Revenue $4.73M

Invest $0 | Revenue Increase

4.3M x 0% = $0 | + $0
0% R.O.I.

New Revenue $4.3M

Why "I don't have the money" may make little sense.

This is how Analyze works. You acknowledge what the customer says and take it seriously... but in seeking to understand what's behind the words that come out of their mouth, you give voice to their emotional world. Remember when we talked about the hidden emotional reasons your employees make mistakes? When prospects or customers hesitate to bite the bullet, they also have hidden emotional reasons. Many of them are valid... but they may also be obsolete. Your job as the salesperson is to gently draw them out so the customer can see the folly of their (emotional) reasoning.

Customers' Perspective

Sometimes, you have to challenge customers' perspectives—while still being honest. I run into this occasionally. A good example is the box products we make at the box company. Some customers become a little cynical: "You're kidding me, right? You actually think I'll sell more of my products if I put them in your boxes?"

Well... *will they?* The answer comes down to whether you can speak with conviction about (realistic) possibilities. If my skeptical customer sells Rolex watches, for example, it's a fair question. A Rolex is still a

Rolex, whether it comes in a sleek, luxurious box from our company or a recycled cardboard box from Amazon. However, what would *you* say when you receive your Rolex in an Amazon box? Would you shrug or even notice? Or would you be a little surprised, given the prestige of the Rolex brand? It's important to help a B2B customer think through the *entire* process of satisfying their consumers' demand, rather than let them fixate on one chunk of it.

On the other hand, let's get into Analyze mode: what if a highly influential writer at *Luxury Watch Magazine* does a review and raves about the packaging on the Cosmograph Daytona this customer sells? How many units would they need to ship before recouping every penny they spent with us and then some? It's all a matter of the customer's perspective, and sometimes customers genuinely need a transfer of enthusiasm, optimism, or confidence from a salesperson. They need to "borrow" faith from you. Maybe business hasn't been so hot for them lately. If you can't muster this energy when you need to, don't plan on making a lot of sales.

Fixes

Move quickly when your customer has an issue with your product or service. Speed is everything. Even if the repair or solution takes a while, don't leave your customer sitting there, wondering if you're making moves or not. Update them. Show them they're on your mind. Text or send an e-mail. Whatever you do, don't keep your customer guessing.

If you can't fix things right away,
you can *always* communicate right away.

"Dear John,

I just want you to know I'm continuing to work on your issue today. I don't have any news to report just yet, but it's better to communicate than keep silent.

I'm committed to getting this fixed for you as soon as possible, and will check in daily until I have something concrete to report.

Regards
Dean"

High-quality vendors fix problems immediately when they occur. Don't make your customers feel like *they* have to follow up on your behalf. If they could manufacture your product on their own, or find time to perform the service for themselves, they would do it. They're paying you because they believe you're better at it than they are or they simply don't have the time or skill.

Hard Selling

Customers reject "soft" selling all the time. I don't believe "hard" selling is obnoxious or invasive—or at least, it doesn't have to be. Most of what you see lampooned or caricatured as "hard selling" isn't "selling"… it's sleazeball tactics from desperate people.

Let's agree: customers want the best product at an affordable price. Well… you have it! Why would you deprive your customer of what they want because you prefer to wait until everything "feels right"? Did Steve Jobs wait until the market knew they wanted the iPhone and asked for it, or did he spearhead its development and launch it?

Customers don't know what they want, as we covered earlier. Part of your job in sales is to believe and articulate that you have the best product in your industry at a price point your customer can afford. I wrote this book, for example, because when it comes to consulting for a business that wants to learn or is in trouble, I have the best product that truly solves the problem. I own numerous companies where I've proved that it works, and I charge a very reasonable fee for what you earn in return.

Make the Customer Feel Important

Remember the contractor I fired when we built our new facility for my manufacturing company? What if that foreman had carried around a notepad and wrote down everything I asked him to do? What if he'd been as proactive as I was about the project's Critical Priority? It would have communicated to me, as a new owner, that he cared deeply about the health and continued prosperity of my business. It would have been his way of saying, "I'm only successful in business when my customers are successful, and that includes you."

When we talk about making customers feel important, it's easy to fall into the trap of thinking about simple things like birthday cards or gift boxes. Those can be helpful for certain personalities, and I recommend doing them after you close your first sale. But if that's all you ever do, you're keeping your customer in "shallow waters." Your customer is a human being, and human beings have problems and issues they want to solve—or at least talk about. (They might have thousands of them if they're a fellow business owner.)

If you become a problem solver for your customer, you multiply your chances of gaining a customer for life. If you create a super-high degree of trust with them, they won't want to work with your competitors. Most leaders fail at this miserably, which brings us back to our famous question: **Are you ready for change?** Are you ready to do what most people are too indifferent or lazy to do?

> Most of your competitors **couldn't care**
> **less** about your customers' well-being.
> And that gives *you* the advantage.

How You Know the Analyze Phase is Working

You know you're deep in the Analyze phase when you suddenly have information you didn't have before—and it answers questions you didn't even know to ask. At first, it's like lifting up a rock and seeing all the bugs underneath. You **identify everything that's broken**— whether it's processes, equipment, systems, policies, or even something as simple as the lighting in your facility. It's all on the table.

But the true mark that you've completed Analyze is this: **you run out of new problems to find**. With the data you've gathered, you can't identify anything other major item left unchecked.

But, in the meantime, what do you do with all the information about the problems you've found?

Document it. Fully. By department, by process, or whatever structure works for your company. Then you rank everything. Critical issues go to the top, medium-priority next, and nice-to-haves go at the bottom. As Stephen Covey points out in *The 7 Habits of Highly Effective People*, your tasks and objectives sort neatly into the "Urgent/Important" quadrant:

	URGENT	NOT URGENT
IMPORTANT	DO	PLAN
NOT IMPORTANT	DELEGATE	ELIMINATE

Once you've done that, you build a path forward. A plan. In today's day and age, you can leverage artificial intelligence (AI) to put this together in *seconds*. That means every critical item needs:

- A clearly defined problem
- A practical, executable solution
- A timeline
- A responsible person or team
- A date it'll be resolved

That's when you'll know you're headed into the next phase—because now you've shifted from *discovery* into *execution*. Don't worry about having every last issue solved. Just make sure the critical stuff has a plan. Start moving on the medium priorities, too, if you can. The rest will follow.

Remember: **Clarity kills confusion**. The Analyze stage gives you the clarity to stop guessing and start leading.

Chapter Eight

Structure
Document Core Processes and
Assign Clear Responsibilities

"Every company has two organizational structures: the formal one is written on the charts; the other is the everyday relationship of the men and women in the organization."
Harold S. Geneen

The Structure phase is more subtle than Brute Force and Analyze. At this point, you've moved past firing bad employees and getting rid of twenty-year old cabinets full of ancient paperwork. You also move faster (in some ways) than you did in Analyze because Structure is where you refine, like going from Ford to Ferrari. You focus like a laser on Critical Priority because you have all the necessary parts for the engine, which you've cleaned, repaired, and oiled. Structure could be called the "execution" of the Analyze phase. You've gathered all the information and research you possibly can,

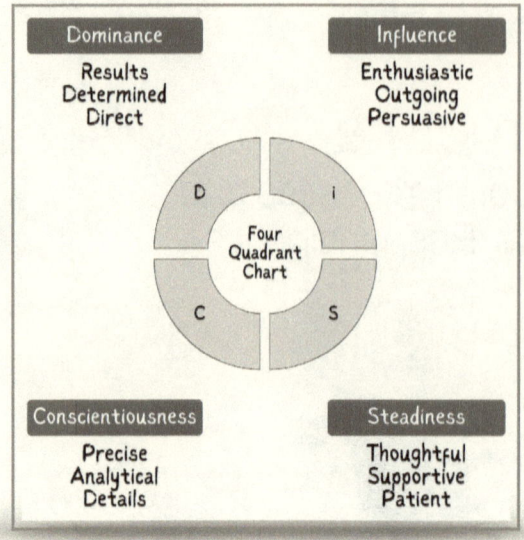

assembled it into a detailed strategy, and now you push the "Play" button.

Structure Your Team

Primarily, you drive forward by putting the most effective person in the right role. Part of the Structure phase identifies who can handle the "non-tangible" parts of the job—stress, team building, cooperation, and unique interpersonal challenges. I've interviewed many people who had technical or mechanical skills to perform a role... but failed to demonstrate that they could work well with others. Knowing what I know now about toxic behaviors from employees and managers, I care more about an applicant's character strengths than their technical aptitudes. I'm not going to put a laid-back personality in charge of collecting outstanding invoices, nor do I put hard chargers in the customer relations role. The more critical the project or task, the more you need both "hard" and "soft" skills to qualify to lead (or even participate).

This is where a working knowledge of personality types helps. Remember the DISC tool we talked about in Chapter 2? Here, it becomes critical. Arrange for your entire team to go through the self-assessment questionnaire... and *review the data* when you get it. You'll learn all about their behavioral style, preferences, and get a custom personality profile for each person. It'll help you predict how they typically show up, respond to situations, and interact with others in the workplace.

At one of my companies, I identified a few key employees who excelled in different areas. One was a tough "D" negotiator who could handle uncomfortable situations. If we encountered difficult vendors or suppliers, she was "the sharp end of the stick." Another was a quiet and withdrawn "C," but he produced the most stunning, accurate, and well-thought out designs I'd ever seen... so I made him one of the top designers. A third one, an "S," was of the sweetest, kindest, most sociable people you could meet. She was in charge of new client onboarding and spreading the word about good things we did.

Moves like this affect your organizational chart, and that's okay. You might hear some gurus say you shouldn't do that, but if you're a small outfit, what choice do you have? More often than you think, the most technically-qualified person is *not* the best person to handle a situation effectively—at least, not as a supervisor or manager.

I've been surprised how frequently the people who *seem* the strongest and most capable... are actually the weakest, and vice versa. Back during my years working in corporate America, I got caught off-guard by one of my bosses. He seemed very soft in comparison to my tougher bosses in the skilled trades. But when it came to handling serious problems, I noticed how much more skilled and competent he was in comparison. The other bosses "acted" tougher, but they struggled to handle complex, detailed problems well. I learned to wait until the right time to judge someone's competency.

Kari, one of my employees at the box company, is like that. At first glance, she seemed timid... but when I began to challenge her to stretch and grow in her role, I found out that inside, she's a lion. She will need additional training as she moves into management, but there's no project or task you can throw at her that she won't overcome.

In my companies, we use the acronym F.A.I.L.—First Attempt In Learning. If you're going to let your employees try something, reassure them that failure is an option. Tell them it's okay to make mistakes. Obviously, you don't want them to make the same mistake multiple times without correcting it... but you can certainly create an environment of safety where employees feel empowered to try things out. Success in the Structure phase frequently depends on your willingness to "test drive" projects with different employees at the wheel. I have a running joke with Kari because she's not a fan of mistakes. We all make them, of course, including Kari. So when I see her on the floor, I say, "I'm still waiting for the day you make a mistake, Kari." When I interviewed her for this book, she elaborated:

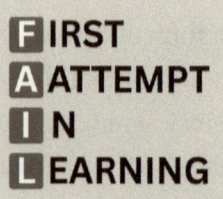

FIRST
AATTEMPT
IN
LEARNING

> *"I enjoy that joke because if you know that your boss, the owner of the company, has every intention of using mistakes as opportunities to teach, learn, empower, and encourage his employees—you don't fear making mistakes. You think to yourself, 'It'll be okay. We'll troubleshoot and figure out what went wrong. Making a mistake doesn't have to be a negative experience.'"*

Some employees may respond to your offer by saying, "No thank you, I'm happy doing what I do." But that doesn't mean *other employees* don't watch or overhear the conversation. Many of my employees didn't know what they were truly capable of doing until we believed in them, and decided to ask.

So give employees a shot at trying their interests under your employment. Let the staff watch you experiment with them, and allow them to make mistakes. Let them see their co-workers move from one machine to another, where they make a huge impact. All of a sudden, productivity and morale take another leap forward. Success and growth are contagious. The big idea here is to build a bench where you can run "two or three employees deep" on all critical roles and responsibilities. We'll cover more on that later in this chapter.

Structure Your Knowledge

Structure is where you put the "rough draft" business plan into action. When you get to later stages like Improve and Sustain, you'll still make changes when you discover areas that need work. But at this point, everyone in the company should have visibility of the map, and staff should know where to find it for reference.

Make a personal plan for yourself, as well as for the company. While you should avoid overestimating what you can accomplish in one year... it doesn't mean you should leave your own sheet blank. Let's say that in five years' time, you want to triple the size of your business, hire a CEO in your stead, and remove yourself completely from the day-to-day. Okay, great! Now you need a plan to get there, which means thinking through the sales increase you need each year, as well as the expense of hiring and training your replacement. That vision won't come to pass if you don't have a plan, no matter how hard you work.

If you know your current revenues and the percentage increase you need for one year, you can break those numbers down to weekly, or even daily, figures. This gives you more immediate clarity on performance. If you gross $5 million per year and you need a 43 percent increase each year, then you know you must earn over $7 million in the first year to be in the ball park. That's just under $600k per month, $150k per week, or $30k a day. **Pro tip**: the daily numbers don't have to hit $30k every single day, so long as they *average* that number consistently.

Marketing professionals have a rule that's helpful for Structure: "Find out what the market wants, and give it to them." When you release your vision and business plan, the company's response and performance will reflect whether you've done your homework, just like when the market responds to a campaign message. But by this point, you should feel more confident about publishing a plan because of all the clutter and chaos you've cleared away. You've spent enough time interviewing and gathering information, fixing and firing, and studying feasibility based on capacity and financial health. You shouldn't feel anxious; the plan should feel obvious at this point.

Structure should also solidify **reviewing the vision and business plan** at regular intervals. There's nothing more motivating than each person *knowing* they hit their daily metric. That starts with knowing the plan for the year, then the quarter, then the month, the week, and finally, the day. If your average line worker knows he's got to make a minimum of twenty widgets that day, and he hits it consistently, you know you're on track. If he misses it consistently… you know it's time to find the bottleneck. If he exceeds it consistently… we'll cover that in the "Improve" chapter.

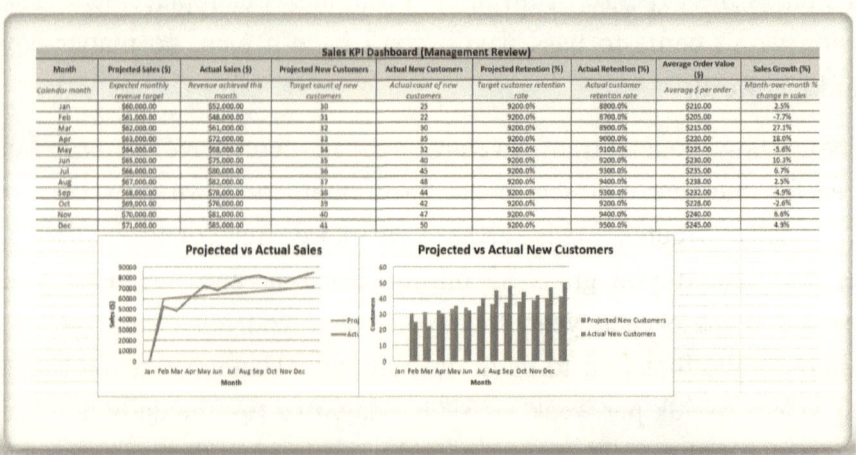

Sales

Your "quote-to-cash" sequence needs defining, especially with routine tasks your team must do in every transaction. If a detail can be seen on paper or grasped with the hand, it's your job to name it, define it, document it, and track it. Is there a checklist of documents, signatures, disclosures, and other discussion items your team needs? Make sure they have one spelled out and ingrained into their heads. Train management to reject incomplete files until you have 100 percent compliance. Is there an order of questions and information gathering reps must follow, to ensure quotes are accurate and final? Put it on paper. Talk about it. Rehearse it. Role play it. Leave as little margin for error as you can. Your growth depends on it.

During Analyze, you studied the sales process in detail. You should know where its worst "chokepoints" are and discuss with your sales team how the process *should* look under ideal circumstances. You might not be able to implement solutions right away, depending on what they tell you. But you can at least be aware of blind corners where salespeople run into the most frequent problems and solicit their input on how to modify or improve the process. Tell them to document these blind corners and unforeseen problems in a notepad as they go, and bring them up at the next meeting.

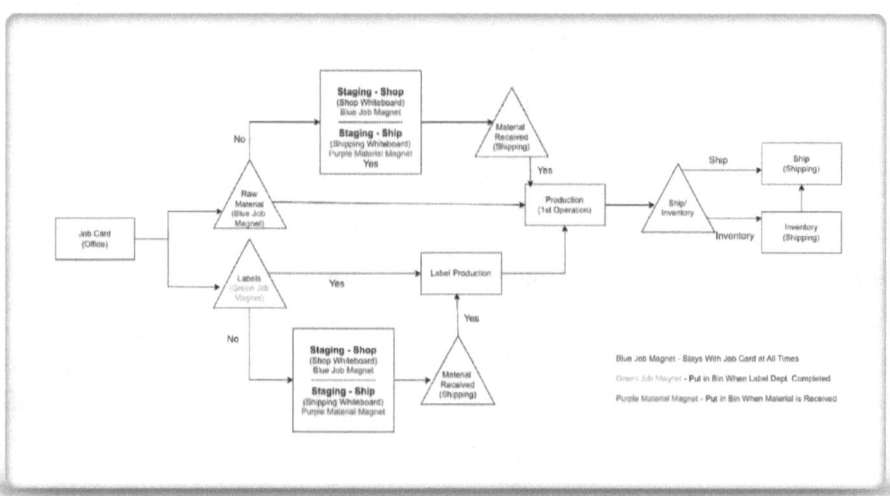

One of my actual Quote-to-Cash flowcharts

Growth

You've identified the people most effective in various roles, particularly leadership and project management. Structure is where you formally integrate them with growth targets in mind. Let's say you have a project lagging behind by a couple of weeks, but Craig, the current senior technician, doesn't strongly drive it forward. He's interested in growth, but not along the lines of leadership and project management. You have three options:

- Lean on Craig to double his efforts.
- Take over the project yourself.
- Delegate the non-technical parts to capable others in your company.

You suddenly remember Sally, a hard-charging "D" manager in sales, and you cross-train her into a temporary, additional role to fulfill this project. Of course, this doesn't mean you send her out to swing hammers or fix air ducts. But it does mean time out of her day to follow up on critical items, check the status of each task, keep the team focused, overcome delays, lean on the subcontractors, and negotiate faster deliveries with vendors.

If Sally needs additional support or resources, Structure is where you give her what she needs. Maybe she needs a more private office where she can drive the project by phone, or perhaps she needs to use a company car to visit job sites. Maybe she needs administrative support —so you offer it from Jessica, a detail-oriented "C" who normally focuses on her role as your executive assistant. You cross-train two employees instead of one. Jessica now benefits from additional exposure to work where, although she may lack experience, she has talent and natural enthusiasm to make up for it.

Hopefully you see how this works: Craig, who is neither a project manager nor an administrator, avoids overwhelm and maintains focus on his role as senior technician. Sally and Jessica, meanwhile, widen their capacities and strengths, and the path to growth becomes more and more real. If you lean on Craig to do all of this by himself, it can easily cause further delays—or worse. Nobody grows, talent and opportunities go to waste, and headaches multiply. The same is also true if you take it over personally… and of course, you sacrifice your time at great cost to yourself and the company.

Structure Your Finances

Once you reach the Structure phase, hiring a controller is a good idea. If you're a small company, hire one part-time. You stopped the bleeding in Brute Force, and in Analyze you traced where your money goes. Now it's time to find an informed source of judgment on the facts you've gathered. Look for someone who's run their own business in the past. If you can find someone from your particular industry, that's even better.

A good controller is 80 percent "rough" and 20 percent "finish." What does that mean? Numbers and accounting are a game of hitting the "refresh" button over and over until all the mistakes, assumptions, and corrections get factored in. The controller you hire needs to be highly detail-oriented and comfortable spending much more time delving into numbers than you. They need to think about those numbers dynamically and help you interpret them as they rise, fall, or stay put. You should treat a surge in profitability with as much suspicion as you'd treat a surge in shrink (losses), and if you have numbers that don't shift when they should… you need to be curious.

Even your average CPA worth their salt knows to reconcile reports several times before they make conclusions. But most CPAs' knowledge falls short of what you need as the owner—they don't dig into analytics or interpret data. They rarely give advice or make recommendations based on how your numbers behave.

> ## Accountants tell you what the numbers **are**; controllers tell you what they *mean*.

George, the controller I hired at my first company, looked over my cash flow and balance sheets and said, "Dean, you're doing several things where you're not making any money." He knew exactly what to look for, how to assess it, and which reports were essential. He could also make recommendations that helped steady the ship immediately. In a few short months, we increased our margins dramatically, from 23 to 56 percent.

People I know have complained that they hired controllers and nothing changed. But remember—if you can't explain your vision and objectives or provide an abundance of detail, controllers can't do your job for you. They can point to numbers on a sheet and say, "This is your sales figure for last month." But the only way they can advise you on what to do about those numbers is if they know *where you want to go* in relation to where you've been and where you are. The same goes for forecasting; a controller can tell you, "You'll gross $25,000 next month." But what does that *mean* if you haven't decided ahead of time what you want?

I spend a lot of time going over business plans with my controllers. Why? Because the business plan that works best is the *one you follow*. I stress to my controllers: "Hold me to this plan. If I wander off the reservation, I want you to tell me, 'Dean, you're wandering off.'" Sometimes, this process reveals where we've failed to follow the plan. Sometimes, our numbers reflect that we've failed to think about the basic risks you can always assume, such as inflation or taxes.

Some discrepancies are due to factors beyond your control, like a spike in the cost of insurance. In that case, the controller who knows your business plan can advise you on how to decrease costs and expenses. As I got used to hiring controllers in my companies, I learned to ask, "Can I afford XYZ?" Previously, I might have had *some* idea of whether I could afford the item or not; today, I am synced up with my controllers like a captain with his chief of engineering. They know my vision and goals, and I trust them to tell me the truth. I can think intelligently about how we've performed and how we'll likely perform because they produce accounts, projections, and forecasts weeks and months in advance of when I need them.

Controllers also advise on investing in the business, which means "money that goes toward making the business earn and keep more." *Read that again.* We're not talking about buying a nice leather chair for your office. Whatever you invest in has to help the company grow and earn greater revenues and profits. It could be equipment, staff, supplies, real estate, or competitor acquisitions. When you **invest** in your business, you do it for the same reason you invest in the stock market—to grow your balance sheet and personal wealth. In business, your capacity to serve more and more customers, whether the economy's booming or going bust, is a strong measure of your business' health and wealth.

How to Implement the Structure Phase

The other key component of Structure is the Critical Path—knowing what to do, in which order. You can make more or less money than others, but you get the same amount of time as everyone else. So, you must become an expert at **scheduling**. Alongside this comes **building the bench**—identifying and assigning contingency personnel for unexpected turns.

Scheduling and Building the Bench

When I bought my first home, we invested $50,000 into renovating and improving it. I don't like long, unnecessary waits, so I also built a schedule—I arranged to have the plumbing, electricity, carpeting,

HVAC, bricklaying, painting, and interior teams arrive within one day of each other over five consecutive days. I knew which order to put them in, so in a space of literally five working days, the home went from unlivable... to move-in ready. My family arrived over the weekend and began moving in on Monday. Under normal circumstances, this takes weeks, or months if you do it yourself. We were done in five days.

When we moved the machining company into its new facility, I knew from the experience of moving to numerous homes that timelines get disrupted easily when people don't understand sequencing and how moving parts overlap. I leaned heavily on my background with project management. I called the contractors who worked on the facility, laid down a specific schedule, and told them, "I need you here at 9AM. I don't want you here at seven, because the plumber's coming at seven and he'll be in your way. I also can't do later than nine, because you need five hours to do the work and my drywaller comes at 2PM, and you'll get in his way. So it's got to be 9AM. Can you do that and be finished by two?"

I called our machine suppliers and the movers, and I nailed down all of their timeline projections well in advance. A normal company making a move like ours would take a month, possibly several. But if you line up electrical, plumbing, HVAC, flooring, painting, and delivery/installation of key pieces of equipment, you can shorten the length of a move dramatically. I also built a "bench" of reserve contractors—I obtained quotes and timeframes from three or four of them per category so I had backup options. The day before we expected them, I'd call each provider to double-check:

"Now, they're going to be here at nine, right?" I said.

"Oh, yes," they replied.

But if something changed and they said, "No," I'd cancel the order, move immediately to the bench, and get a replacement as fast as possible. That's how you weave together Critical Path, "right person, right place, right time," and building the bench. First, you identify the work you need to do and think through the sequencing. Next, you delegate the work to the most *effective* people—not necessarily the most qualified! Then, you train and line up second- and third-string options in case anything disrupts the progress.

Sometimes, building a bench takes a lot of time, effort, and energy—more than you bargained for. One of my companies had such a dysfunctional purchasing department that, during Brute Force, I terminated all six people working in it. I took over all of their jobs and learned them for myself for the following three months... without a customer list, vendor list, pricing, or any useful information. (I called the bad purchasing manager to ask where she'd kept her list. When she told me and I didn't find it, she said, "Well, I guess somebody stole it." Hmmmm...)

The moral of the story is—avoid *irreplaceability*. If you don't, you'll end up with a different set of problems where employees become aware that you need them. They'll turn on you by saying, "I need a raise, or else I'm leaving." And guess what? Unless you can replace them in under two weeks, you will be forced to give it to them. As much as possible, get information, processes and data out of people's heads—particularly people who've worked at your company for a long time. Document what they know so you don't get caught off-guard by their sudden absence.

Don't ignore me on this! Get it done. Don't sit back and say, "Well, I can't afford to train people. I don't have time to train them to pitch in if we lose the top employee." *Right...* and when you lose that top employee, what will you say then? Will there suddenly be thirty-two hours in a day instead of twenty-four? Will you have double the disposable income? Where's the logic in that? It's the same as those bad owners who thought they'd save money by not buying employees a coffee maker!

Choose the lesser of two evils.
Invest the time and money, now, while you have it.

We've approached a good time to mention information security. I've come across companies where only one person knew all the passwords, calendar entries, and managed all the contacts in the computer systems... document this stuff, or it'll come back to bite you! Trying to unlock a computer system without the password is like having surgery without anesthesia, while going through probate without a will. If your employees control that information and circumstances change, you could end up in a situation where your company's security and ability to operate and grow gets compromised. Put all your infosec in a password-protected document where only certain people have access. Have your IT guy do a system-wide evaluation for every possible password and security code you might need.

Meetings

We've all seen *Dilbert* comics and cultural parodies of "death by meetings" in corporate America. I have worked in the past for companies where I can honestly say that my job was to attend meetings—all day,

every day. (That wasn't why they hired me, but that's what I did.) This is your chance to structure meetings so that you avoid debacles most companies have. They're not even real meetings! It's just a bunch of employees who get together and talk informally about random topics without solving any problems.

During my time in IT in corporate America, I took forty-plus training courses over thirteen years. From these, I learned much of what I know about leadership, project management, psychology in the workplace, communication, and people skills. It also included a course on running successful formal meetings. I consider that by far the most valuable course I took because I could implement what I learned very quickly and see the results for myself. You can make meetings count, and being a facilitator means more than simply showing up.

Most leaders know enough to know that meetings work best with a clear direction and purpose. You should have an agenda for everyone to read, but you should do several other things to keep confusion and distraction to a minimum. Here are some habits I developed over years of organizing and facilitating meetings:

Invite only people who need to be there. I believe in seeking input and building consensus throughout my companies. But that doesn't mean every one of my top management employees needs to be at every meeting. Unless I'm running a meeting that impacts their roles or departments, I leave people off the invitation.

Prepare and distribute an agenda. If I call a meeting on a Wednesday, I set aside fifteen minutes a day or so beforehand to draft an agenda. If you leave it too late, the chances increase that you'll forget important topics or details. Doing a draft ahead of time allows you to remember other details before you start. Once you're settled on what you want to discuss, either add it to the meeting invite or print out copies for attendees. If you're running a more informal, blue-collar company where you don't use conference rooms, handouts, or slides, you can still put up a post or notice to announce the meeting and the topics you plan to cover. Whatever you do, *document* what you intend to talk about.

Discuss the agenda before the conversation starts. Take a couple of minutes to go through the agenda and preframe the meeting for attendees: "We'll start with the budget, then we'll cover the hiring freeze. After that, we'll provide an update on the office Christmas party, and round it out with any subjects not covered in the agenda." Depending on your company's size, you can set the time limit in the calendar invite, or announce it verbally.

Keep the meeting on track. People sometimes veer off-topic or start talking about subjects outside the scope of the meeting. This chews up valuable time when you're trying to stick to an agenda. If an attendee starts to go off-track or down a rabbit trail, I usually interrupt and say, "I appreciate what you're saying, and I hear you. If it's okay with you, I'd like to put that topic in the parking lot, for the time being, so we can focus on the agenda for today."

Beware of "game-changers." Let's say you're trying to build consensus over a limited range of options—red notebooks versus green notebooks, for example. Some attendees will use the occasion to impose their "outside-the-box" opinions and suggest gray notebooks instead. They *appear* to be on topic… but they actually delay the process of deciding between the two viable options. The facilitator must now steer the meeting back to its agenda without dismissing the person. I learned to do this by saying, "I hear you, John, but we're trying to decide between green and red notebooks. Let's parking-lot the gray notebook option and discuss it after the meeting."

Avoid "stolen" interactions. Quieter and more reserved attendees might feel awkward or go very slowly, either when asking or answering questions. One of my pet peeves during meetings is when I ask a question of one attendee, and another attendee (usually their manager) interrupts to answer for them. It takes tact and patience to refocus the question onto the employee without humiliating the manager or raising the tension in the room. When this happens, I acknowledge the manager, but continue to ask the employee for their thoughts and opinions.

One other angle on meetings: there's a different way to handle them when you try to solve the real, hidden problems in your business. If you schedule a meeting to discuss the *symptoms* of a problem, that's fine—but I call those "discovery phase" meetings. If that's the case, you should be clear up front: "We know there's a problem, but we don't know where the bottleneck is just yet. So the purpose of today's meeting is to dig and find out as much information as we can to try to locate the source of the problem."

Lastly, **end your meetings with purpose**. Sometimes, you can end with a round-robin review and ask each person to restate back to you, out loud, something they take away from the meeting. Restate back to them any concerns they brought to you, along with your plan to fix it or provide them with the resources they need. Also, document action items, decisions, discussion points, and parking-lot items. If there's a follow-up meeting or fixed date for reviewing results, make sure everyone knows and has the checkpoint on their calendars. Meetings are caricatured in culture because of mismanagement; you have the chance to redeem them as meaningful moments where you solve problems and make decisions together.

Delegate

Get it through your mind right now and put it on "repeat" until you can accept it:

> Your employees will *NEVER* do things
> as fast or as well as you do them.

I could write an entire book on delegation. One day, maybe I will. Next to mindset, this is the top struggle for owners and managers, because now they have to let go and trust others to do important work they've always done for themselves.

Personally, I work very hard at delegating. I'm an effective and efficient worker; nobody has ever had to tell me to stay focused. But I delegate tasks in my companies anyway, even small ones that take minutes of my time. It takes *much more* time to be an effective *leader* than it does to be an effective employee.

I occasionally come across things so simple that they would take longer to delegate than to do. Fair enough. But if you're going to act

like a leader who knows the value of your time… I'm sorry, there's no other way. Trust your employees and accept that if they can do 60 percent or better at the same work you've done… it's good enough—especially if you follow my 90 Percent Rule and only stress quality where it counts. You can delegate just about anything, and if you have work that can be done for $20 an hour or less, don't leave it up for discussion. Assign that work to someone else and focus on what only you, as the leader, can do.

That purchasing department where I terminated all six employees became an exercise in delegation. The manager performed poorly, argued a lot, and resisted my new systems and processes. She entered orders incorrectly, failed to track her activities, and routinely kept us behind schedule by not getting her work done in a timely fashion. I tried to work with her for several weeks, including putting her on a Performance Improvement Plan (PIP). But after a while I could see—she remained committed to doing things her way. She also exerted strong influence on the other two purchasing representatives, one of whom was her friend.

So I took over purchasing for a while and documented the steps as I mastered each aspect of the job. When the time came to hire a replacement, I had very clear expectations and a description of the qualities and competence I needed. I hired a new purchasing agent, whom I trained extensively, and then delegated the entire department to her. She assumed managerial duties, hired new agents, and made most of the purchasing decisions independently from me. At last, I could refocus my energy on building and working on my business. Today, she runs the entire purchasing operation, hires new staff, and only consults with me when necessary.

Remember—you can't compare a $20/hour job to the value of your time and energy. But there's another reason to delegate—and this one goes beyond the money. If you tracked your entire day in fifteen-minute increments, I'd bet you could delegate three quarters of everything you do. This would leave you with a surplus of time to do the most important thing leaders can do: **think**... and teach employees (especially managers) to think.

Thinking is hard, and it takes time. You can mop a floor or plunge a toilet in mere minutes. Fixing chokepoints in a production line or eliminating bottlenecks in a quote-to-cash system are much more difficult. Thinking requires focus and minimal distractions, which makes it difficult for "doers" who got their start with physical tasks. They're used to doing work with their hands or bodies all day. But few receive proper training when they rise to the ranks of management.

Every company I've owned or managed became successful on the strength of *many* people, not just one. Yes, I provided leadership... but my employees did the hard work of change and learning to think differently. I want to delegate more than tasks to my staff; I also want to delegate *how I think* because the results are in: it works!

Employees get paid to *execute*, but influenced to think.
Managers get paid to *think*, but influenced to lead.

That's why I was so opposed to the vice president who filled the soda machine and the production manager who plunged the toilets. They felt uncomfortable, like they needed to prove to the employees that they still did physical work. I had to teach them that their work is much more complicated; a manager's job is to think and solve problems so employees can remain focused on their tasks. That includes asking lots of questions, documenting tons of information, and delegating every non-essential task to employees along the way. To develop these skills, managers need a good example to follow from the owner or senior managers.

Facility

My favorite part of Structure is "flow," where we think through the A-Z process of converting raw materials into finished products and the positioning of each machine and piece of equipment. This works really well if you have a balcony level in a factory, but if you don't, you can always make diagrams and flow charts. You watch the flow and analyze how the process unfolds from one step to the next. Then you draw out on a whiteboard what it would look like to rearrange the equipment—ideally, so the process flows from one side of the building to the other.

One of my companies used to receive raw materials and outside services through a large bay door. When we'd complete our manufacturing, we'd ship our finished product and dump our garbage out of the same door. Nothing was "wrong" with this, necessarily, but I noticed that the finished products and garbage took up valuable space in the doorway. The building had eleven of those doors, so I changed the flow. From then on, we received new materials and services through one door, and we shipped our finished products and dumped trash out of another. As you can imagine… we doubled the space where we could receive new materials, as well as the space where we could stack up exports. Sales also increased because we could meet higher demand.

You can call it "Feng Shui" if you want, but my philosophy is that factories and offices are just like vehicle engines I worked on when I was young. Some parts just need to be at the front of the car, like the headlights. What sense would it make to put the windshield on the undercarriage or the brake lights in front of the steering wheel? Why on earth would you keep an old transmission in the backseat when you replace it with a new one? Yet when you walk into the average plant today, spectator-leaders do exactly that. Equipment and machinery get strewn about the floor, wherever they can find space. Old equipment sits idle, collecting dust. You can't run a plant effectively that way; you have to structure your building to create flow.

How You Know Structure is Working

You'll know you're wrapping up the Structure phase when you've taken a hard look at how the company currently functions, you've compared it to how you *want* it to function—and you've **mapped a clear plan** to get there.

At this point, you go beyond just identifying problems. You build the foundation. You make structural changes that weren't addressed during Brute Force. You place the right people in the right roles, with clear responsibilities. You map out what roles are missing. You adjust how invoices get processed, how materials get received, how checks get sent and signed, and how bills get paid. You put form to the chaos.

If you've documented these processes—or at least created a working outline—and you're executing on them, then you're likely coming to the end of Structure. You've set big shifts into motion. You've got systems taking shape. You're addressing the high-impact areas: personnel, equipment, policies, procedures—down to how you track Accounts Receivable and Accounts Payable.

Let me be clear: if you *don't* have your AR/AP process documented and running, you're *not* done with Structure. That's not a "someday" thing—that's a *right now* thing.

But once your critical and medium-priority items are identified and in progress, you can taper out of Structure and prepare to move into the next phase: Improve.

Sure, you might still have to order more garbage cans or fine-tune office supply systems—and, yeah, that stuff's important. But if you only have that left on your list, you've probably done the heavy lifting already. Structure is about turning vision into mechanics. When the mechanics are moving and your systems have traction— you can know you've built the framework to scale.

Chapter Nine

Improve
Modify Policies and Procedures Based on What's Essential vs. Outdated

"The biggest room in the world is the room for improvement."
Helmut Schmidt

T he Improve phase is where you start to see real traction, but let's not kid ourselves. Improvement isn't a clean, straight line. It's more like turning over rocks. You've already bulldozed through Brute Force, done the homework in Analyze, and built the Structure. *Now,* you're seeing how all that plays out in real life.

You've analyzed your company in depth. You know the major problems, and most of them are either solved or have a resolution in motion. But fair warning: as you fix issues, new concerns will pop up. That's normal. It's like pulling weeds—some are surface-level, but some have roots you don't see until you start digging.

By the time you hit Improve, the company's running. You've got your org chart built with detailed responsibilities. The right people are in the right roles. You've let go of the wrong ones. Your systems are up. You've put processes, policies, and workflows into place. You've built the Camaro. It runs, it moves, and it'll win a few races. But it's not the Ferrari yet. The Improve phase will deliver that. Here, you stop asking, "Does this work?" and start asking, "Is this *the best way* to do it?"

Structure focused on getting things functional. Maybe you had a four-step process just to run a report. It worked, so you moved on. But now's the time to slow down and ask, "Why are there four steps? Could this be done in two? Or one?" Improve is where you look at what works and ask, *"Could it work faster? Easier? Smarter?"*

For example, your AP clerk spends thirty hours a week managing invoices. With a cleaner process, it could be five hours. That's Improving. You're not rebuilding anymore—you're refining. Think of Structure like putting up the drywall and wiring the house so the lights come on. Improve is the finishing work—adding dimmers, better fixtures, painting, and making the whole thing run on a smart home system.

During Improve, you might:

- Streamline workflows
- Automate repeat tasks
- Update training documents for clarity
- Shift work to lower-cost labor without sacrificing quality
- Cut redundant processes
- Eliminate bottlenecks and time-wasters

You couldn't do this during Structure—you were too busy building. Now, you've got room to breathe and optimize. That's how you get from Camaro to Ferrari.

Team Improvement: Accountable vs. Responsible

Accountability and **responsibility** sound like the same thing, and have several attributes in common. But the two have subtle differences, as well.

At each of my companies, employees learn that they are *responsible*. We assign tasks, and we expect them to perform them in exchange for their pay. Responsibility is a more immediate, task-oriented, daily idea: "You do ABC action, to XYZ standard. If anything is incomplete or unsatisfactory, you go back and do it again. You are responsible for completing *these* tasks, on *this* list."

But the higher they climb up the chain into management, the more employees become *accountable*. Accountability is a lengthier, broader emphasis on the entire field of battle. Managers and owners enjoy a de-emphasis on the daily tasks of employees, but they accept accountability for interviewing, hiring, training, challenging, educating, rewarding, recognizing, paying, supporting, correcting, reprimanding, and terminating those employees. They also accept accountability for supplies, machinery, equipment, cleanliness, timeliness, responsiveness, functionality, legal compliance, finances, marketing… the list goes on.

Owners take full accountability for *everything* in their organization, including the dysfunction, errors, bottlenecks, breakdowns, inefficiencies, waste, and toxic residues in the culture—just like when the box company coordinator dilly-dallied on the refrigerator for the break room. I could easily have blamed her in front of the entire staff, and I'd have been (factually) correct. She made the decision to delay on it without consulting me or asking for guidance. But I am *accountable* for what led to her decision: she worried I would behave just like my predecessors, who were too stingy to buy a fridge. She made that assumption because I didn't think to ask how well she understood my request. I assumed she knew what I meant because I had given simple, plain instruction in English that most people have no problem following.

But just because people speak the same language... *doesn't mean they understand each other.* As the famous playwright George Bernard Shaw once said:

> "The single biggest problem in communication is the **illusion** that it has taken place."

So teach employees the difference between "responsible" and "accountable." "Responsible" means your obligation to perform a task. "Accountable" means you answer for the results of that task, often to others. Aside from your own responsibilities, you're also accountable for outcomes of others' work, which can lead to reward or consequence from an external source.

The best outcomes I get from conversations like this are when employees begin to take responsibility in their roles. I show them how an accountable leader behaves... and they get inspired to become responsible leaders themselves. They move beyond simply following instructions, and they begin contributing to the policies and procedures we write together. Leadership is more than a title, and you can exercise it in the most entry-level roles.

Bridge the Gaps with Retirees and Part-Timers

Improvement sometimes requires testing and "sampling" before you jump into something full-throttle. In software development, they call it "beta testing." One way you can improve without overspending or endangering the company is to hire retirees and/or part-timers as you expand an offering.

Instead of hiring a full-timer to implement an add-on, you might look for a retiree in your network who has knowledge and experience, but who doesn't want to work forty to sixty hours a week. It's worth asking around, especially if you can find a retiree who knows the product *and* understands people.

Other alternatives include part-timers or contractors. Many working adults seek additional work to supplement their main source of income, or they look for roles that offer them more flexibility than a full-time one. You might even find a fellow business owner who's looking for a way to share their knowledge gained over the years— they might know how to manage people, direct operations, understand finance, or beef up your marketing strategy. In exchange, working for you can broaden their skill set, secure a small benefits package, or keep them busy during a slump. These people don't require the same volume of overhead as a full-time employee, and they often prove more valuable with their work ethic and how their skill sets cross over into your industry. Stay on the lookout: you may have better options than hiring more full-time W-2 staff.

Training to Improve

You don't know what your employees don't know... and often, they don't know either. It's like if I stopped you on the street one day and said, "Tell me everything that happened on your tenth birthday." Unless you just turned ten yesterday, you "know" quite a bit in your subconscious mind... but by now, you've probably forgotten most of it. You'd have to see a video replay of your entire tenth birthday to answer the question.

If you don't know where your employees are deficient in their knowledge, how can you possibly train them? It turns out, some things we do in school work equally well in the workforce, if we use them. The best way to assess an employee's knowledge is... to test it! At my companies, we administer regular knowledge and skill assessments to measure employees' capabilities and capacity. The data they provide through those assessments dictates the kind of training we create.

Remember my unionized gearbox company? What a headache that was, going hour by hour through hundreds of training modules, all lasting twenty minutes or more. It's painful, especially if you're getting "trained" on topics you've already mastered or covered. I despise "tick the box" trainings like that and avoid them wherever I can. You can't bypass some legally-required trainings—but for everything else, we go the opposite route. We do the assessments *first*, and then we provide the training. This gives us astounding results.

Think of your random thoughts throughout the day and how quickly we've learned to turn to Google to get the answers. Now—imagine yourself, the owner of your company, behaving the same way Google does when people enter information in the search field. Firstly, Google records that data and ranks it. So if you administer an assessment to your employees, and it comes back that a majority of them don't understand Task ABC, you have acquired a data point. You can observe their deficient areas. By contrast, almost all of them score at 90 percent or better on Task XYZ. Great! Train them on the remaining 10 percent they don't know, and focus on other content your employees really need to learn.

Like satisfied searchers on Google, my employees walk away from our training sessions saying things like, "Wow, that was super helpful!" or "I didn't realize what I didn't know! How did you know I needed that?"

I smile when they ask. We know… because they took the assessment, and they revealed to us where they're struggling.

Don't forget about the benefit to the company. When your employees go enthusiastically through training, soak up knowledge, take detailed notes, and apply what they learned, what does your company get? If you guess "better-quality workers," you're on the right track.

Goals for Improvement

In Structure phase, you laid out Key Performance Indicators (KPIs) as part of your business plan. Improve is where you measure daily, weekly, monthly, and annual performance against your targets. Most companies grasp this idea for sales, but in my companies, we set KPIs for most employees, managers, departments, and sometimes for me as the owner. KPIs give managers and owners clues about how the employees respond to the vision and business plan.

Improve phase is also where you sometimes have lengthier, more "negotiated" conversations with employees about their goals and performance. This is the time where I ask an employee, "It seems to me like you could handle multiple projects every day, based on the average number you do now. Is that realistic? What do you think?" Setting goals for improvement, or improving the goals themselves, should be collaborative at this point. You want your team to take as much ownership in their goals as possible.

By measuring KPIs, you can dialogue effectively with employees. If you agreed on a goal of twenty-seven jobs per week, and the employee starts slipping and turns in subpar numbers, put your Analyze hat back on and ask, "Why?" If a salesperson agrees to meet with one hundred customers for $40,000 of sales, and they record fifty meetings and $20,000 of sales, go back to the original plan and hold them responsible for what they committed themselves to do. Clearly communicated expectations reduce the variables you have to think about when things don't go according to plan. Either the goals are unrealistic, circumstances have changed, or the employee didn't truly understand what you required from them.

Set expectations for your team, and
follow up on them.
Don't just give them work and say,
"Let me know how it goes."

Remember: set expectations so you can follow up and *verify* that the company fulfills the vision and business plan. **Follow through** to make sure they meet your expectations! Don't just tell them to employees, and then walk away. Seek employee input, set the expectations, and document them. It pays here to think a little bit like an attorney, even though you're not suing anyone. Setting and following up on expectations allows you to get concrete answers to the question: "Did you do what I asked?"

Let me tell you a quick story about how we got serious with our invoice terms. When I first took over the box company, our customer payment terms were all over the place. It was chaos. One customer was on forty-five-day terms, another on sixty, someone else on ninety, some at net thirty—it was a mess. We had no consistency, and we struggled to get paid on time. So we made the decision to clean it up.

We kicked off a full-scale project to standardize all of our invoicing terms to **1% 10, Net 30**. That means customers get a 1 percent discount if they pay within ten days. Otherwise, the invoice comes due in thirty. It took us a solid two months—digging through contracts, cleaning up systems, reaching out to customers—but we did it. Now we have everyone on the same page. We have a clean and predictable process, and it's had a massive impact on cash flow and operational efficiency.

I later found out: one of our team members accepted 24 purchase orders with 75-day terms, because she completely skipped reviewing the terms. I asked her, "Did you ever look at the terms on this PO?" She said, "No. I didn't understand I was supposed to check the terms." So we put the Analyze hat back on and dug into it. It turned out the documents didn't clearly explain that she needed to review the terms. The process was unclear. It wasn't her fault—but it became our problem.

As a result, we had to sit on a job we already completed, and wait nearly *three months* to collect. That's **$400,000** we wouldn't see for a quarter. That doesn't just delay a deposit; it could drain the business. That kind of cash sitting in limbo cripples momentum. It could impact payroll, purchasing, and growth. It bleeds the business quietly until something big forces the leadership's eyes open.

When you run a business, this is the kind of work that matters. Think of it like washing behind your ears or flossing between your teeth. It's not always flashy, but it's foundational. If you don't set the terms, someone else will—and that usually doesn't end in your favor. Hopefully, you discover issues like this in Brute Force and Analyze, but I've had them slip through the cracks into the later stages. Bottom line: fix it, or you'll end up with more headaches.

Improve Issue Resolutions

During the Improve phase, the speed and efficiency of fixing "bugs" and maintaining a safe workplace take center stage. You've worked very hard to reach this point. The company's on its way to self-sufficiency. But if you eventually want to step away and let it run on its own, you must make sure you have trained, empowered, and "certified" (in a sense) your employees to prevent and fix all the basic issues that can derail your progress. They must demonstrate that they can handle common, everyday issues, like maintenance and malfunctions. They must exhibit a strong proficiency for preventing trips and falls, misuse of equipment, and shortcuts that lead to injuries.

The larger your company, the more challenging it is to drive home a culture of safety or of speedy, efficient issue resolution. By now, you should have created an environment of psychological safety and a workable method for employees to report issues. Remember how I told my team to use tags to report issues instead of coming into the office over and over to ask questions? You may have started that trend during Brute Force to fix problems. Now, encourage employees to use it—not only when something ceases to function properly, but also in areas where ordinary function slows things down or has the potential to do so. The issue log is your employees' #1 tool to serve as your "eyes and ears" for "good, but not (necessarily) great" processes."

Safety

Additionally, your employees should document safety hazards. Most modern big box retailers equip their employees with Zebra technology —handheld smartphones staff can carry with them everywhere while at work. When they assign daily safety checks, this makes it very simple to photograph, upload, and report possible hazards. Any business with a large facility, vehicles, machinery, equipment, chemicals, and so forth, will benefit from this worthy investment. Start a monthly safety meeting, collect data like this from your employees, and review it with management at each meeting. Keep your eyes open for patterns, just as you did in Brute Force with the employee issue tags. Wherever the most issues occur, start digging, until you get to the root cause of repeated safety issues, and change the policy or process.

The safety issue came back to bite me at one of my manufacturing companies after I terminated a disgruntled employee. He called the Occupational Safety and Health Administration (OSHA) and reported us. As a self-funded wing of the federal government, OSHA can cause tremendous difficulty for a business, using all kinds of laws and regulations to impose fines, restrict your operations, or even shut your business down if they want to. I made the mistake of assuming we'd complied with all OSHA laws, only to find out later that some of the laws and regulations we'd obeyed were obsolete. One of their rules is known as "lock out, tag out" (LOTO), a procedure to ensure dangerous machines get shut off and can't be restarted until you perform proper maintenance, service, or repair.

While we did our due diligence with our equipment, we didn't realize that OSHA had changed their rules to require *each individual machine* to need a LOTO procedure. They'd also updated to require that every machine come equipped with safety shut-offs; some of our machines predated those regulations, and the factory didn't install shut-offs on them. Our forklift certifications, which management thought to be necessary to renew every five years, turned out to be every three years.

> Have a real safety discussion with your team
> so you don't have to have one with the government.

It's simple math, the bigger your company gets. Don't waste opportunities to protect yourself in the name of productivity. OSHA regulators *do not care* if their decisions put you out of business. They are *trained* to be skeptical of you, kind of like a police officer who pulls over a suspicious vehicle with "probable cause." It is much better for you to occasionally give your team a few days of inconvenience rather than deal with an OSHA bureaucrat who has the power to put you out of business.

Improve Your Finances

During Analyze and Structure, you took a good, hard look at your "cash cows" (profitable products and services) and your loss leaders, and you directed your sales team to emphasize the cash cows. The Improve phase gives you the chance, in partnership with your controller, to reduce (or discontinue) underperforming products—or, if they sell well enough, to change your prices on them so it makes sense to continue stocking and fulfilling them.

Margins

No company will ever have a 100 percent rating on profitability of every product or service they sell. But if your HVAC company earns a high margin on furnace installations and very little on routine AC inspections, you have to figure out a profitable way to provide both services. Routine inspections are the "gateway drug" for your customers to higher-ticket services, like furnace installations. Many HVAC companies today encourage customers to subscribe to an annual service agreement, where the provider visits the home one or two times a year to inspect the air conditioner in exchange for prioritized service if their HVAC system needs repair. This is a good example of how you balance out low-margin activities so you don't lose money on them. You might not even need to raise the price; if you charge $250 for an AC inspection, simply annualize the bill ($500 for two inspections a year) and bill the customer $42 per month.

When George came aboard as controller at my first company, he looked closely at the profit margin on each individual part we sold. The previous owners had raised prices inconsistently. Some parts continued to sell at a loss, while others broke even—which was just enough to cover payroll. Once I understood this, it was a no-brainer: we discontinued several parts that cost more to make than we earned in revenue. We set a new, across-the-board pricing strategy that caught us up to market standards and rapidly increased our margins. From then on, my attitude was, "If we're going to make something... we have to make a profit on it."

Expenses

Direct your controller to prepare a list of *all* of your company's expenses, from greatest to least. Now, you have a green light to make cuts everywhere you overspend. When I take over companies, all contracts under the old company name get nullified. This provides me a good excuse to negotiate new terms or find less expensive options. Money isn't everything... but you have to play a numbers game if you want to stay in business and be profitable.

Employees are still the #1 overhead cost for most companies, and while this part isn't pleasant, somebody has to examine it for the health of the organization. If you're the leader, that "somebody" is you. I once took a machine shop I bought through the Analyze phase and discovered several employees got paid to work on tasks that *lost* money for the company; their tasks didn't earn a shred of profit. I always try to hang onto employees if I can, but after we'd increased prices and discontinued unprofitable services— some of them had to go. I couldn't reassign them elsewhere or find any work for them to do.

Remember the stories of owners overpaying for services? The key to improve your finances is **to look at them**, and then ask: "What could we do differently?" You have to figure out ways you can get the same (or better) labor, supplies, equipment, and so forth... without paying more than you need to—or, if unnecessary, to pay for them at all.

Get the Money Through the Door

We all have our preferred payment methods, but we don't sacrifice a customer because they want to use a different one. When it comes to getting paid, a bird in the hand is worth two in the bush. The more choices you offer people, the more often money lands in your hand— and stays there.

Let's say a customer wants to pay their $3000 bill using a credit card instead of a bank transfer. Credit cards have processing fees, usually 3-4 percent. It doesn't take more than a few extra seconds to calculate 3-4 percent of your total price and tack it onto your invoice. Then, when the customer asks you for the price, you just say, "This is my fee, and it fluctuates a little here and there depending on how you want to pay. You mentioned using your credit card, so that's an extra $120 for processing fees. Your total will be $3,120."

There's only two ways the conversation can go from there. If your customer balks at the processing fee, you say, "I can drop the surcharge to just $20 if you want to do a bank transfer, or to zero if you want to write a cashier's check." Now the ball's in their court. But if they shrug and say, "Fine, I'll pay the surcharge," why not accept their credit card? You're still going to get paid in full. The additional $120 just covers the processing fees.

How to Implement the Improve Phase

As someone who's spent a lot of time creating policies and procedures, I'm excited to live in the age of artificial intelligence (AI). You can now draft documents that used to take hours to write in no time at all. You can voice-dictate the parameters and upload it to a system like ChatGPT or NotebookLM, and it will create the draft document for you in seconds. Then you can spend your time fine-tuning the language.

Make It Official

As quickly as AI can generate those documents, however, be prepared to spend time communicating them to staff. Even though you've done a ton of research and set up the appropriate procedures, documenting policies and procedures forces you to think in *even more* detail. Management, in particular, needs to know the process you want them to follow, especially if someone gets sick or injured on the job. If you don't go carefully through these documents, and (in some cases) discuss them out loud… you can easily confuse employees. You know (in your head) what you want to happen… but spelling it out on paper is another matter.

Outside of the manufacturing industry, I also own a real estate investment company. We purchase, rehab, refurbish, and rent or sell residential and commercial properties. In the world of tenants, building codes, civil authorities, and estate agents, you need to respond quickly when something's out of whack. We spent over a year creating procedures from scratch: pre- and post-acquisition steps, handling utility shutdowns, evictions, remodeling, managing communication, etcetera. All of it needed to be spelled out in a step-by-step process in clear, plain language.

Policies and procedures provide the "grease" that keeps your delegation "engine" running. If you want a sure way to improve your company's self-sufficiency, publish these documents, especially if you can get to the point where the language is so clear that it's impossible to mess it up.

Sales

Remember: this is not a sales book, but the mark of a company that's truly improved (from a sales standpoint) is when its prices become less relevant to its market and audience. We all know you can purchase a smartphone that performs just as well as an Apple iPhone for half the price... but on the day they launch their newest model, Apple stores have people lined up around the block.

> You are not selling on price!
> You sell on everything *but* price.

Ever heard the saying, "One man's trash is another man's treasure"? We know it's true, but we act like prices are some kind of "scientific number," maybe because of what we're used to seeing in retail stores. Guess what? Retailers have negotiable prices, too. They're just more formal about it than car salespeople... but clothing stores have racks marked "Clearance" and "Up to 30% Off" for a reason. They drop the price on those racks because the market refuses to pay full retail price. It's ideal to make $20 from selling a t-shirt... but if you can only get three dollars in profit, that's still better than zero.

Sell based on the impact or benefit it will have for the customer, not the price. Nobody wants to "buy" a price! They want to buy things they believe will make a noticeable, tangible difference in their lives. So as you pursue improvement in your sales strategy, aim to have fewer and fewer conversations focused on price. Talk about your speed of implementation, the quality of your product, and the level of service your customers expect... but price should fall from the #1 spot in the customer's mind.

I once hired a salesperson based on future growth potential, as opposed to present-day salary and earnings. I had a case of hiring the right person at the right time; we had an undeveloped local market, and despite over forty years in business, the company never had a formal sales department. He liked our culture, which emphasized positivity above performance; even top performers couldn't expect to hold onto their roles if they used their performance as an excuse to have a bad attitude. I often joked, "We didn't have a single jerk in the building."

He seemed eager to discuss the possibilities. In addition to the position, he had the opportunity to build our sales department from scratch. All of our business up until then came from out-of-state customers, but he loved the idea of building an entire new customer base in our own backyard. Despite the obvious performance implications of his role, he appreciated the greater emphasis on character and attitude. He bought the *impact* of the role more than the compensation or benefits.

So whether you sell someone on a job opportunity or your product/ service, focus on the impact and benefit toward the "buyer." Think of it the same way you would if you were the buyer… would you want to invest in something if you didn't feel confident that it would enhance or benefit you? Of course not. Assume the same for everyone else— and do your due diligence to learn what's truly important to them.

Follow-Up

Do you think I'm going to remember this person's name if they call me? If you don't recognize the names, numbers, or emails of all the salespeople trying to get your attention… don't be surprised if your potential customers don't recognize you. Especially if you don't do any follow-up.

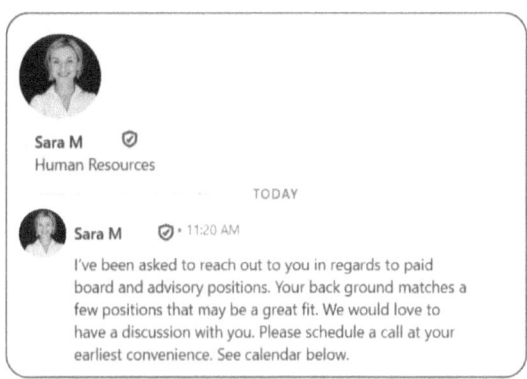

I don't blame salespeople for assuming that the answer is probably "No" after the twentieth time they dial a number and get no answer… but remember, people are busy. Like you, they have to prioritize what their focus. Your sales follow-up call probably won't rank high on their list. Make your business memorable by showing how well you understand the customer on the first interaction. If they currently buy from your competitors, why are they buying? What do they like and dislike about them? Ask questions like these so that when a problem comes up, they remember you.

One of the employees at my manufacturing company, Cara, embodied this principle during the process she went through to get hired. She performed well in her initial interview, but she truly distinguished herself in the follow-up. She could have sent a generic thank-you letter, but she instead chose to send a link to a sales video that touched on our previous conversation. This demonstrated to me that she understood and appreciated the role she wanted to play. She stood out as a strong candidate and a valuable asset to the company.

Credit (Where Credit is Due)

Nothing helps cement trust with customers like the perception that you and your team are "Johnny on the spot" when it comes to satisfying their needs. In this area, you can leverage the inner workings of your company to your advantage in the eyes of the customer.

While writing this chapter, I got wind of a deal brokered by the vice president at one of my companies shortly before he left town for a vacation. When the initial email came through, I made a mental note of it and moved on with my day. But a day or so after my VP left town, the customer emailed to ask how soon they could have the materials delivered; they needed them sooner than they'd anticipated.

Tom, my VP, had his email auto-responder on, but it was after-hours and the customer hadn't received any correspondence to let him know whether the order had shipped or when it would arrive. I don't normally intervene with these matters, but in this case I made an exception. I wrote back to him, "Let me see what we can do for you." I logged into the system and checked—sure enough, it had shipped. Everything was in order. So, I wrote back to the customer and said, "I double-checked with the factory, and they said they can expedite it."

This is a subtle way of letting the customer know—"We've got your back." Even though Tom had already done his job and the order was well on its way, hearing personally from me made the customer very happy.

Leverage the excellence you already deliver… to make sure your customer truly appreciates it.

Just because you already do these routine interactions and tasks doesn't mean you can't take credit for doing them well. Don't chest-thump or demand trophies… but it's okay to make a slightly bigger-than-normal deal about good things you do every day. Look at it this way: no one else will do it for you, so don't pass up the chance.

Hard Close

To definitively close is better than not closing. People either want to do business with you, or they don't—but not every prospect is good at saying "No thanks" and moving on with their day. I've chased plenty of "maybe" clients in the past and concluded they're not worth it. These days, I prefer to cut to the chase, and if they drag their feet after three attempts, I politely move on. (Not everyone agrees with this approach. Some prefer to persist forever, and that's another way of doing it.)

Sales is an occupation, not a hobby or pastime. If you don't sell, you won't succeed in your occupation, and you'll become a liability to your organization. It's perfectly okay to demand that people respect your time by saying, "Call me when you're ready to do a deal." In the meantime, focus your energy and attention on the people interested in buying. You can socialize and let loose after quitting time; while you're on duty, make up your mind quickly about whether someone's worth talking to. It would help you to have a "move on" number for all your interactions… for example, after three attempts.

So size them up quickly, and get to brass tacks: "When? What time? What day do we get together to sign the agreement? When do you want the first delivery? How soon can we get this off your plate?"

How you phrase things has a huge impact on sales–for example, using the word "agreement" versus "contract." But if customers hem and haw too long on these questions, move on. You have bigger fish to fry.

How You Know the Improve Phase is Working

Here's how you know Improve is nearing completion: You no longer just throw stuff at the wall to see what sticks. You've stopped reacting and started **refining**.

Sometimes, even after doing a great job through Brute Force, Analyze, and Structure, you'll still uncover something *massive* that slipped through the cracks. It happens. The key: don't panic or blame. Instead, adjust, fix it fast, and keep moving.

You'll know you're coming to the tail end of Improve when:

- You spend your time refining and improving, rather than fixing problems.
- You don't have to fight daily fires—you tweak to sharpen processes.
- The systems you put in place hold up and produce results.

Improvement isn't about perfection—it's about **progress that sticks**. When your changes stop being disruptive and start becoming *the way things are done*, you'll know Improve is working. And once your team can operate with clarity, consistency, and confidence, you've got your cue to move forward—to make your systems permanent through Culture.

Chapter Ten

Culture
Instill Accountability, Urgency, and Continuous Improvement

"To win in the marketplace,
you must first win in the workplace."
Doug Conant

I remember watching that TED Talk by Simon Sinek where he said the most successful companies all start with "why." At the time, it struck a chord. But I didn't fully understand what it meant until I compared my first company with the ones I've acquired *since* I did the hard internal work.

Think back to the first few chapters of this book: you are the nucleus and the captain in your business. That still applies. Your company's culture starts with you and your "why." But if you don't predetermine your why, a default kicks in. Usually, it's money. And trust me— money alone is a terrible motivator over the long haul.

But once you've pushed through those earlier stages like Brute Force, Analyze, Structure, and Improve—you're different. You're not the same person who started out. You've seen how personal growth leads to business growth. You've built something sustainable. You've built something that matters. It's time to solidify the culture and lock in the values that will last, because this is bigger than just you. Culture is what carries your company into the future—long after you step away.

Build Team Culture

Back in the early days, money was a bigger motivator for me than it should've been. I still worked my tail off to be a good leader and run the business right, but I had my priorities out of balance. When I did the tough, uncomfortable, personal work, it changed everything. It gave me the clarity and the fuel to start leading from a place of purpose, not just performance.

> "We're a company that changes lives.
> We just happen to make boxes."

That's my why. And it doesn't matter which of my companies you go to—just switch out the product we make, and that same purpose holds up. I went through a transformation, and now I teach what I've learned to my team. I don't just talk about it; I live it. At work, at home, with my family. That's what keeps the fire burning when the pressure's high.

You can tell when a company's culture is at work, whether good or bad. It'll show up in how they communicate with one another—*if* they communicate at all. At each of my companies, I lead employees to the point where they change *other* people's lives in the same generous and holistic way. Along the way, they become best-in-class at what they do for a living.

Motivation

You've got to understand what actually motivates people. You could easily assume money is the primary driver—and for some, it is. But I've found that most people aren't incentivized by money alone. What really lights a fire under them is **recognition**: being seen and appreciated. The moment when someone says, "You did a great job" or "You made a real difference here"—that hits deeper than a bonus ever could. Learn what matters to each person on your team, and speak *their* language when it comes to motivation.

Recognition isn't fluffy; it's *powerful*. Use it well, and you'll build loyalty, momentum, and a culture people want join. I've seen it time and again: what people value more than a bigger paycheck is *time*. Time off work. Balance. Recognition. Appreciation. Here's the truth—most people know they can get another job making about the same money somewhere else. That's not what keeps them around.

If they don't feel appreciated, they're more inclined to leave. Simple as that. But if they *do* feel seen, valued, and respected? They'll stay—even if the money isn't quite as high. Why? Because culture and appreciation go a lot farther than a few extra bucks.

If you want to build a team that sticks, learn to value what they value. Find the people who want to work *with* you, not *for* you. If they believe in your vision, they'll go the extra mile. Sell your employees on where the company is going, and show them they have a future there.

Pay people what they're worth. This doesn't always mean paying the most. It means paying a fair market rate based on ROI. My goal is to always pay people 10 percent over their market value.

When I visit the office or shop and walk through the changes we've made—and reflect on how far we've come—it fuels me. But it also fuels the team. They feel like they're part of something real.

Something growing. Something successful. Everyone wants to be part of a winning team.

Do Your Job Better

Whether we're talking about your business, family, or team—*you set the tone.* They'll do what you do, period. If you show up to check boxes and do the bare minimum, guess what they'll do? The same bare minimum. They watch you, whether they say it or not. Children, spouses, employees, teammates—they all pick up on how you carry yourself. If you drag, they'll drag. But if you push hard, lead with integrity, and set the example... you'll pull more out of them than any motivational speech ever could.

You don't get better results until *you* do your job better.

Here's the reality—*even if you give 100 percent,* most people on your team are going to give 60 to 70 percent in return. That's just how it works. Sure, you might get lucky and hire someone better than you in a certain area—and when that happens, great! But don't bet the farm on it. Your employees need to *see* what good work looks like. They won't learn it simply because you bark orders from the office.

When I started out, I was willing to do anything, including cleaning the bathrooms at my companies. Now, thankfully, I don't have to—but I made a point to *never* act like I was "above" any task. Why? Because I was setting the standard. That's what leaders do. You can't expect someone to work hard, take pride in their job, or operate with excellence if they've never been trained how to do it. And I don't mean technical training—I'm talking about how to *carry yourself like a professional.*

So if you look around and wonder why nobody gives their best effort even though you pay them—stop and ask: *Have they ever even seen what "great" looks like?*

If the answer's "No," your job is to show them.

Let's go back to the beginning—*are you even ready for change?* Is your company ready for change? Because if you're not showing up energized, dialed in, and motivated to crush it... *why not?* That's a question worth asking. And I'm not talking about surface-level stuff like "Oh, I'm tired" or "The job's boring." No. Dig deeper:

- Do you even like what you're doing?
- Do you have some baggage from your past that makes this kind of work feel like a drag?
- Do you have confidence issues like bad memory, poor time management, or burnout?
- Are you trying to live up to someone's expectations instead of what actually lights you up?

If you're not motivated, something's off—and it's usually personal. I know owners who walk around checked-out and uninspired, and it shows. You think it's a business problem? It's not. *It's a personal one.* If you're not satisfied in life—spiritually, relationally, emotionally—you won't lead well. You won't build well. You won't inspire anyone to follow you. So before you talk about incentivizing your team, ask yourself: *Why aren't you incentivized?*

If you can't answer that, you know... you're not ready for change! I hate to say it if you've come this far, but it's Chutes and Ladders time: you've landed at the top of a chute, and you need to slide all the way back down to the beginning. That's not easy to hear... but it's better than crashing and burning after all your hard work.

Model and Reward Loyalty

If you want to build a good company that actually matters, make it one that *changes people's lives for the better*. That's what I do. I don't just make boxes, tooling, or run payroll. I change people's lives—positively, intentionally, and consistently. Who would want to turn quickly on an employer who cares that much about you?

A life-changing culture is a breeding ground for loyalty.

Honestly, *why wouldn't you want to change people's lives for the better?* What's stopping you? If you're going to build something, build it to matter. Build it to leave people better than you found them. That's the kind of company worth running. It's the only kind I'm interested in.

Here's the funny part: people ask what all this effort "costs" me. I'll tell you: **practically nothing**. As the old saying goes, "It doesn't cost a nickel to be kind." But I get back more than money can buy. The payoff is internal and personal. You feel *good* when you do it. You know you did something right. And to be clear: I don't fake it. I don't hand out fluff. If I say something, I mean it. It's real. That's why it hits so hard. Recognition doesn't have to be expensive. It just has to be *honest*. You know you're doing it right when employees say, "I want to stay. I don't want to leave this company." Or even better: "I couldn't be happier here. I've got a friend who's sharp—I'm going to tell him to come work here, too."

Recognition and attentiveness build respect and trust among your employees because they see your sincerity. You know Culture is clicking when it shows up at home. I've had employees tell me, "My wife noticed I'm different. Happier. Less stressed. I actually look forward to coming in." True success happens when the people whose lives you've changed... now go on to change others' lives. You effectively "reproduce" parts of your character, ethics, and attitude in others.

And, please, for the love of all that is holy... If you find someone loyal and who wants to work, **find them a job**! If you don't have one yet, create a new one. A person like that is rare! You can train people on tasks, but not loyalty.

Legacy: Cultural Goals

Ray Kroc passed away in 1984, but to this day, you can still expect predictable, consistent food served to you within minutes at any McDonald's restaurant you visit. That's a cultural legacy.

J.W. Marriott, founder of the Marriott hotel chain, died one year after Kroc... but whenever you stay at one of his company's hotels, you still expect the same levels of hospitality and quality that made them famous, along with the Bible in the nightstand drawer. Another cultural legacy.

One day, the business giants we've all looked up to in the last thirty or forty years will be gone. When that day comes, how will their companies behave? This goes back to knowing your "why." If I want to leave a legacy of companies that change lives... I need to set a tone of standards and ethics my employees will follow in my absence, even if I'm gone for good. When I think of legacy, I try to think like a real estate developer—I want to create a high-end neighborhood where people pay good money to live because they know the caliber of people surrounding them, and it has standards of behavior both expected and enforced.

When ownership changes hands, legacy can be touchy. What kind of future do you want for your company when the time comes to sell or transition your business to your children? Spend time considering why you started or bought your company. What did you notice in the marketplace that was missing or handled poorly? How did you figure out a better way to provide people with your product or service? Maybe you worked for someone else and disliked the way they did things, and you vowed that one day you'd show them how it should look. Whatever reasons you had for going into business… they make up a huge part of your legacy.

Keep It In the Family

A warning to family-owned businesses regarding legacy: an owner who strings an adult child along for decades refusing to let go of their business builds a disaster waiting to happen. When the parent finally retires or passes away, the kids ruin what the parents built. One situation I know of stands out—owners in their sixties, still running the show, while their forty-something sons were stuck in mid-level roles, waiting. The result? Resentment, stagnation, and missed potential. Don't plan to leave your business to your kids—it can hold them back. Let them build their own path. I've seen too many second-generation business owners never truly step into their own because their parents never stepped aside.

If you decide to involve your kids in your business, let them first build their own path. Let them experience working for different bosses, learning what they like and dislike so they can decide what kind of future they want. If you try to plan your kids' future before they make their own way, you steal their pride, self-respect, and ability to develop confidence in their own abilities.

This reminds me of a buddy I'll call "Bill." He worked for his father-in-law's business—a big operation, thirty million or so. He had zero experience, yet his father-in-law brought him in as a sales manager. Right out of the gate, he sat under the father-in-law's thumb. How much respect do you think his wife had for him, knowing he worked for her dad?

Instead of carving his own path, starting at the bottom and earning his way up, Bill shortcut the process, which deprived him of the skills, experiences, and insight he needed to grow and improve the company.

At one point, Bill even told me he was "an owner" in the company. I asked him flat out: "Really? Do you own stock?"

"No."

"Got any money in the business?"

"No."

"So how do you come out as an owner?"

"Well, I do everything my father-in-law does when he's not around."

Bill later left and "started" his own company. But he borrowed equipment from his father-in-law's business, and he also used the company's admin resources. He liked to say, "See? I finally did it!" But he never actually built anything on his own.

I see this with a lot of kids who work for their dads. They have no real power. They sit around, waiting for dad to either die, sell, or hand the company to them. In the meantime, they never test themselves or risk failure; they never find out what's actually possible. As you know— you need to get comfortable with failure and pain if you want to grow and scale your business.

You can't live up to your potential in your parents' shadows. You won't find out what you're made of propped up by other people's success. Isn't this obvious from our cultural jokes about "trust fund babies"? If you want to become the best version of yourself, you've got to step out, fall down, get your teeth kicked in, and build something that's actually yours.

Remember my story of winning Manufacturer of the Year? Most of my peers at that ceremony didn't like that I'd won. They were similar to me in age, but they worked for their parents (who owned the companies). I had the freedom to make decisions and improve how my business ran, whereas they always had to get mom or dad's permission and agreement.

So push your kids out of the nest and challenge them to go and make their own luck. If they eventually come back and still want to work for you, make them prove their commitment by starting at the bottom, working under your supervisors, and earn their way to succeeding you through merit and leadership. Only when they take your company and make it "their own" (in practice) are they ready. And if you're fortunate enough to see that happen… you get to begin your transition into chairman emeritus. Negotiate your passive income stream from the business (or sell it to them), and step aside.

Cultural Knowledge – The Floor

Walk the shop floor. Don't just visit or pass through—*engage them genuinely*. You unearth the real problems in the walk, not from behind your desk. Talk to employees and ask how they're doing. Notice and understand what's happening. Eventually, teach your managers to do the same. Do this because many issues don't show up in reports or meetings. You discover them when you're out there, walking among your people.

When I engage like this, the number one comment I repeatedly receive is how much it means to employees that I show up. Even if I only interact with them for a few seconds and a handshake, asking them "How are you doing, today?" made them feel cared for and important, as opposed to just another number on the payroll.

The opposite also surfaces: when I *don't* walk the floor for a while, they notice. I'm not saying you absolutely must do this, but it's necessary if you want people to feel like they matter. You'll find the same principle with family: some people think plopping on the couch for five hours with the TV on counts as "family time." It doesn't.

That's *existing*, not engaging. What matters is the (usually much shorter time) you spend face-to-face, laughing, talking, connecting.

Make room for quality time on the shop floor, just like at home. It makes people believe they matter. Of course, you'll discover mechanical and process problems this way. Sometimes, you'll also get a glimpse into how employees respond as they mature through the B.A.S.I.C.S framework. Cultures—even good ones—create environments of expectations and pressure, which some employees handle well from the start. Others grow into handling it more slowly, and sometimes they benefit from guidance and clarification.

One day, I stopped to talk to one of my employees and see how she was doing. As we spoke, she got emotional—I could see it on her face. I didn't want her breaking down on the floor in front of everyone, so I said, "Hey, can I show you something real quick in my office?" She agreed, came in, and I asked her, "What's going on? You seem like you're carrying a lot, today."

She let it out and wept—*"I'm trying so hard. I've got a ton to do, and I feel like I'm not making any progress."* Here's an example of someone who did their best to adapt to the change but needed help from time to time. I didn't dismiss how she felt; I affirmed her hard work and reassured her that everything would be all right. I said, "Let's walk through this together. Let's itemize what you think needs to get done, and I'll help you prioritize it."

She laid out all of her tasks, and we talked them through, one by one. By the end of it, she was back on her feet, in control, and it turned out to be a really productive day for her. Sometimes, people don't need you to fix everything—they just need someone to stop, listen, and help put things in order. We should remember that the people who work in our companies typically come from previous bosses and environments. They're not accustomed to virtuous, growth-oriented workplaces where high performance is the natural output.

That evening, I got a text message from my employee. This is what she wrote:

> *Good evening, Dean. I hate to bother you for nothing too important, especially. I know you're trying to rest. I've been sick for days here. But I wasn't sure it could wait until tomorrow.*
>
> *I just wanted to say thank you for not getting upset with me today, understanding what I needed to do, and getting me back on track. I just hold myself to a higher standard now, and I do not want to let you or the company down!*

She wasn't afraid for her job. She was bothered because she didn't want to let me down. This is when Culture is in full flow: employees think and behave like they own the company.

Would you like to receive a message like this from one of your employees? I know leaders whose jaws drop wide open when they read them. But this happens to me all the time. It's not because I'm special, exceptionally good-looking, or lucky. It's because I believe in building a great culture, and I hire people who prefer to work in one.

So walk the floor, talk to people, watch for the cues, and take time out of your busy schedule to help them re-center or process events that go on in the background.

Quitting

When you change a culture, you will lose some people. It happens.

Sometimes it's the old-school guy who just refuses to adapt. He doesn't want to play by the new rules. He doesn't fill out the new forms. He refuses to put his timecard where it belongs. He insists on using the old system.

You change a process—something as simple as digitizing paperwork —and that's enough for him to walk out.

Let him go. You've got to be okay with that. Cultural growth isn't for everyone. If someone's committed to staying stuck in the past, you're better off parting ways. Other times, people just move on because of circumstances outside your control or influence. Maybe they have an aging parent, a sick child, or their priorities change... but to you, their timing makes it feel like a conspiracy. It's not; people come, and people go. Hold onto them... *loosely*.

When I took over the box company, it felt like the place was booby-trapped. During the first hour of ownership one of the key guys in the department, the only guy left who really knew how to run the machines, pulled me aside and said, "Hey, just wanted to let you know... I'm quitting in two weeks."

What?!

His decision had nothing to do with me. He'd already made it before I showed up. It was about working hours, personal stuff—just bad timing. He split from us amicably, and there was nothing I could say or do to make him change his mind.

Thirty minutes later another guy, equally essential, told me he was retiring (which meant "leaving in a week"). That would have been nice to know before I completed the purchase! Right after him, a third guy quit because he didn't want to go through another ownership change. He said, "I'm done. I'm not going through this again."

Which—honestly? I get it. Before I bought the company, it had already gone through *another* ownership change (a rough one) for about eleven months before I stepped in. The morale was already shot. The team had been through the wringer. That transition was brutal, and it taught me quickly to be ready for chaos, whether you step into a company mid-stream or set about reforming it from the ground up.

Three key employees vanished in the first sixty minutes I owned the company!

(By the way... the guy who retired got wind of how the company was run after he left. He came back and now works part time on an "as-needed" basis.)

Just a reminder—not all chaos is cruel or toxic. People change, don't they? Kids, like my own, grow up, and employees become grandparents who want to make time for their grandkids. Marriages sometimes end in divorce, and people want to rebuild their lives elsewhere. Once in a while, you do so well at helping people grow and mature in their careers that they decide to start businesses of their own, modeled on what you taught them. Who are you to stop *that*? People get old, they feel the weight of their years, and they retire. Be prepared and expect it so you can adapt quickly.

Work is Theater of the Mind

I have many great memories from working with my unionized gearbox company. A labor union truly is a "culture within a culture." You have more than a simple 1:1 relationship between the employer and employee, so an extra set of dynamics affects the whole environment.

All workplace cultures create "stages"---a context, setting, and series of relationships that play off of each other. As the leader, you have a big role to play in how these "stages" take shape. As Shakespeare famously said,

> "All the world's a stage, and all the men and women are merely actors."

You're an actor in your company, but you also have a directorial role to play. To give you an example of just how theatrical workplaces can be, I find this story helpful:

After a year of working together, the union president (I'll call him Chuck) called a meeting one day with me and the union representatives to discuss a minor issue. During the meeting, he suddenly exploded in my face, screaming and swearing at me. I couldn't get him to calm down; no matter what I said, he got more upset and irritated. He turned around, stormed out of my office, and slammed the door.

I couldn't believe what had just happened. The union guys in the office were caught off-guard, too.

"What just happened?" I asked them.

None of them could give me a satisfactory answer, so I eventually went to Chuck's office and said, "What happened? We've never had that kind of confrontation before. I don't know what I said or did, and I had no intent to offend you. Were you having a bad day? Did I say something that pissed you off?"

He looked at me for a moment, and then he said, "You really don't know?"

"No," I replied.

"I had to do it."

"Okay, but why? What caused the problem?"

"Dean," he said, "I had to do it to show face in front of the union."

It turned out that Chuck wasn't upset with me at all; his concern was *other unions*. When unions learn of another union that has a strong and productive relationship with management, they typically suspect that the union leadership is "in bed" with the employer. So Chuck had to make it *appear* as though we were adversaries, even though we weren't—kind of like in politics.

I was relieved, amused, and a little ticked, all at the same time. "Can you tell me next time, a little bit in advance?" I said. "I would've yelled back, told you to get out, and kicked you out of my office. I didn't know! I couldn't participate. Just tell me next time in advance that our meeting is 'not going to go well,' and I'll make sure it doesn't."

I walked away, conjured up my best "I'm not taking this crap!" attitude, slammed his door, and stormed down the hall, pretending to huff and puff like the Big Bad Wolf. I'm sure there were a few more whispers among the rank-and-file once I closed the door to my office.

Maybe it upsets you to read that. Maybe you don't like the fact that I let them carry on the charade. But a grievance rate of zero is hard to beat. As President Harry Truman said:

> "It's amazing what you can accomplish
> if you don't care who gets the credit."

But the story stuck with me. All these years later, I still encounter situations where things go "off-script" because of human and relational dynamics. Remember when Tom, my VP, was out of town and his customer wanted an expedited order? I'd normally stand back and let the sales team handle things like that, but it was an opportunity to drive home to the customer the value of working with our company. It was like ad-libbing; I interrupted the normal flow of conversation because I saw that doing so would earn additional "credit" for our company in the mind of the customer.

So remember, no matter how "hard" your skill or tangible your product, running a company requires an appreciation for theater. Maybe you could do with some acting classes.

Thoughtfulness

Remember the coffee maker story? One of my first actions in a low-morale shop was installing a commercial-grade coffee maker. No more McDonald's coffee runs! That small change said, "I care." Culture begins with the little things. From the employee's perspective, this was much simpler than paychecks or benefits. All they wanted was a coffee maker.

The previous management had money. They had the means. But for whatever reason—call it apathy, penny-pinching, or whatever—they decided a decent coffee maker was "too expensive." So, every morning, people either brought their own coffee or went without. No one expected anything to change.

When I took over, no one filed a request, filled out a survey, or asked me for a coffee maker. But I made it a point, especially during the Analyze phase, to walk around, observe, and most importantly, *care.* I asked questions. I listened. I noticed what was missing—not just in process or performance, but in morale.

When I bought the coffee maker, I made it a permanent part of the facility—basic institutional decency to suit modern expectations. I supported, stocked, and made sure the coffee maker wasn't just a one-time gesture. It's a real part of how we do things. That may sound small, but to the employees, it sent a loud message: *I thought about you before you had to ask.*

When an employee hears their boss say, "Hey, guys—I know you don't have this, but I think you should, so we're going to do something about it," that employee feels seen, like someone actually gives a damn about them. It tells them: *You're not invisible. Your comfort, your well-being—it matters.*

Here's another example: simple, over-the-counter medications and medical supplies like Advil™, Tylenol™, rubbing alcohol, and Band-Aids™ (*yes, you can use Band-Aids™ in this context*). You know people sometimes develop headaches or get minor cuts and bruises, don't you? Before I took over, the company acted as though this never happened. Managers went out-of-pocket and bought the supplies, themselves, just to take care of their teams. As soon as I heard that, I said, "Nope! Not anymore! From now on, we stock them on the floor. Order everything you need. We'll pay for it."

And how does that make people feel? They feel respected, like they're more than just a body punching a timecard. It tells them the culture has changed, and leadership cares about more than dollars, numbers, and metrics. They care about *people*. When you lead like that, employees remember you. They show up differently. They care more, because you cared first.

That's the difference between a boss running a company versus a leader leading the people.

Perks

Tell employees, "Thank you." Not just a passing "thanks," either—make them *feel* it. Buy lunch a few times a year. Hold company events, like cookouts, away from the factory floor. Bring donuts on Saturdays. Hand out gift cards to those going above and beyond. Celebrate birthdays with cake or cards.

Put yourself in an employee's shoes: you're on the floor, grinding every day. No one notices. Maybe you've put in extra effort just because it's the right thing to do. How do you think you would feel if the owner walked up, handed you a gift card as a gesture of appreciation, and said:

"Hey, I noticed what you did. You went above and beyond. That means a lot to me. Thank you very much!"

These moments stick. For some people, like Ron, you've just handed him a *world-changer.* It says, "I see you. What you do matters." That's culture-building at its core. You don't always have to give a big bonus check or a massive ceremony—just a few words, a small gift, and the decency to stop what you're doing and make someone feel valued. If you do this consistently, you'll have a team that wants to go to war with you. Not because they have to; because they *want* to.

Money Culture

If you're building a commission-based sales program, make the structure clear and consider removing the cap. A mentor once said, "Why cap what someone can earn if you're both making money?" Look, it's different depending on the industry, but you'll miss out if you don't pay attention here.

Imagine you have a guy in sales who's a hard worker, but he's capped at $120,000 a year. That's his ceiling. Would it surprise you if he busts his tail until he hits that number, and then shuts down? Why shouldn't he? As far as he's concerned, he met his goal for the year; all the rest of the money he might make goes only to you. You'll get this result when you cap earning potential.

Now, contrast that with companies like Gateway Computers. They went from $300 million to $7 billion. Why? Well, one reason was they had an open sales compensation plan with no cap. If somebody sold like crazy, they could out-earn the CEO. I'm okay with that; the company wins, the leader wins, and so does the salesperson. I don't get why people cap it. What's the logic? They think they're saving money… but in fact, they limit drive. My sales teams can outearn me if they have the drive. That doesn't threaten me.

Removing the cap doesn't mean you forsake accountability, either. Set KPIs. Say, "Hey, you need to hit 3 percent growth, month over month." If someone closes a monster deal in March and rakes in $100k in commissions, good! Celebrate it. But don't let that be the finish line. The structure still holds them to performance metrics. If they stop hitting KPIs amd coast, you dig into why they've stopped performing. If this doesn't work, consider a reprimand or termination if you have to.

Don't cap earning. Keep the pressure on with expectations, not limits. That's how you scale from millions to billions.

Implement Culture

Communication is one of the biggest gaps in most companies, especially small and mid-sized ones. People think an annual meeting checks the box. It doesn't. A company can't thrive off of the bare minimum, occasional communication. Employees need to know what the plan is. *What do we want to accomplish? Where are we going?* You can't just walk in and dump a bunch of updates on them.

Before you even start rolling out messaging, do some groundwork. Run surveys and get a feel for people's mental and emotional states. *Acknowledge what you heard.* That alone builds trust. At a minimum, have a monthly company-wide update—just a "here's where we're at" talk covering wins, losses, where we hit goals, where we missed. Don't make it fancy; just make it real.

Now with your **management team**, you should meet at least every week or two. Make these formal, scheduled, and no fluff. You're looking for highlights:

- Any safety issues?

- Any employee issues?
- How are sales?
- Any quality issues?
- Overall company financials

You should set the expectation that <u>you don't have to ask</u> for this information; they should come prepared to give it to you.

Have them update you about current and future projects.

- "Here's what we're working on now."
- "Here are some projects we're planning in the near future."
- "Here's why we're moving this machine to a different area."
- "Here's why we bought that new truck."

One time, one of my old bosses told me to post a slew of company metrics in six different spots around the shop—walls, time clocks, bathrooms, whatever. The notices contained a bunch of sales and data that only pertained to executives and managers.

I said to them, "I don't think the employees will find value in this. You didn't ask them about what matters to them."

They told me, "You're wrong," and then they walked away.

That's the problem with a lot of upper management and owners. They make decisions without checking in. You have to talk to your people. They'll tell you what matters.

Don't leave managers guessing. When people don't know the story, they rely on past experiences or their own viewpoint and assume. And when they assume, fear, speculation, and bad morale get in. By the way, this kind of communication protects your reputation. If someone's frustrated and doesn't feel heard, they'll more likely go post about it on social media. If you want to prevent that, keep them in the loop.

Even small things, like changing the wall color from red to blue—explain to them why you want to do it. Maybe red felt aggressive, and blue's more calming. It doesn't matter. The point is that your team feels like they're part of the journey.

And don't forget internal job boards. There could be opportunities inside the company no one even knows about. Share that stuff. People want to grow, and if they don't see opportunity, they'll find it somewhere else.

Communication is a culture, not a meeting. If you don't build it deliberately, you'll spend a lot of time addressing rumors and plugging leaks.

What to Implement

Effort doesn't always equal results. I learned this running payroll. If someone doesn't get paid, your effort doesn't matter; the *result* is what counts. Build a culture where results are the standard.

As a young man, I worked for a pharmaceutical company. One day, our CEO had a companywide meeting and said, "Your effort doesn't matter. Results matter." At the time, this floored me. I thought, *What a rude, disrespectful thing to say. Doesn't he see how hard I work?*

Fast-forward a few decades. As a business owner, I get it now. He was right.

You can have someone run around the shop all day, busy from start to stop. But if they don't actually produce—if they work inefficiently, focus on the wrong tasks, or avoid important work in favor of what they *prefer* to do, the results show it. Most people fall into that trap. Remember my employees who walked around all day looking for tools and parts? Or the guy who walked back and forth across the floor every hour to get to the shipping office? Recognize these as examples of being *busy*, not productive.

In business, results are measurable. You need X amount of invoices processed, parts produced, or jobs completed. If people fail to meet those expectations, their efforts don't count for much.

What if the roles were reversed? If your boss didn't hand you your paycheck on Friday like he promised, you wouldn't care how hard he worked with the accountant or the payroll company. You wouldn't want excuses. You'd want results: your paycheck, on time, as agreed.

That's the reality. In the end, results matter. Effort only has weight if it produces the outcome you committed to deliver.

Let me give you another example: at my unionized gearbox company, I had two shifts—day and night. They each ran exactly the same machines on the same setup. Nothing changed about the equipment or nature of the work.

The day shift averaged twelve parts a day. That's a little more than one per hour. Night shift only did six parts... but both shifts got paid the same. Is that fair? No! And it wasn't because the night guy was lazy. He stayed at his machine all night. The problem was *he didn't trust the results he produced.* He'd check and re-check, fifteen different times, because of OCD or some other mental block. So the work crawled.

I worked with him and got his numbers much closer to the day shift's output, which was a big improvement—even though there was still room for more.

Do you see how effort alone doesn't matter? That night shift guy produced exactly the same quality in the same amount of time. But somehow, his work resulted in less output.

And that's why I took that plant's efficiency from 71 percent—a number they could never break—to 85 percent in just two months. I focused on results, not how busy someone looked. The profit margin they made from that productivity increase recouped every single cent of the salary they paid me.

Effort is nice, but results pay the bills.

Opinions

Ask for opinions, but not from specialists. Seek feedback from someone who supports you but isn't afraid to tell you what they honestly think. Invite a peer business leader you know through networking to visit your plant or office, and ask them for feedback on what they observe.

(I excel at this, by the way. It's another good reason to contact me once you've finished reading this book.)

My friend Jason, a business consultant, always says you should make a list of four types of people to evaluate the condition of your business:

- Champions
- Supporters
- Resistors
- Bystanders

A **Champion** supports you unconditionally. A lot of moms fit into this category. Champions will cheer for you no matter what. You need them to help pick you up when you're down… but don't count on them for a healthy critique of your culture.

Supporters are more like business coaches or peers—they generally support you and what you do, but they can also provide honest advice and save you a lot of trouble. Have people like this observe and give feedback about your company's culture.

Resistors might sound like "opponents," but the better word to describe these people is "indifferent." They aren't yet convinced they should pay attention; their resistance manifests more like cynicism. They might think, "If you've seen one culture, you've seen them all."

If you can win these people over with your culture, you've made good progress.

Bystanders bring a critical role to this because they watch what you do, even though they appear preoccupied with their own activities. If you convert a bystander into a supporter or champion, you have a good sign your culture has become magnetic.

This points back to the original question: **"Are you ready for change?"** By now, you should be... and the proof will show by how you engage outside, unbiased opinions and feedback on your culture.

How You Know the Culture Phase is Working

You'll know you're tapering off the Culture phase when the environment feels significantly different from where you started—and when the people start to reflect that shift.

Let me break it down.

If you've done Brute Force right, your team should have seen early, noticeable changes. If they resisted the changes, that's your first sign: they may not be the kind of team members you want long-term.

During Analyze, ask: *Were they helpful? Did they contribute what they could based on their role?*

During Structure you ask, *Did they lean into the new systems? Were they eager to implement, or did they drag their feet?*

During Improve you ask, *How did they respond as you worked toward maximum efficiency and effectiveness?*

If you had to come up with all the improvements by yourself...

it might need more work. But if the employees themselves made contributions to processes, policies, and procedures... you did your job.

Culture gets refined after you've laid all the hard groundwork. Then, you stop brute-forcing big changes and tend to the environment— getting into what really matters to your people. You've done the heavy lifting. Now, you're building an environment they'll want to stay in.

What do they value?
What keeps them motivated?

Here's what I've found: the smallest gestures make the biggest waves. One of the most common pieces of feedback I get is how much employees appreciate it when I walk around and say good morning. That simple act of presence has more impact than you'd think. It builds relationships and trust.

You're not just doing the "big boss" stuff anymore—you're asking better questions:

- What motivates these employees?
- What do they need to feel appreciated?
- What kind of recognition actually lands?

It includes things like:

- Holiday meals for every shift
- Summer cookouts on company time
- T-shirts or gear that reflect company pride
- Public recognition for going above and beyond
- Asking how someone's day is going—and actually caring about the answer

These tools sharpen your cultural edge.

When can you know you've truly approached the end of this phase? When you can honestly say:

- You've asked everyone for feedback—through surveys, one-on-one talks, or team discussions.

- You've responded by taking real action: installing lights over dark workstations, adjusting break areas, or tweaking shift schedules based on employee input.

- You've earned enough trust that employees tell you what they need because they know you'll listen.

It never really ends—culture is ongoing. But the turning point comes when you walk the floor and ask, *"Can I help you with anything?"* That's the sign your people matter to you. It's also the sign you're doing it right.

Because once they know you care about them, they'll start caring even more about the company.

Chapter Eleven

Sustain
Secure Success, Seek Significance, and Review Where You Stand in the Daily Operations of Your Company

"When you reach the peak, you'll realize—the mountain wasn't the obstacle. You were."
Briana Wiest

C ongratulations, captain. You've steered the ship into better waters.

Maybe you think you've reached the point where you walk away and the company runs itself while you sit on your yacht. Or perhaps you've learned a thing or two and developed a passion for leading people well. Either way, I strongly suggest you go back to the beginning and take another complete pass through this book.

Remember when you were a kid, how you saw a movie in the theater and then saw it again later when it came out on DVD? The same principle works here. Go back and read again, multiple times. Write notes in the margins, underline, and let whatever you missed on the first pass hit you in the second or third round. Growing usually happens this way—you absorb it best through repetition and reinforcement. Make it tangible with your notes. You know how I handle things: "If it's not documented, it didn't happen." That's also true for the amount of study and effort you put into your work through *Trojan Horse*.

If you've gone through the degree of change necessary to revive, grow, or scale your business... you've become a very different human being from the one you were when you started. Your priorities shift when you do deep, remedial work on yourself. If money was your chief motivator when you started, that should look different now. If it doesn't, *you're still not ready for change*, never mind sustaining it. It's time to go back to Square One.

On the other hand, you may have developed the confidence to take your enhanced skills and apply them in other places. I applaud anybody who goes through significant personal change and realizes along the way: "It's not just for me." If you want to reach out and help others succeed, good for you!

But before you set the auto-responder email and head for the exit... you've still got some work to do.

Set Goals to Sustain Success

In Chapter 2, you learned how to articulate the vision for success to your team. If that vision included removing you from all daily business operations, now's the time to lay it on thick. Have you discussed with your management and team members about how you want them to operate without you?

I'm not saying you should remind them every time you talk to them, but you'll benefit from keeping a track record, maybe in a journal somewhere, of occasions you discussed it. The newer the idea seems to the team, the longer it will take to sell them on it. But if they're used to you talking about it every couple of months for the last three to five years… they expect it.

Remember: though it's mainly management's job to think, you need to make clear to employees that you expect *them* to think on the job, as well. Since they know their jobs at a more granular level than management, express that you count on them to help management make better decisions.

This is easier to talk about in the pages of a book than to do… but it's still *simple*. Success lies in the repetition, discipline, follow-through, checks for feedback, and documentation, just like a coach with athletes on a sports team:

- First, you show the athletes how you want them to move.
- Then you get them to repeat it to you verbally.
- Then you watch them perform it, monitor for consistency, and make adjustments.
- Then you check with them verbally, to see if they understand the concept mentally as well as physically.
- Then, you make note of who can execute the move correctly and consistently.
- Then you keep a close eye on how they perform working with others.

How much difference do you really think there is between athletes in the professional leagues versus in the minor leagues? Minor league athletes are *tremendous* athletes compared to the average person on the street. They can run very fast, jump explosively, shoot accurately, and make great plays. Physically, they're just as gifted, strong, fast, and skilled as anyone else. So what separates them from the athletes who get drafted and called up by the pros?

It's discipline and the ability to *think*. Not every athlete can make the right split-second decisions and moves in real-life situations. Not everyone can do it day in and day out. Not everyone can remember every detail and principle they need to in the moment. Fortunately, your employees usually have more time to think than the average pro athlete. But you still need to make sure that they move in the same direction as everyone else and that your instructions and procedures are clear. You still need to make sure everyone understands how to respond and prioritize day to day, whether you're in the office or not.

Are You Needed?

Every once in a while, you'll get that playful comment from a rockstar employee: *"Boss, we got this. You go do your thing."* It sounds great, and if you hear that, it means you've built trust. But don't fool yourself—rarely will anyone in your shop know *every* corner of the business well enough to run it without you for long.

So, what do you do? Simple: **interview your people again**. Why? Because the gap between what you think the business needs from you and what it *actually* needs can be a mile wide. I'll give a short list of areas where, typically, you still matter:

- **Deliverables.** Stuff you haven't delegated yet. List them out daily, weekly, monthly.

- **Technical know-how.** Some knowledge can't be Googled. You might not be "hands-on" anymore, but you're still the attending physician, the one people look to when it's mission-critical.

- **Emotional support.** Don't underestimate this. Your people notice the deep personal work you've done to lead with patience, empathy, and grit. Your presence matters more than you think.

Open Doors

Here's another thing: when you don't walk the floor every day, can your people comfortably reach out if things go sideways? Or do they stay quiet, afraid of breaking the "don't bother the boss" rule? Imagine this: Someone spots a problem with a forklift, reports the problem to management, and nothing happens. Do you want that person second-guessing whether to come to you, or do you want it fixed? Don't cut the lines of communication just because you're off-site. Make sure they know they can reach out to you.

Communication

It doesn't just stay inside your four walls. Customers and stakeholders will still reach out. If you've stepped back, that means someone else monitors your inbox. Train them. Spend time teaching them judgment. Spam and sales messages? Of course, they go in the trash. A note from your biggest customer's CEO, however, may need to come straight to you or the VP. Within the messy middle, trust in your gatekeeper makes or breaks your focus.

Training Management & Employees

Remember the story of how I trained the three managers to make decisions together? At first, the process was clunky, but over time they learned to anticipate each other's concerns. Eventually, one of them could make a call on his own because he already knew how the other two would react. Trust gets built this way—shared reps, shared decisions.

Tell your managers straight up: "The buck stops with me." Let them know: "You'll make calls. Some I'll agree with, and some may be questionable. That's fine. If I wanted to make every single decision, I'd be in here every day doing it myself. But I believe in you."

Back up your confidence with accountability. Remind them: their decisions are only as strong as their diligence with the weekly issue log, the P&L, and the metrics. When things go wrong (and they will), you're not going to lose your mind, judge, or reprimand. You will analyze, drill down, and find the root cause, just like you do now.

Safety and Discipline

Don't wait until chaos hits to decide who handles what. Write it down, now:

- Who handles injuries, fire, flood, or structural damage?
- Who is the safety officer, and what's their process?
- Who deals with OSHA, and what steps do they follow?

Don't kid yourself into thinking you're "up to date." Remember my story about the outdated lock-out/tag-out machines? You think you're fine... until you're not. Contract a third party to train your people and inspect every couple of years. Everyone may find it boring, but I'd rather be bored than face the "excitement" of OSHA showing up unannounced.

Do your due diligence: sprinkler certifications, emergency exits, generators, active shooter protocols. Get your insurance company to walk through—many offer inspections that catch blind spots you'll never think of. Safety isn't optional; it's binary. You either do it, or you don't.

The same goes for discipline. Appoint leaders with the authority to enforce standards, even when you're gone. Make it clear to the whole team: the rules stand whether you're in the building or not. And spell out the gray areas—when does management handle it, and when do they loop you in? Clarity now prevents chaos later.

Sustain Employee Cohesion

Beyond all the systems and processes, ensure your people actually work as a team. They don't need to just "show up for a paycheck," but have them function the way championship teams or elite military units do it: *for each other.* If you haven't nailed the Culture piece, you've still got work to do. I want to know my employees have each other's backs, that they'll pull together and keep the team strong, no matter what.

And here's another question... do they trust management? Sometimes, employees might trust you, but not Joe Schmoe, the manager. Joe isn't a "bad" manager. He's just wired differently. My employees got used to a high-energy "D" personality walking the floor, calling it like I see it, watching everyone's back. But if they worked with more reserved "C" or easy-going "S" personalities as managers, the interactions would be different. As the leader, you have to ensure employees understand that managers with different personality types still take their concerns and safety seriously.

That difference matters. Your team may keep performing in your absence, but don't kid yourself. They notice when you're not there. They feel it, and it changes the way they think about their job, day to day.

Sustain the Money

I'm a big believer in "checks and balances" when it comes to money. Unlike the government, I can't just print cash when I run out. In my companies, every dollar has to go through multiple sets of eyes and signatures before it leaves the account.

Remember that story about the administrator who ordered those giant aluminum pillars for $48k and we couldn't even use them? After that, I locked down spending authority. But here's the thing about limits: they're not handcuffs. You can always raise or waive them when it makes sense. In the meantime, though, your managers need to know exactly where the line is—what they can spend, what they can solve—before they involve you.

You can also keep money from "mysteriously disappearing" by splitting the duties of handling and processing it. One person prints or writes checks. Another person verifies and signs them.

Get yourself a weekly financial rundown. Nothing fancy—just the basics on one sheet:

- Current bank balance
- Accounts receivable this month
- Accounts payable next month
- Sales month-to-date
- Sales orders last month
- Invoiced month-to-date
- Any special purchases planned

That's it. If you don't know these numbers, you're flying blind.

Sustain Sales

In no version of reality can your business grow without income. You can have all kinds of problems inside your company, but if you don't have money flowing and growing, you won't have the time or resources to fix them. You can trust management to track other metrics. But sales? You'd better know those numbers yourself, and not in some fuzzy, once-a-quarter report either. I'm talking real-time data, updated weekly, laid out on a ninety-day timeline—forty-five days back, forty-five days forward.

A million bucks in sales this month might sound great. Or it might be below target. Or maybe you had a fluke that's not sustainable. You can't judge unless you know your KPIs. And you can't build leverage unless you know where that money came from. Was eighty-five percent of it just cross-selling to existing customers? That tells you something very different than a million in brand-new accounts.

Don't stop at your own understanding. Whoever you leave in charge of sales has to know the same numbers, track the same way, and care just as much about the fortune in the follow-up. Too many reps leave money on the table just because nobody holds them accountable.

Set the expectation for your sales manager: when should they call you? Do you plan to stay close to the calendar and watch sales cycles while you're out? If not, you'd better put a communication rhythm in place. Otherwise, dips and spikes will drag on too long without explanation. By the time you discuss it, emotions have already worn thin.

Sustain the Facility

You could waste time imagining a million "what ifs" for your facility, but let's focus on the big ones you're guaranteed to face:

- **IT outages.** When the internet or systems go down, who's the first person you call? Don't leave employees guessing.
- **Machine or equipment failure.** When a machine breaks or starts acting up, who's the go-to? Make sure you have a clearly designated chain of command, or you'll lose hours while everyone stands around. If the team can't fix the problem, who should they turn to?
- **Vendor screw-ups.** Wrong material, late delivery, or no delivery at all—what's the process? Who makes the call, and do you have a sequence for keeping production on track?
- **Invoicing/Payment failures.** Customers try to pay, and the automation breaks down. Now what? What backup do you have in place to keep cash flowing steadily to the business?

These aren't optional scenarios; they're certainties. The only question is whether you've got a plan or you prefer to make up solutions on the fly.

Projects

Ever lose your place while reading a book? That's exactly what happens when a facility failure hits. You don't just stop the work; you throw off the rhythm. And depending on how long the interruption lasts, you can feel like you've lost your place entirely on a project.

For this reason, you need a dashboard. Something digital you can monitor that keeps the big-picture projects and issues in view. Whiteboards on the shop floor are fine. I like them, but if you have a fire, a flood, or some kind of accident, they're gone. Digital dashboards don't burn, especially in the cloud.

Shop Task List

Priority: 1=High, 2= Med, 3= Low, 4= Later

	Order	Due	Status	Notes
nent machine issues	1	7/1/25	Completed	
ooards and chairs in office	1	9/2/25	Not Started	
phault in front of building	2	6/4/25	In Process	Supplies r
glass can be removed from bulb in pump warning	1	7/1/25	Not Started	Need par
excess grease on gate rollers	3	9/2/25	In Process	Supplies r
chain with dry rag and clean oil off asphault	2	6/4/25	Not Started	
n thermostat on A/C	3	7/1/25	Completed	
all cables properly and safely	4	9/2/25	Not Started	Supplies r
ers for blower, clean at least	4	6/4/25	Not Started	Work wit!
wire properly over Journyman and etc	5	7/1/25	Not Started	Supplies r
ugs to open boxes	5	9/2/25	In Process	Supplies r
r venting to water closet to stop mold	1	6/4/25	Not Started	
black pipe for downspouts	6	7/1/25	Not Started	Supplies r
r storage shed	2	9/2/25	Not Started	Work wit!
garbage in storage shed	7	6/4/25	In Process	Work wit!
2 bulbs in pump station warning system	1	7/1/25	Not Started	
all machines off wall 1.5 ft	8	9/2/25	Completed	Work wit!
machines around	9	6/4/25	Not Started	
lown all plastic pipe	6	7/1/25	Not Started	Need siss
e maker water feed line not working?	10	9/2/25	In Process	Maybe so
ce security cameras	11	6/4/25	Not Started	Need par
celing in office	3	7/1/25	Not Started	
ugs to each machine	12	9/2/25	Not Started	
fown hanging supports over machines	13	9/2/25	Not Started	Need sice

Office Tasks | Data | ⊕

Now, how much detail should you track? That depends on how "removed" you plan to be. But you still need a working intelligence of the projects. You should know expected time frames, their progress, and who holds the day-to-day responsibility. You don't have to remain in the weeds, but you can't afford to be blind either.

Conclusion

I'm proud of you for making this journey, but let me stress one more time: *one round isn't enough*. Go back and re-read this book, and then re-read it again. In the same way you see a movie differently the second and third times than you did in the first... so goes this book. Write in the margins. Take notes. Highlight. You need to get this stuff deep down in your soul for it to truly work.

If you're challenged and encouraged by this book, would you consider buying it as a gift for other leaders and managers? They would appreciate your thoughtfulness. If it's helped you, why keep it to yourself? It can help others make those big changes and improve performance, too. Head over to deansvarc.com to get copies.

For some readers, this book looks like a fantastic blueprint... *and you have no idea how to implement it.*

I get it. What's instinctive and obvious to one leader feels like rocket science to the next. As a "D" leader on the DISC profile, I excel at getting things done and galvanizing people. But what feels instinctive and obvious to one leader is challenging to the next. Everybody has their own strengths and weaknesses.

That's why I make myself available for consulting to owners and management teams. If you own or manage a business you want to scale, or you're at a crossroads and not sure what to do, I want you to:

- Subscribe to the Dean Svarc Podcast at DeanSvarc.com. I release episodes every two weeks that break down the stories I've lived and the strategies I've created to start, grow, and scale my businesses. If you got a lot of value from this book, wait until you hear me talk about these and similar topics in a live, conversational format!

- Reach out to me and schedule a complimentary chat to see if we'd be a good fit to work together. Due to running multiple companies and limits on my time, I can only work with so many clients at a time. But I promise you: no matter the outcome of the call, you will leave with value. In no time at all, we will chip away at the root of your problems.

Now, it's time to get back to the B.A.S.I.C.S, and the basic question:

ARE YOU READY FOR CHANGE?

All the best as you seek to answer that question.

Dean Svarc

Acknowledgments

Dominique, you were my partner during some of the most defining chapters of my life. Those years shaped who I became as a person and as a business leader. You believed in me when few others did, and you trusted my vision even when the path forward wasn't clear. Your faith gave me strength when I doubted myself, and your love reminded me what it meant to build something meaningful in business, as well as in family and life.

Thank you for your patience, and for trying so hard to reach me during the moments when I was lost in the storm. Thank you for creating a home filled with warmth, laughter, and memories that will always be part of who I am. The years we shared taught me lessons about love, commitment, and growth that guide me to this day. You will always have a place in my story, and the memories we created will never fade.

Justin, a lifelong friend. Nearly five decades of shared history, loyalty, and unwavering support. You've been there from the very beginning, long before the businesses, the success, or the chaos that unfolded. During the hardest parts of my childhood, when stability was hard to find, your friendship was a constant source of comfort and belonging.

As the years went on and I began building businesses from the ground up, you were right there beside me offering your time, expertise, and patience. You helped me set up servers, phones, and systems when every dollar mattered, and you never once asked for anything in return. Your generosity and loyalty have meant more than I can ever express. Thank you for being not just a trusted professional, but a true brother in every sense of the word.

George, as both a controller and a friend, you were far more than a colleague. You were a mentor, teacher, and the closest thing to a father I've ever had. You brought wisdom, steadiness, and perspective to every challenge we faced. In moments when I needed help the most, you showed up without hesitation, offering guidance that kept both me and the business grounded and moving forward.

Your influence shaped not only how I ran my companies but also how I grew as a person. You reminded me that leadership isn't just about numbers and strategy. It's about integrity, patience, and heart. Thank you for being a constant source of balance and clarity throughout the years. Your presence was foundational to every success we built together, and your impact will never be forgotten.

Jason & Paul, thank you both for your incredible support, creativity, and belief in this project. From the early stages of development through the long hours of editing, refining, and promoting, you each brought energy, insight, and commitment that helped transform this book from an idea into a reality.

You believed in my vision when it was just a concept, and the idea that my experiences could help others rebuild, refocus, and reignite their businesses and their lives. Your guidance and encouragement pushed me to refine my message and reach further than I thought possible. This book is as much a reflection of your faith and collaboration as it is of my journey. I'm deeply grateful for your partnership, your friendship, and your belief in what this work could become.

Dean Svarc

About The Author

A builder at heart and a strategist by training, Dean Svarc has done everything from turn wrenches on the shop floor to leading teams in the boardroom. Before advising owners and management teams, he trained and worked across multiple skilled trades—auto mechanic, machinist/journeyman, electrician, plumber, and carpenter. He acquired a rare, ground-level view of how products, processes, and people actually come together. That hands-on foundation, combined with years managing manufacturing operations and construction projects, informs the practical, no-nonsense approach at the core of his work.

Dean's career spans manufacturing leadership, engineering environments, and corporate IT and software development. He has taught Policies, Process, and Procedures courses; completed more than fifty professional trainings in project management, financial analysis, business management, and meeting facilitation; and has formal training in Six Sigma, Lean Manufacturing, and Project Portfolio Management. He also studies human psychology inside and outside the workplace. For Dean, sustainable performance is ultimately a "people" question, rather than just a process chart.

A pivotal moment that shaped Dean's perspective came during his tenure as the owner of a manufacturing company. Despite strong results in many areas, he noticed the bank balance drifting downward. With payroll approaching and only about $10,000 left in the account, he hired a highly experienced controller to perform a deep analysis. The findings were blunt: the company was losing money on certain parts, pricing and cost inputs were inconsistent, and employee efficiency had slipped to the point where some work was being done at break-even. That conversation—equal parts financial autopsy and leadership mirror—crystallized Dean's conviction that the most dangerous business problems are the ones you can't see, and they originate in the mind (and hands) of the man in the mirror. Driven to reverse the spiral, Dean built methods for exposing hidden costs, standardizing decisions, and aligning people, processes, and prices so that every role contributes to the mission.

In recognition of his operational excellence and leadership, Dean received numerous awards in previous roles, including Manufacturer of the Year from the Chamber of Commerce in Rockford, Illinois. He brings the same discipline he learned as a pilot—checklists, situational awareness, and calm decision-making under pressure—to the way he diagnoses and resolves organizational bottlenecks. Whether he's mapping a pricing workflow, re-engineering a production cell, or coaching a leadership team, Dean's emphasis is consistent: clarity first, then execution.

A driven entrepreneur, Dean is passionate about continual self-improvement and the health of family culture. He believes businesses can be both high-performing and deeply human—places where people are treated with dignity, equipped with clear processes, and measured by meaningful outcomes. That belief powers his work with owners and executives who feel the weight of responsibility and want a straight path from unseen problems to durable solutions.

In *Trojan Horse: The Unseen Solution to Critical Business Problems*, Dean distills the lessons of a career spent bridging trades and strategy, data and judgment, metrics and morale. The result is a practical framework for leaders who are ready to find what's hiding in plain sight—and fix it for good.

www.ingramcontent.com/pod-product-compliance
Lightning Source LLC
Chambersburg PA
CBHW030911120626
46554CB00001B/106